From Start to Finish

Microsoft Word 2.0 for Windows

Anthony Lewis

PITMAN
PUBLISHING

PITMAN PUBLISHING
128 Long Acre, London, WC2E 9AN

A Division of Longman Group UK Limited

First published in Great Britain 1992
Reprinted 1994

British Library Cataloguing-in-Publication Data
A catalogue record for this book is available from the British Library.

ISBN 0 273 03814 1

Printed in England by Clays Ltd, St Ives plc

The Publishers' policy is to use paper manufactured from sustainable forests.

Contents

Preface

Microsoft Word for Windows is much more than a basic wordprocessor. It is described as a 'compound document processor' by Microsoft Corporation as it is able to incorporate an extensive range of text, graphics, spreadsheets, graphs and charts into documents. It is also able to display an exact image of a document onto the screen, and is therefore closer in many ways to desk top publishing, than to the traditional concept of wordprocessing.

Microsoft Word for Windows operates from within the Microsoft Windows 3.0 (and above) environment. Although it is possible to operate the Microsoft Windows environment by use of the keyboard, it is assumed that a mouse is attached to your system, which provides a much more convenient method of control. An assumption has thus been made, that a mouse will be available for use with the Microsoft Word for Windows program. This does not preclude use of the guide with keyboard-only systems, since reference to keyboard control is made throughout the text. Indeed, the most efficient control of the program is made using a combination of mouse and keyboard actions.

This book has been structured in such a way as to enable you to learn quickly how to use the Word for Windows wordprocessing program, at a number of different levels, according to your requirements. The text may be used to take you from an elementary, to an advanced level of use, whether it be within a business or educational context.

For examination purposes, the guide has been divided into three main Parts: Elementary, Intermediate and Advanced. These correspond approximately to RSA, PEI, City & Guilds and BTEC examination levels. Since examination syllabuses vary in content, and are constantly undergoing changes, there may be some overlap across Parts within the text. The demarcation of skills required at the various levels has been made at a logical point, using an average syllabus requirement. It is important to note that Part III (Advanced level) goes very much beyond current Advanced level syllabuses, however for 'real production', an appreciation of the additional techniques leads to more efficient, flexible and time-saving document processing.

If you are already familiar with the basic Word for Windows screen layout and the various methods of controlling the program, you may choose to omit 'Getting Started' and Chapter 1, 'Finding your way around'.

The guide has a 'hands-on' practical bias, as it is believed that this provides the most appropriate method of learning to use the extensive facilities offered by the program. An emphasis is placed on understanding what you are doing and why, rather than a 'which button to press' approach.

The sample disks, referred to in the text, are available from Pitman Publishing (*see* order form at the end of the book). They provide the means by which you may carry out any of the exercises in this book, in any order, according to your needs. These disks contain all the sample documents and graphics used within this text, with the exception of certain graphics supplied with the program. They also contain solutions to exercises.

The disks are not necessary if you intend to carry out all exercises in sequence throughout the book, although they may save you considerable time in text entry.

Getting started

Mouse controls

Throughout this guide, the following terms will be used to describe **mouse operations:**

Point Move the mouse to control the cursor position on the screen to 'point at' and select menus, menu options, buttons etc.

Click Press the left button on the mouse quickly and release it (the right button has only a small number of functions in Word for Windows). Assume that you should press the left button on the mouse unless otherwise indicated in the text.

Double-click Press the left button on the mouse twice in quick succession.

Drag **Click** and **hold down** the left mouse button while moving the mouse to a new position.

Highlight **Highlight** describes the use of reverse video (the normal screen colour white becomes black and vice versa in a particular area of the screen) to indicate a current menu option or currently selected text. This process may involve click, double-click or click and drag mouse operations.

Select The action of selecting involves pointing to a menu option, button etc. and clicking.

Accept Some options present you with a menu in which there is an **Ok** button. Point to this and click the left button on the mouse. Pressing **Enter** on the keyboard has the same effect.

Cancel Some options present you with a menu in which there is a **Cancel** or **Close** button. Point to this and click the left button on the mouse. Pressing **Esc** on the keyboard has the same effect.

Left-handed?

Left-handed people may find it more convenient to use the right button as the main action button on the mouse, rather than the usual left button. It is possible using Microsoft Windows to 'swap left/right' mouse buttons. This may be accomplished by using the *Mouse* dialogue box, accessed by double-clicking on the **Mouse** icon in the *Control Panel* which in turn may be accessed by double-clicking on the **Control panel** icon found in the Windows **Main** menu. Consult your Windows User's Guide for more information.

Keyboard controls

It is recommended that a mouse is used for control of the Microsoft Word for Windows program and the Windows environment in which it operates. The result of this method of operation is that far fewer commands need to be remembered and the program, as a result, becomes far easier to handle.

As you become more confident in the use of the program, you may wish to combine mouse and keyboard controls, which leads to the most efficient operation of Word for Windows.

It is assumed that a mouse is present. However, equivalent keyboard controls are shown in brackets throughout the text and are summarised in *Appendix A*.

The following conventions are used to indicate **keyboard controls**:

Function keys — You may have 10 or 12 function keys, to the left or above the main keyboard, marked F1 to F12. These will be shown throughout the text as **F1** to **F12** .

Alternate key — The **Alt** (Alternate) key is used in association with other keys. A sequence such as: **Alt F A** would indicate that you press and hold down the **Alt** key, press the **F** key and then press the **A** key.

Control key — The **Ctrl** (Control key) is used in association with other keys. A sequence such as: **Ctrl F** would indicate that you press and hold down the **Ctrl** key and then press the **F** key.

Shift key — The **Shift** key is used in association with other keys. A sequence such as: **Shift F12** would indicate that you press and hold down the **Shift** key and then press the **F12** key.

Enter key — The **Enter** (or Return) key, in the context of program control, is used to signify the completion of an operation. This is the equivalent of accepting using a mouse. Throughout the text, this key will be shown as **Enter**.

Backspace key	The **Backspace** (or delete) key is used to delete characters to the left of the current cursor position. Throughout the text, this key will be shown as **Backspace**. This key is found at the top right-hand side of the main keyboard and is often marked with just a left-pointing arrow.
Delete key	**Del**. This key is used to delete characters to the right of the current cursor position and should not be confused with the **Backspace** key.
Cursor keys	◄ Left cursor control key shown in the text as **Left**
	► Right cursor control key shown in the text as **Right**
	▲ Up cursor control key shown in the text as **Up**
	▼ Down cursor control key shown in the text as **Down**
Page up key	**PgUp**
Page down key	**PgDn**
Insert key	**Ins**
Escape key	**Esc**

Memory problems?

Word for Windows is capable of working on several documents at the same time, the maximum number being determined by the length and complexity of the documents, as well as the amount of available memory in your computer system.

If you work through a large number of exercises within this guide in one session, it is possible for 'Not enough memory' messages to be reported by the Word for Windows program. Whether or not this occurs, will depend upon the size of memory that you have installed in your computer system.

In the event of memory problems, close any or all of the currently opened documents, thus releasing the memory used for other documents.

A document may be closed by double clicking on the *Document Control Menu Box* (see the illustration on the next page) or by selecting **Close** from the **File** menu.

Loading and running Microsoft Word for Windows

Getting started may vary enormously from system to system. Most systems however, may be started conveniently as follows:

1 At the system prompt C> (or similar e.g. A> or N>) type: **WIN WINWORD**

2 Press **Enter** to carry out the command. This will load Windows and Word for Windows in one operation. An 'hour-glass' symbol will indicate that the computer is busy during the loading process.

Wait a few seconds for the Word for Windows Copyright screen to appear. This will be replaced by the opening screen after a short pause.

The various parts of the Word for Windows screen are shown below:

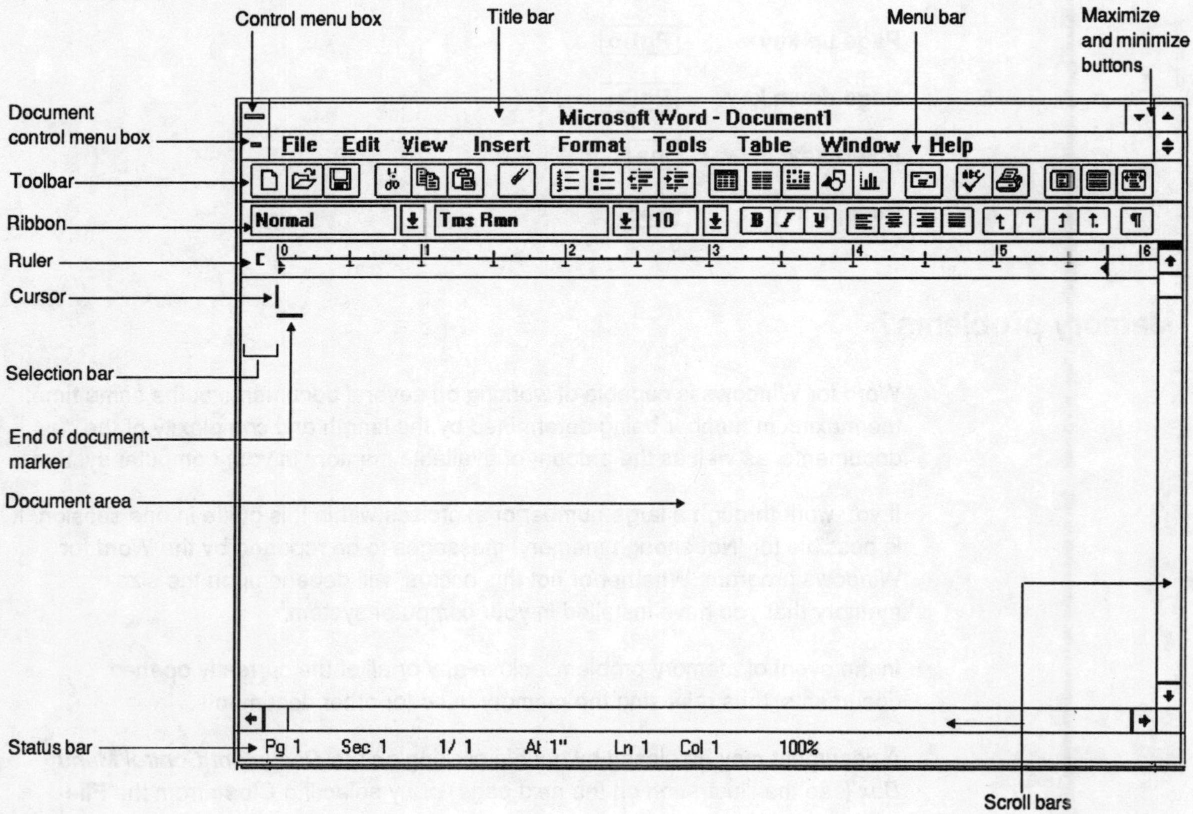

Part I

Elementary level

Introduction

Wordprocessing traditionally involves three basic stages:

1 Typing in the text.

2 Editing the text (removing typographical, grammatical, syntactical and other errors).

3 Formatting the text (making the text appear exactly as you wish it to be displayed on the printed page).

This Part of the guide provides a practical introduction to the basic features of Microsoft Word for Windows Version 2.0 and has been organised in such a way as to explore the main tools and facilities available at each of the three wordprocessing stages in turn.

The exercises within this Part of the guide are based around one substantial piece of text, which forms the basis for a whole range of practical activities. These exercises concentrate on the development and practice of essential skills, without the necessity to continually type in new pieces of text.

The main sample text has been deliberately chosen to offer reinforcement of the many skills and techniques developed throughout the exercises within this guide. All the main aspects of controlling and manipulating the Word for Windows program for the purposes of wordprocessing and document production, are practiced more than once. Further practice and experimentation with your own documents is actively encouraged as you progress throughout the text.

It is important to note that this Part of the guide is not directed at specific standard document layouts and production tasks, but is designed to develop an understanding of techniques which may be applied to any of your documents, irrespective of their content and layout.

1 Finding your way around

1.1 Title bar

The top line of the screen shows the window (or application) title. In this case, the program running is 'Microsoft Word' and the document title is 'Document1'. Since no new document has yet been produced, Word automatically defaults to the name Document1. Once a document has been given a name, it will appear in the Title bar.

1.2 Maximize and minimize buttons

To the extreme right of the Title bar are two arrow buttons.

An *icon* is a graphic or drawing which represents some kind of operation, or function within the system. Word for Windows icons are sometimes referred to as *buttons*.

- Clicking on the **Maximize** button (upwards pointing arrow) causes the program to occupy the full screen.

- Clicking on the **Minimize** button (downwards pointing arrow), reduces the whole application to an icon which may be re-activated by double clicking on it. This icon may be difficult to locate (depending on how your Windows system has been set up) since there may be other windows lying on top of it. In this case, the simplest approach is to reduce all open windows to icons by minimizing them, until you locate the icon which represents Microsoft Word for Windows as shown.

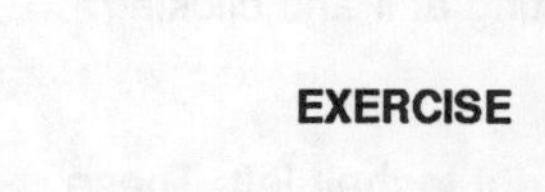

Once the application fills the whole screen (has been maximized), the maximize button changes to display both up and downwards pointing arrows (this is referred to as the *Restore box*). Clicking on this button again will cause the application window to be reduced to its default size (less than a full screen).

EXERCISE

1 If the **Maximize** button shows an upwards pointing arrow, point at it and click to maximize the Word window (with the keyboard, press **Alt F10**). The application should now occupy the whole screen. The Maximize button should now display both upwards and downwards pointing arrows.

2 Click on the **Restore** (previously Maximize) button. Alternatively, press **Alt F5**. The Word window will occupy less space on the screen.

3 Maximize the application again (point at the maximize button and click *or* press **Alt F10**).

4 Click on the **Minimize** button (*or* press **Alt F9**). The whole application will be reduced to an icon.

5 If you cannot see the icon which represents the Microsoft Word application, reduce any other open windows that you may have on the screen in turn (by clicking on their Minimize buttons) until you find it.

6 *Either:* double-click on the icon to restart the application *or:* click on the icon and point at **Restore** in the pop-up menu which appears and click (using the keyboard, press **Alt F5**). The application should be restored on the screen exactly as you left it (in this case maximized), including any document on which you may have been working.

1.3 Menu bar

The second line on the screen shows the nine 'pull-down' menu options which are used for controlling all the functions of the program. This line of menu commands is called the *Menu bar*.

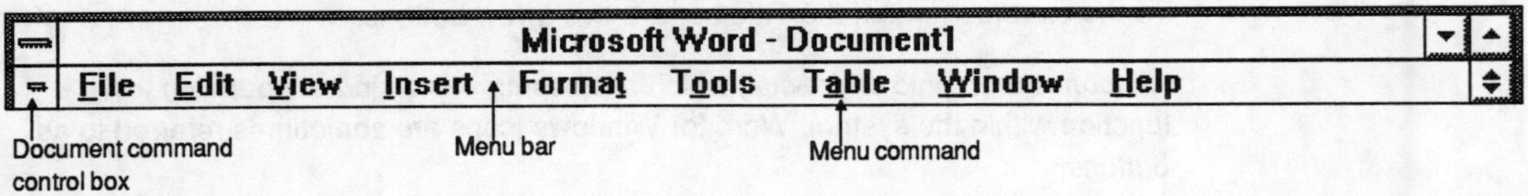

EXERCISE

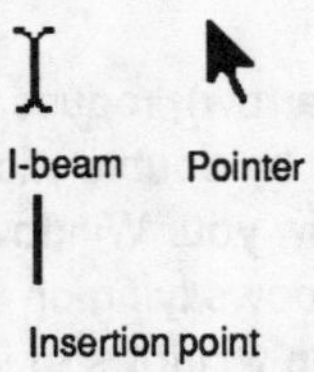

1 Move the mouse (and thus the screen pointer/cursor) around the screen. Note that the pointer follows your hand movements. As you move to the edges of the screen, the cursor changes from an I-beam to a pointer and back again as you move towards the centre of the screen. A second line-shaped cursor (known as the *insertion point*) should be flashing in the top left-hand corner of the document window indicating the position where any text typed in will appear.

2 Point at the **View** command in the Menu bar and click. A 'pull-down' menu will appear as shown on the next page. Notice that certain items in the View menu are shown in black and some in grey. Black indicates the only options that are available at this time. As you use the various wordprocessing functions, other options will become available.

Any item from a pull-down menu may be selected by pointing at it and clicking with the mouse.

Certain items in the pull-down menu may have a tick or a dot to their left. These selections are those currently in operation.

3 Point to an area outside the menu and click (or press the **Esc** key on the keyboard). This cancels/removes a pull-down menu.

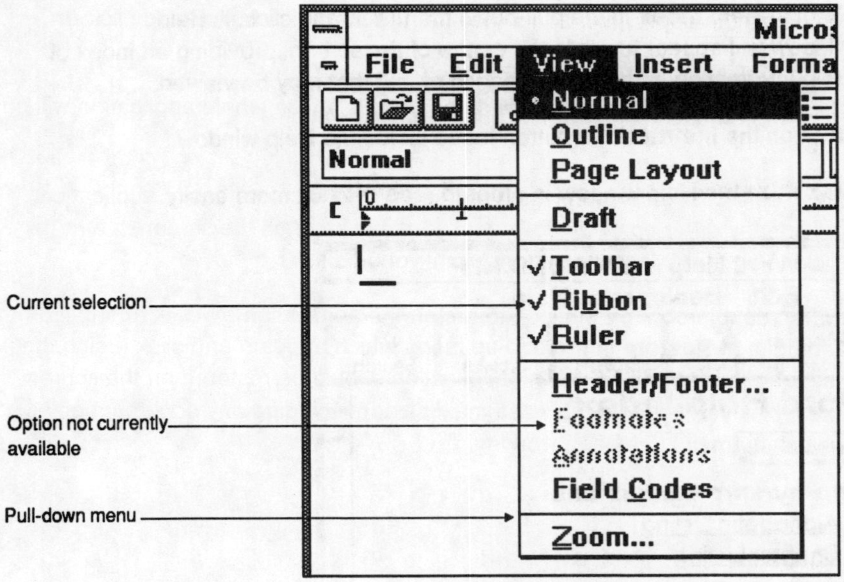

4 Point to the **File** command in the Menu bar.

5 Move the mouse from left to right across the Menu bar, clicking on each of the commands in turn.

6 Examine each pull-down menu briefly to get some idea of the groupings of options within the menus.

7 Remove any pull-down menu by pointing to an area outside it and clicking (or press **Esc**).

1.4 Help

Help on a full range of wordprocessing topics is provided in Microsoft Word for Windows and may be accessed by using the **Help** option in the Menu bar (or by pressing the **F1** key on the keyboard). In addition, help may be obtained for any individual command, key combination or screen area by pressing **Shift F1** and selecting the required element on the screen.

Computer-based tutorials ('Getting started, and 'Learning Word') for both keyboard and mouse control of the program are also included within the Help menu. You may wish to use these facilities in conjunction with this guide.

EXERCISE 1 Point to the **Help** command in the Menu bar and click to activate the pull-down menu.

2 Point at **Help Index** in the pull-down menu list, and click. A Help window will appear towards the centre of the screen, providing an index of Help information in the form of pages of text that may be viewed.

3 Click on the **Instructions** button found inside the Help window.

4 **Maximize** the Help window in order to read the text more easily.

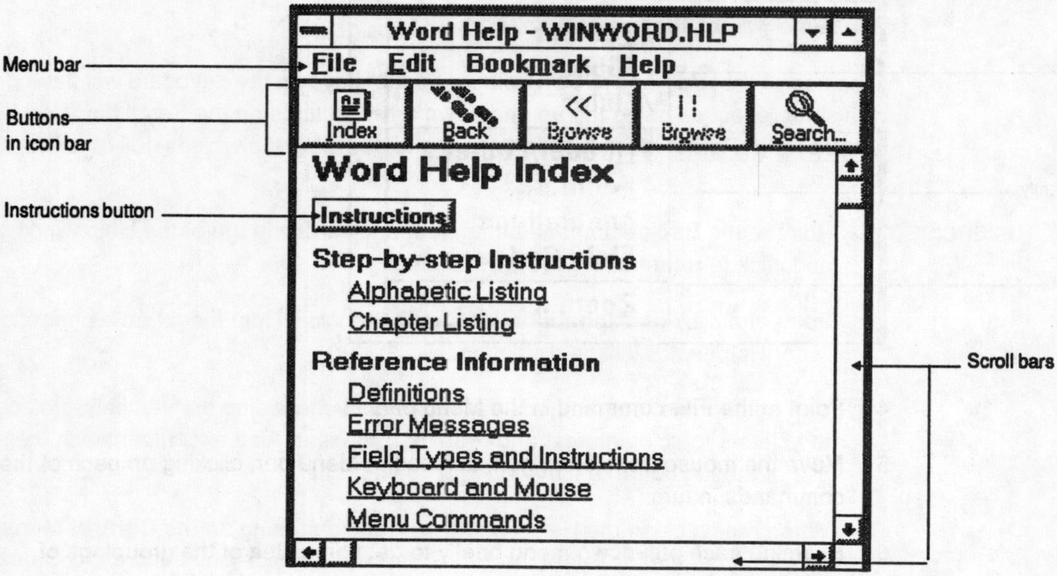

5 Read as much of the help text as you wish. The next exercise explains the use of Scroll bars for moving through text within a window.

1.5 Scroll bar

To the extreme right and bottom of the Help window may be vertical and horizontal Scroll bars which allow you to move different sections of the text into the viewing area.

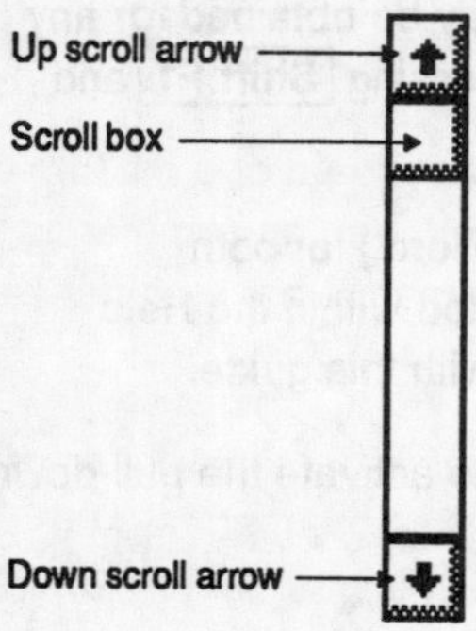

Towards the top of the vertical Scroll bar you should see a darker shaded button (called the *Scroll box*), which marks the position of the text currently on view in the window, with respect to the whole text i.e. if this button is at the top of the Scroll bar then you are currently viewing the beginning of the text, vice versa if the button is at the bottom.

There are numerous ways of controlling a Scroll bar using a mouse:

- Click on the up or down arrow found at the ends of the Scroll bar to move the text up or down one line at a time.
- Click and hold the mouse button on the up or down arrow to scroll the text up or down.

- Click on the Scroll bar, above or below the Scroll box, to move the viewing area up or down by a window-full of text at a time
- Click and drag the Scroll box up and down the Scroll bar (hold the mouse button in) to the part of the text that you wish to view, then release the button. This is the most efficient way of moving up and down the text.

Movement through a document in Word for Windows may be achieved in exactly the same way by the use of Scroll bars.

The use of the **Up** and **Down** cursor control keys on the keyboard will have the same effect as using the up and down arrow buttons on the Scroll bar. Using **PgUp** and **PgDn** will move the text up and down by one window-full of text at a time.

EXERCISE

1 Point at the **Back** command button found towards the top of the Help window and click to return to the Word Help Index.

2 Point and click on **Alphabetic Listing** in the Word Help Index. An alphabetical list of Help topics will be displayed.

3 Use each of the four methods described above for using the vertical Scroll bar to locate a topic of interest and read the Help text. Also experiment with the use of the keyboard to move up and down the text.

4 When ready, close the Help window by double-clicking on the **Control Menu box** found at the top-left of the Help window, *or* select (point and click) **Close** from the pull-down menu which appears.

1.6 Keyboard 'quick keys'

As with most large-scale applications such as Microsoft Word for Windows, there is usually more than one way of carrying out a particular operation. In the previous exercise, the mouse and the keyboard were used to control text scrolling and pull-down menus were used to access the Help command. In other exercises, *icons* will be used to activate particular functions. To remind you, an icon is a drawing, or graphic which represents some operation or function within the program. Icons are sometimes referred to as *buttons.*

All commands may be operated by either the mouse, the keyboard or a mixture of the two. The next exercise shows the use of the keyboard in issuing commands from the pull-down menu system. The main keyboard commands are summarised in *Appendix A.*

Keyboard control (sometimes referred to as using '*hot*', '*quick*' or '*short cut*' keys) requires the operator to remember the key combinations. Use the method(s) of controlling the program that you prefer but note that initially, it is far more convenient to use a mouse. As you become more proficient in handling the program, you may wish to introduce certain aspects of keyboard control.

EXERCISE 1 Point at **Help** in the Menu bar and click as you have done before.

2 Examine the pull-down menu items closely. You should notice that each item in the list has one letter underlined. Note also that each command in the Menu bar has one letter underlined on the screen. This is the key letter and is at the heart of controlling the menu system from the keyboard, as will be demonstrated below.

3 Click outside the Help menu *or* press the Esc key to remove it.

4 Press and hold down the Alt (alternate) key and press H (the initial, underlined letter of the command Help. Upper or lower case letters may be used in conjunction with the Alt key. The same Help pull-down menu should appear.

5 Press I for the underlined letter in the **Help Index** option. This will display the same Help window that you have seen before.

Alternatively, you may use the cursor control keys to move up and down a menu list, where each item will be highlighted in turn. When the desired command is highlighted, press Enter to activate the command.

6 Press Alt F (the underlined letter of the **File** menu found in the Menu bar) and press X (the underlined letter of the **Exit** command). This will close the Help window.

1.7 Toolbar

The *Toolbar* contains a number of buttons which represent many of the most commonly used Word for Windows commands and functions. These buttons are accessed by use of a mouse.

The buttons (icons) displayed in the Toolbar are shown below. Their uses are described later in the text.

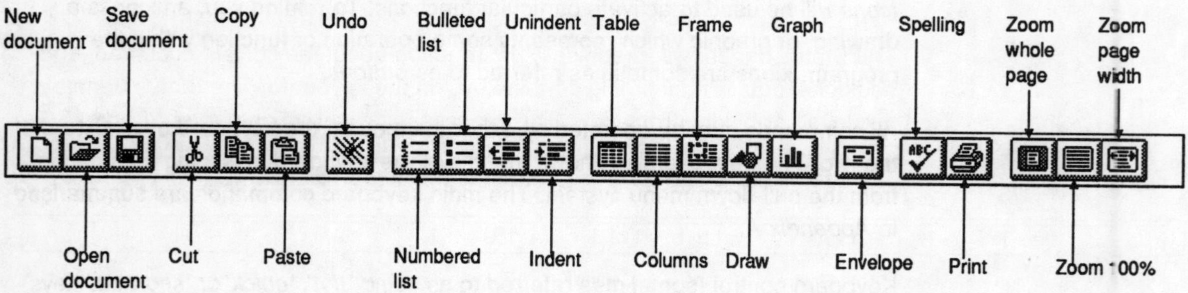

It is assumed that you have the Toolbar displayed on the screen. If not, select (point and click) **Toolbar** from the **View** menu (Alt V T).

1.8 Ribbon

The Ribbon shows, graphically, the character formatting of individual sections of text. The Ribbon may be displayed or hidden by selecting **Ribbon** from the **View** menu (or by pressing **Alt V B**). This option acts like a switch (*toggle*) turning the Ribbon display on or off.

The buttons (icons) displayed in the Ribbon are shown below. Their functions are described later in the text.

It is assumed that you have the Ribbon displayed on the screen. If not, select (point and click) **Ribbon** from the **View** menu (**Alt V B**).

1.9 Ruler

The Ruler displays, graphically, the paragraph formatting of sections of text. The Ruler may be displayed or hidden by selecting **Ruler** from the **View** menu (or by pressing **Alt V R**).

The Ruler is shown on the screen as follows:

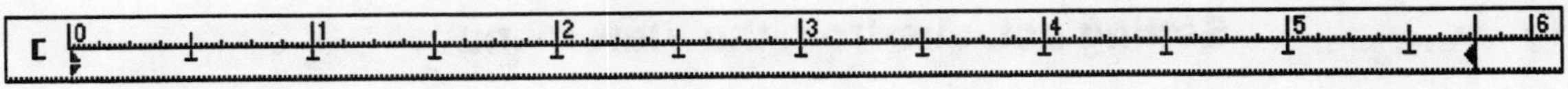

It is assumed that you have the Ruler displayed on the screen. If not, select **Ruler** from the **View** menu (**Alt V R**).

1.10 Status bar

The Status bar shows, graphically, information about the current document and additional details concerning certain keys on the keyboard. The Status bar may displayed or hidden from view. This process is described on pages 11 and 13.

The Status bar is shown at the bottom of the screen as follows:

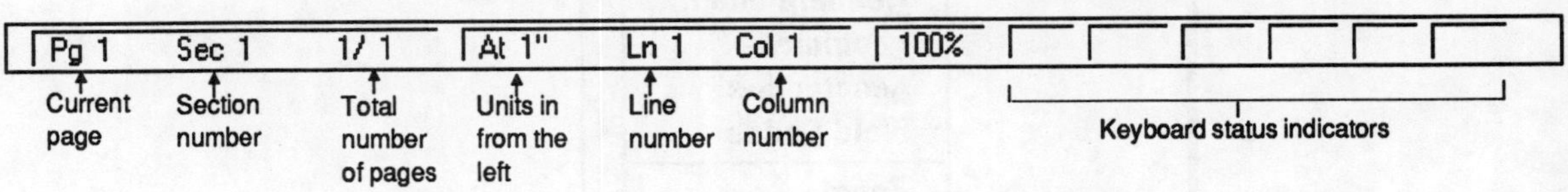

It is assumed that you have the Status bar displayed. If not, the next chapter will describe how to show the Status bar on the screen.

2 Setting defaults

When Word for Windows is loading, it takes up certain default values. These will establish: the way(s) in which you will view the text in a document on screen; whether scroll bars are displayed; whether any text formatting or graphics will be shown; whether the document will be automatically saved to disk after a standard time interval; and many other values.

Whenever you exit from the Word program correctly, values set during a wordprocessing session are stored as defaults for a subsequent session, including a list of the documents last processed.

In Chapter 1, you ensured that the Ribbon and Ruler were displayed on the screen. These will also be stored as default values.

To maintain consistency throughout this guide, further default values will be set using the **Options** command found in the **Tools** menu. In addition, this Chapter will introduce a range of screen elements which you may use to control the program. These include: *ellipses*; *dialogue boxes*; *check boxes*; *text boxes*; *drop-down lists*; and *command buttons*.

2.1 Setting defaults from the View menu

EXERCISE 1 Select the **View** menu (Alt V) and set the options as shown below:

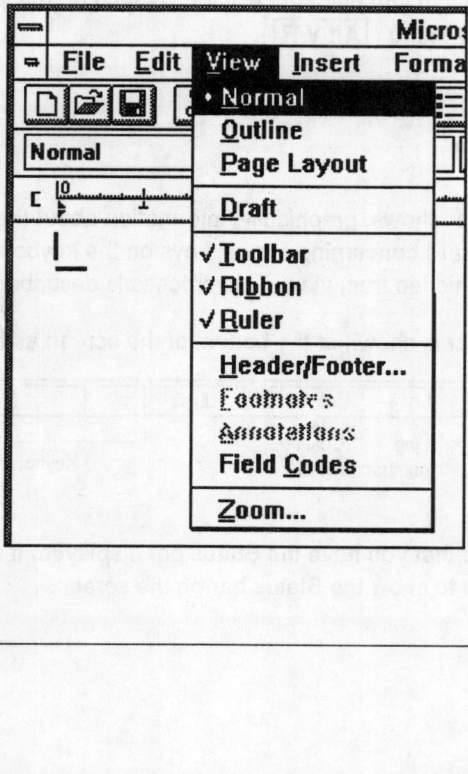

Remember that a tick or a dot to the left of an option indicates that it is active. It may be necessary to return to this menu more than once to activate (and/or deactivate) all the options shown.

2.2 Setting defaults from the Tools menu

EXERCISE 1 Select the **Tools** menu (Alt O). Note that many of the commands in the pull-down menu have three dots (called an *elipsis*) after them. This indicates that if the command is selected, then a type of form known as a *dialogue box* will be displayed on the screen, in which you may select (or de-select) any of a number of options.

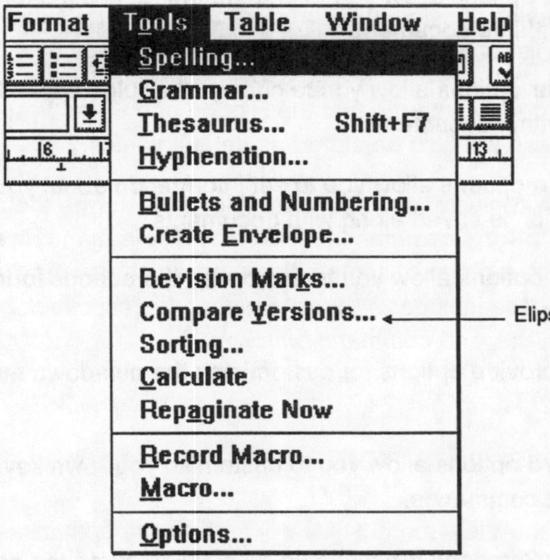

2 Select the **Options** command in the **Tools** menu. The following *Options* dialogue box will be displayed:

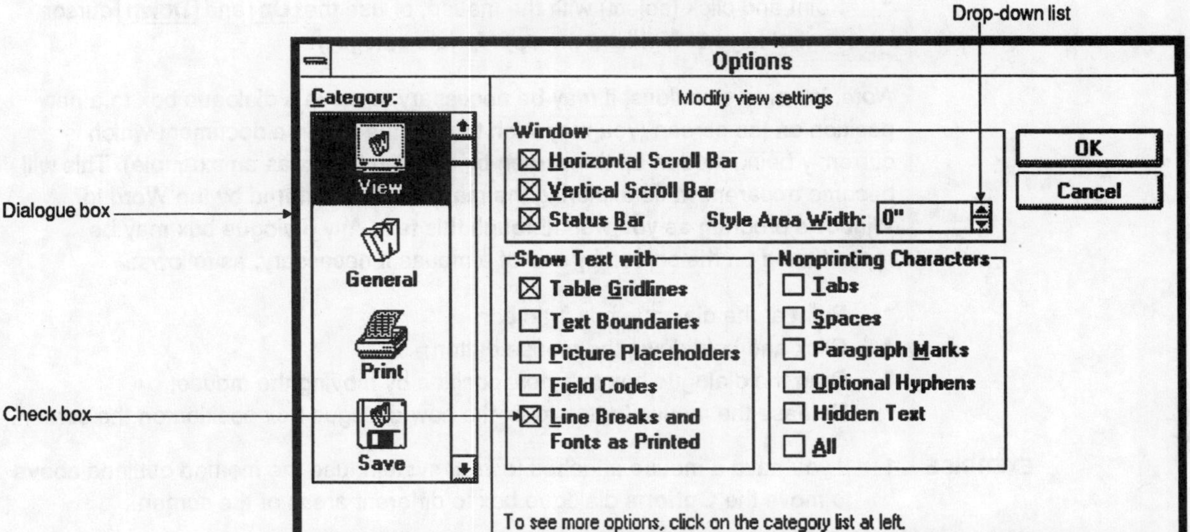

This dialogue box is divided into two sections. The left-hand part is labelled Category: and contains 11 different groups of default values. The right-hand part contains numerous options for the highlighted Category:.

View options specify how you will normally (by default) see your documents on the screen.

General options set the default typing and editing values, including units of measurement.

Print options allow you to specify the default printer settings.

Save options set the default way in which documents are saved to disk.

Spelling options allow you to change the rules used for checking the spelling of words within a document.

Grammar options allow you to change the rules applied to checking the grammar of text within documents.

User Info options allow you to set information about you, as the operator. This information is saved along with documents.

Toolbar options allow you to customise the buttons found in the Toolbar and their functions.

Menus provide options for customising the pull-down menu structure of the program.

Keyboard options allow you to customise your own keyboard key sequences to carry out commands.

The first *Category:* **View** should be highlighted on the screen. To choose a different *Category:*

- Point and click (select) with the mouse, or use the **Up** and **Down** cursor control keys to highlight the appropriate category.

Note: In some situations, it may be necessary to move a dialogue box to a new position on the screen (you may wish to view the text in a document which is currently being hidden on the screen by a dialogue box as an example). This will become apparent while exploring the many facilities offered by the Word for Windows program as you work through this text. Any dialogue box may be repositioned on the screen by use of a mouse if necessary, as follows:

- Point at the dialogue box Title bar;
- Click and hold down the mouse button;
- Drag the dialogue box to a new position by moving the mouse;
- Release the mouse button to fix the new dialogue box position on the screen.

EXERCISE 1 If you have a mouse attached to your system, use the method outlined above to move the **Options** dialogue box to different areas of the screen.

View options

EXERCISE 1 Select the *Category:* **View** from the *Options* dialogue box if necessary.

2 Set the **View** options as shown on page 11. A cross (X) in a box (known as a *check box*) to the left of an option indicates that it is active (if using the keyboard only, do not select the Vertical or Horizontal Scroll bars).

To **set an option**, point to its check box and click and a cross should appear. Alternatively, press **Alt** followed by the letter on the keyboard which corresponds to the underlined letter for the option.

To **remove an option**, point to its check box (containing the cross) and click. Alternatively, press **Alt** followed by the letter which is underlined for the option. The cross should disappear leaving a hollow box.

These settings will instruct Word for Windows to:

- Display horizontal and vertical Scroll bars.
- Display the Status bar.
- Display *Table Gridlines* which are helpful in viewing tables.
- Display any pictures or graphics (instead of rectangles called *Picture Placeholders*) that have been placed into a document.
- Display any text on the screen exactly as it will be printed. This will generally restrict Word to those typestyles (fonts) and sizes that the printer attached to your system will support.

General options

EXERCISE 1 Select the *Category:* **General** from the *Options* dialogue box.

2 Set the **General** options as shown below:

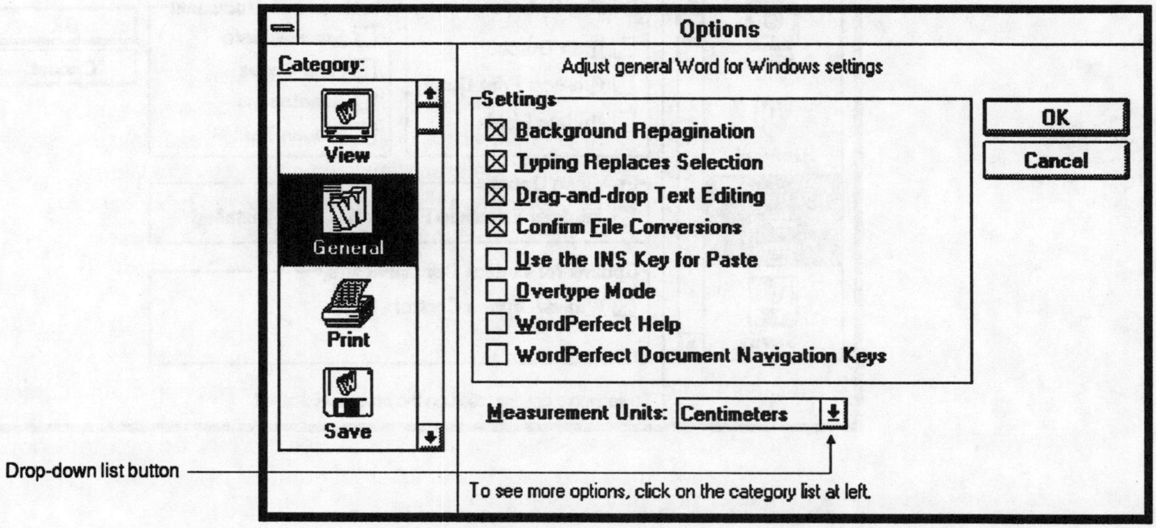

To the right of the **Measurement Units** option is a *drop-down list* button. This operates in a similar fashion to pull-down menus. To choose different units of measurement: point and click with the mouse on the drop-down list button, and select the required units. Alternatively, press Alt M and press the Down cursor control key to activate the drop-down list with the keyboard. Then press the letter which corresponds to the first letter in the word for the required units (in this case C for centimetres).

Another method using the keyboard involves displaying the drop-down list as above, using the cursor control keys to highlight the required option in the list and pressing Alt Down to close the drop-down list.

- **Background Pagination** will instruct Word to automatically paginate your documents as you work.

- **Typing Replaces Selection** allows you to replace text that is highlighted with new text that you type.

- **Drag-And-Drop Text Editing** allows you to move text and graphics conveniently to a new position within the document using a mouse.

- The *Measurement Units:* text box allows you to choose from a range of units of measurement that may be adopted by the program. The ruler will reflect the units chosen. For the purposes of this guide, select **Centimetres**.

Print options

EXERCISE

1 Select the *Category:* **Print** from the *Options* dialogue box.

2 Set the **Print** options as shown below:

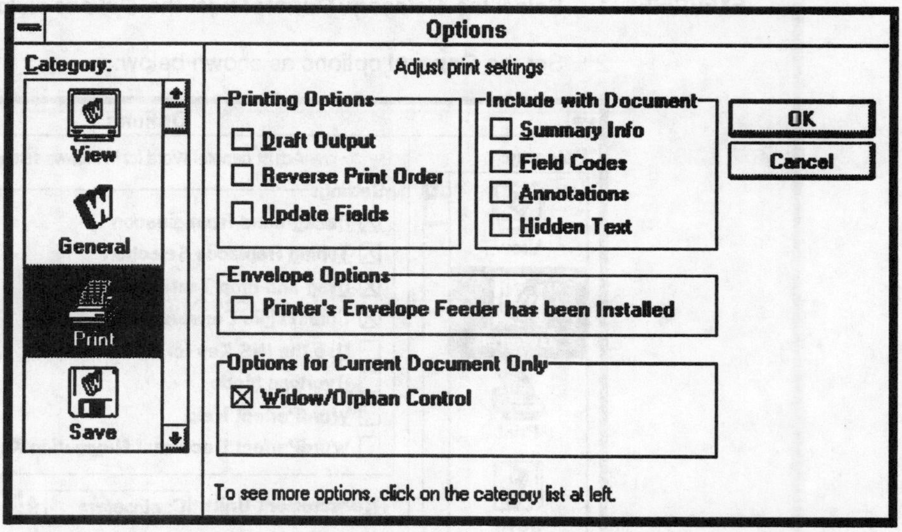

The **Widow/Orphan Control** option prevents the last line of a paragraph (which starts at the bottom of a page) from being printed on its own at the top of a new page. This is known as a *widow.* Additionally, the first line of a paragraph is prevented from being printed on its own, at the bottom of a page. This is known as an *orphan.*

Save options

EXERCISE 1 Select the *Category:* **Save** from the *Options* dialogue box.

2 Set the **Save** options as shown below:

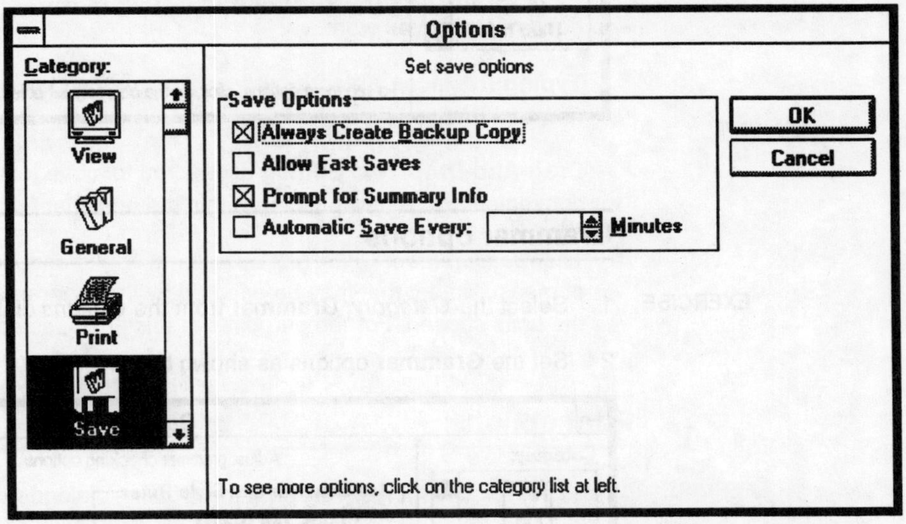

These **Save** options will be explored (and explained) later in the text.

Spell options

EXERCISE 1 Select the *Category:* **Spelling** from the *Options* dialogue box (use the Scroll bar to the right of the *Category:* area or the cursor control keys if necessary).

2 Set the **Spelling** options as shown on the next page.

These **Spelling** options will be explored (and explained) later in the text.

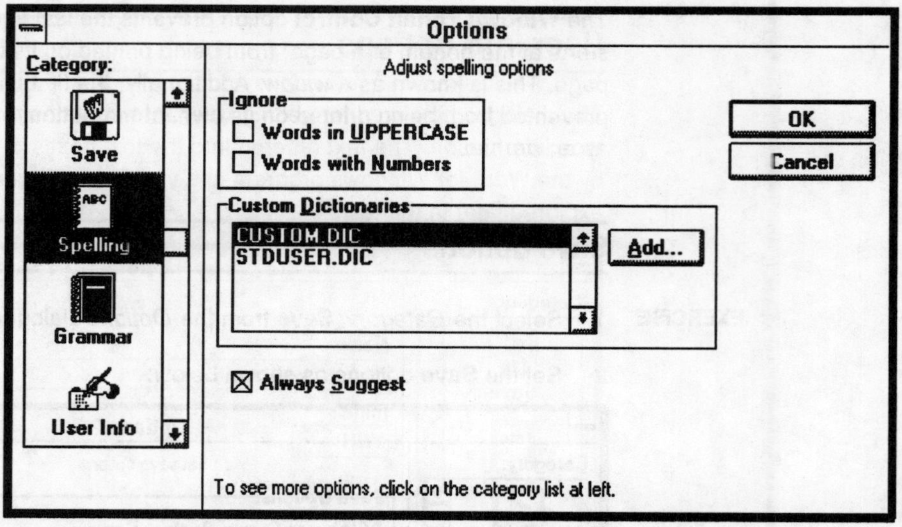

Grammar options

EXERCISE

1 Select the *Category:* **Grammar** from the *Options* dialogue box.

2 Set the **Grammar** options as shown below:

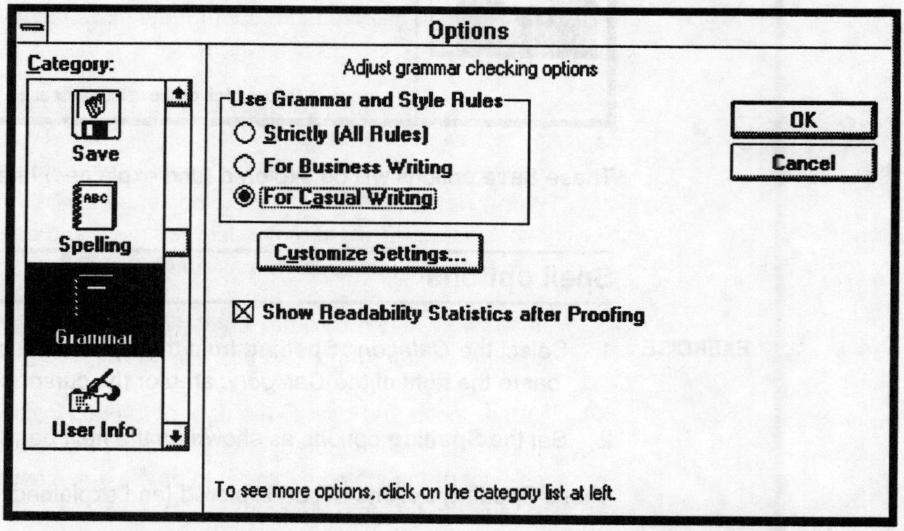

A circular check box containing a dot (◉) indicates that an option is active. The reason for a second method (other than a cross inside a square check box) of displaying active options is that, in this case, only one of the options in a particular range of alternatives must be chosen.

These *Grammar* options will be explained later in the text.

User Info options

The dialogue box used for setting **User Info** contains text boxes in which you may type information. The text entered into the text boxes in the dialogue box is used by the Word for Windows program in a variety of different ways. These will be explored later in the text.

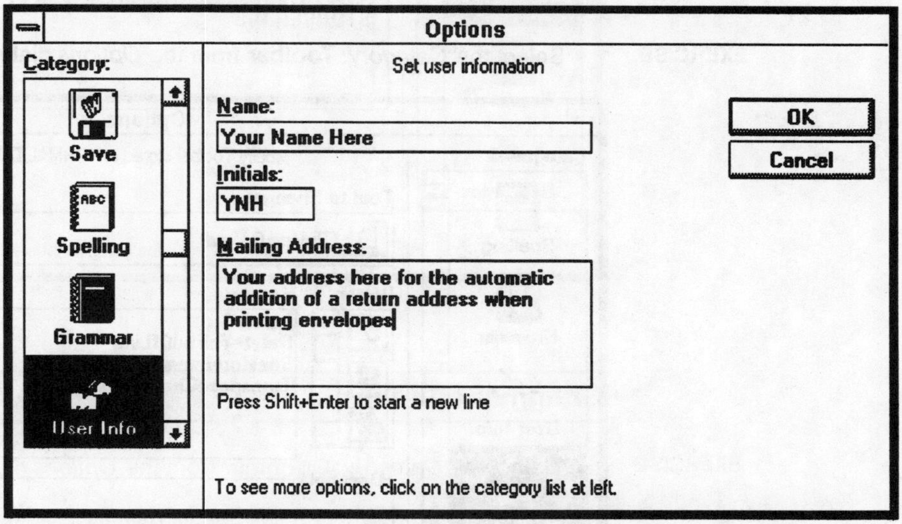

A text box may be selected and appropriate information entered, in the following ways:

- **Keyboard**: press the [Tab] key to select the first text box in the dialogue box. Any text within the text box will be highlighted. Type in the required text. Any existing text will be replaced by the new text automatically. This illustrates the **Typing Replaces Selection** option set earlier in the *Category:* **General** options. Press [Tab] to move onto the next, and subsequent text boxes. [Shift Tab] will move you to a previous text box.

  Alternatively, a text box may be selected by pressing [Alt] followed by the underlined letter for the text box title.

- **Mouse**: point and click to the right of the text inside the required text box. A blinking vertical line/cursor should appear. Press the [Backspace] key (top-right of the main keyboard) to delete any existing text if necessary. Type the required text into the box.

  Alternatively, point to the left of the text contained within a text box, click and hold the mouse button and drag (move the mouse) across the text to highlight it. Release the mouse button when the text is highlighted. Type the required text (this will automatically replace the highlighted text).

EXERCISE 1 Select the *Category:* **User Info** from the *Options* dialogue box.

2 Using one of the methods outlined above, enter the text for your **Name**, **Initials** and **Mailing Address**. This information will appear every time you save a document and will also be saved along with the document. An example is shown on the previous page.

Toolbar options

EXERCISE 1 Select the *Category:* **Toolbar** from the *Options* dialogue box.

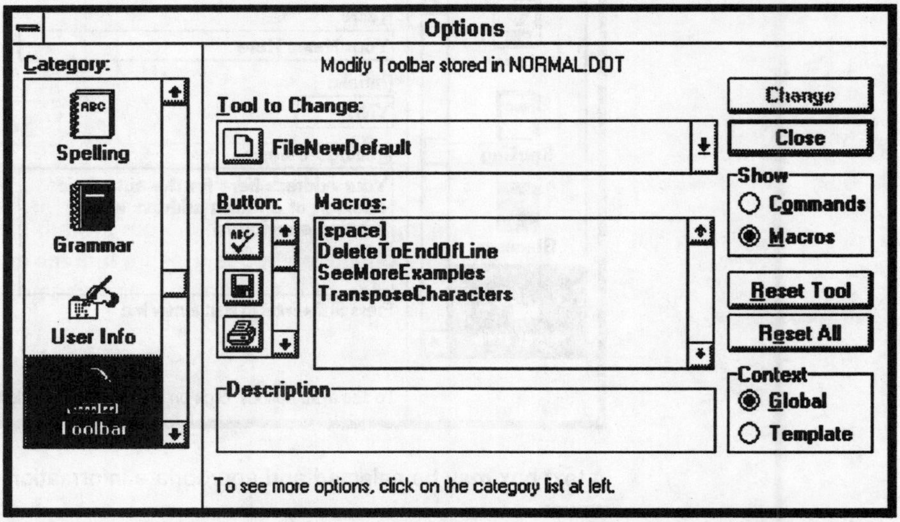

2 Select the **Reset All** command button (point and click *or* press Alt R) to reset all the buttons in the Toolbar to their original values.

Menus and keyboard options

EXERCISE 1 Select the *Category:* **Menus** from the *Options* dialogue box. The result is shown on the next page.

2 Select the **Reset All** command button (point and click *or* press Alt R) to reset all the menus and menu commands to their original values.

3 When ready, click on the **Close** command button, *or* press Enter) to return to the document window.

4 In the same way as above, select the *Category*: **Keyboard** and reset all the keystrokes to their original values by selecting the **Reset All** command button.

At this stage, all appropriate default values via the **Options** command in the **Tools** menu should have been set. Those for *Category:* **WIN.INI** will remain as currently set.

2.3 Setting defaults from the File menu

EXERCISE 1 Select **Print Setup** from the **File** menu (Alt F R).

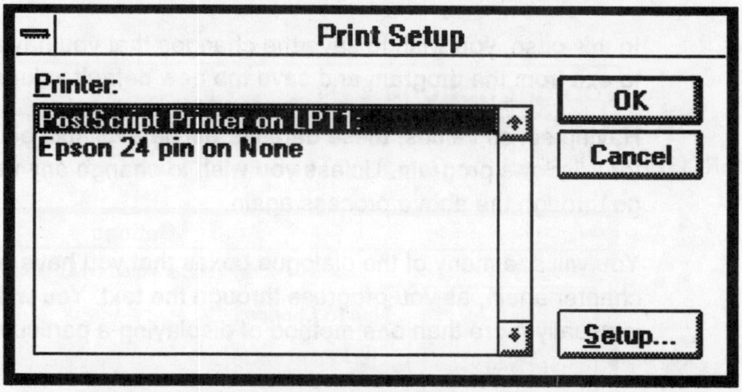

2 The range of printers available for your system may be different from those shown in the illustration above. Ensure that the correct printer for your system has been selected by clicking on the appropriate entry in the *Printer:* area and accept (or use the cursor control keys to highlight the appropriate choice and press Enter).

It has been assumed that the appropriate printers and their **Setup** have been installed correctly for Windows.

2.4 Exiting from the Word for Windows program

In order to save the default values, you need to exit from the program correctly. This may be accomplished in one of four ways:

- Using the mouse, *either* double click on the **Control Menu box** at the top-left hand side of the Word window/screen *or* select **Exit** from the **File** menu
- From the keyboard, *either* press Alt F X *or* Alt F4.

You are advised to use one of these methods now. Prior to exiting from the program, an information box will be displayed as below:

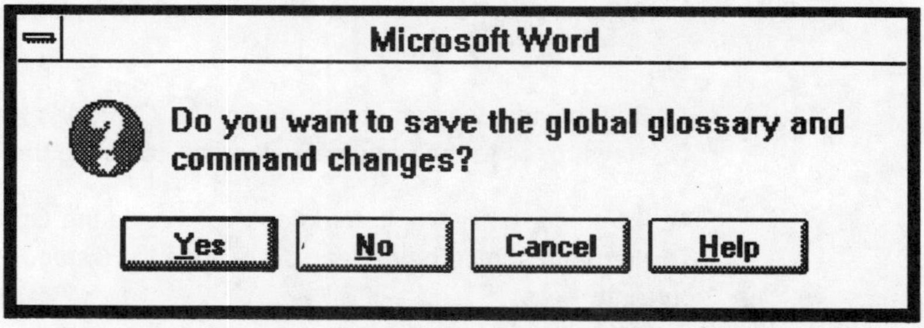

Since you have changed some of the default values, Word for Windows displays this message as a double-check to determine whether you wish to save the new values. If you have been using the program and not attempted to change any default values, this message would not be displayed.

In this case, you wish to save the changes that you have made, therefore accept to exit from the program and save the new default values for future use.

Having set all values, these defaults will be available each time you use the Word for Windows program. Unless you wish to change any values, you do not need to go through the above process again.

You will see many of the dialogue boxes that you have encountered during this chapter again, as you progress through the text. You will also discover that there is usually more than one method of displaying a particular dialogue box.

3 Starting a new document

Now that you have an idea of the screen layout of the program and you have set the default values, you are in a position to make use of the extensive wordprocessing facilities offered by Word for Windows.

You will begin by preparing a reasonably substantial section of unformatted text (which extends over a number of pages) on which numerous further exercises will be based.

The text itself is written in a 1920's style and provides a light-hearted content which has no factual value. In Chapter 4, you will edit the text to make it read the way you wish. The writing style will also be examined by a Grammar-check and archaic words and phrases will be changed using Thesaurus and other facilities offered by the Word for Windows program.

3.1 Entering text

EXERCISE 1 Load Word for Windows if necessary (double click on the Word icon if you are operating from within Windows).

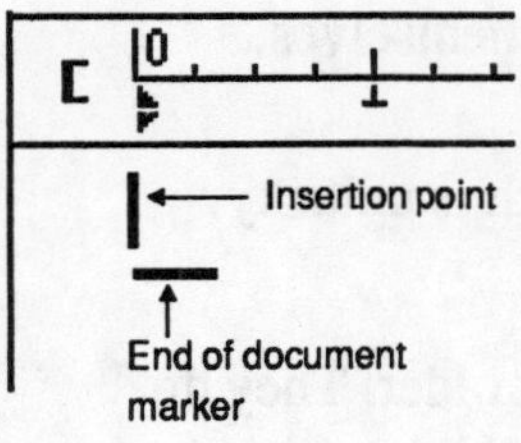

You should have a flashing straight-line cursor (referred to as the *insertion point*) at the top-left of the document window (underneath the Ruler). This indicates where the next text to be typed in at the keyboard will appear on the screen. A short, horizontal line immediately below the insertion point will indicate the end of the document (currently in the same place as the insertion point).

2 Key in the following section of sample text, keeping the line spacing the same. Press the **Enter** key once only at the end of each paragraph. Ignore any typing errors that you may make. When you have typed the equivalent of one page of text, the bottom of this page and the top of the next page will be indicated with a grey line drawn across the document window (this was a default option set in Chapter 2 - **Background Repagination** from the *General:* **Options** category).

3 If you need to save your work before you reach the end of the text, skip to Section 3.2.

MONTHS AND THEIR FORTUNE

APRIL

The April-born are headstrong, erratic, fond of being in the limelight, and are fickle. They are over-easily "up" and too soon "down". But they make good travellers, for they love change, and despise the commonplace and the ordinary in every connection.

They do not think things out, but they can, and do, advise others wisely. All too often they complicate their own lives and are unfortunate in their relationships with people in general, in spite of being very sympathetic.

They ought to dress in blues, greys, greens, and reds; but for evening wear even when older, white is their most lucky colour. They should make important changes in April, and wear their own stone always, this being the glorious diamond.

They should marry persons they have known for years (hasty marriages are never good for the April-born), and should choose their life-partners from those born either in July, August or September.

AUGUST

August-born people are steadfast and truthful, but vindictive when really vexed. Their strong sense of family leads them to shoulder burdens that do not properly belong to them, and they are too often imposed on by the selfish and the lazy. This fact makes them become over-suspicious in later life.

They ought to dress in greys and all the shades of tomato red, also deep yellows. They must take special care of their eyes; and wear a sardonyx, which is their own stone. An August woman rarely marries the first love, nor does an August-born man either. They are old for their years and marry most successfully, partners older than themselves, preferably those born in May or December.

18th August is a good day for everybody. The first Monday in this month is unlucky.

DECEMBER

Those born in December put business before love, especially as they get older. They do not easily forgive any wound to their self-esteem, and should resolve to think generously as well as to act considerately. They are not very strong and, as they look well, they do not get much sympathy in illness. December people do not easily recover from ill-health.

December women are too apt to get into a rut and to stay there, but they are always excellent organisers. They love to help, to give, and to advise others. October is always a lucky month for the December-born people, and Tuesday is their best day. They should marry either on a Tuesday or a Friday. New enterprises entered into on either the 5th, 6th, 9th, 17th, 23rd, 25th, or 28th will turn out well.

31st December is the only "bad day" in this month. December people ought to dress in light blues and pinks; to see that they do not overtax their strength; and always to wear a turquoise, which will turn faintly green as a warning of illness. This stone brings together lovers who have quarrelled. December people should marry those born in June.

FEBRUARY

February-born folks have good memories and are imitative and quick-witted; with acute understandings, although they are apt to run away from "stiff thinking." They love dress and crave authority. They often suffer from rheumatism.

They should wear purples, bluish purples and black if born in the first part of the month; those born in late February will find the red purples more lucky for them than the blues; and should always wear an amethyst. Those born in the first part find 3 their lucky number; but those born in the latter half may take the number 9.

Tuesdays and Saturdays are good for the February-born, and March is a good month for them to enter on new enterprises. They happily marry partners born either in January or October.

JANUARY

Those who have a birthday in January are ambitious, proud, loyal, careless as to appearances; reserved, averse from showing their feelings. They have good business ability, if born in the second half of the month. The women are interested in engineering. If born on or after the 21st, the men make good professionals.

3rd and 13th January are among the twenty-eight outstanding good days of the year; these dates are auspicious for every one, though nobody ought to become engaged in this month.

The January-born people should dress in browns, greys, and black. They ought always to wear a garnet, which is the stone for their month. But it must be given to them with love, and not bought. They marry most happily, partners born either in February or July.

JULY

July-born people are generous and big-hearted, but they are over-anxious for pleasure and crave wealth, power and authority. They are patient, persevering, and very thorough in all they do. Those born in July are not helpful in emergencies, for they require time in which to think things out. They never neglect appearances.

July-born people often have a hard time in their youth. They are great workers, also lovers of music of every description. They ought to take care of their health and check their love for flattery. They may dress in all the colours of the roses but never in blue, and wear a ruby all the time. Mondays and Thursdays through the year are favourable days for them, especially for love.

Good dates in this month are the 5th, 6th, 15th; the 15th and 18th July are particularly good for the July-born. They happily marry, those born in January or March.

JUNE

Those who have birthdays in this lovely month are "born Rovers"; travellers, adventurers, and pioneers, loving to wander far from the land of their birth. They are restless, magnetic, impetuous, over-apt to act on impulse; eloquent, dramatic, nervous, and, if born before the 20th of the month inclined to be dreamers and even "work-shy". They influence other people but are not easily influenced themselves.

June is a favourable marriage month for anyone. These dates are good for all: the 5th, 13th, 17th, 26th, 28th, and 29th. The 3rd and the 8th are especially good for June-born people to start new ventures.

June folks ought to dress in soft shades of red, yellow, and especially white, and to wear an agate on the third finger of their left hands; for this is said to give them the power to attract to themselves the love of any one on whom they set their hearts. They marry happily, people born either in November or December.

MARCH

These people are generous, impressionable, easy-going in money matters, apt to let good chances slip past them. But they can fight when they are really up against it, though they do not always, even then, hold what they gain. To wear the noble bloodstone, which is the month-stone of March, ought to help the March-born to cultivate that steady courage which they lack.

They may wear all shades of green and will look well and feel happy when dressed in green and red together. Good days for the March-born are the 3rd, 22nd, and the 30th; the Fridays in their own month are propitious for them to embark on voyages or enterprises. March people are rarely strong, though they are healthy.

March engagements do not last, as a rule. March people marry happily, those born either in September or July.

MAY

May-born people are vivid, hopeful, and eager for adventure. They are somewhat obstinate, yet neither persevering nor patient; affectionate but not generous. Destiny plays a big part in their lives; it is the unexpected that happens to them. They are fascinating, with a flare for dress and a real talent for art in any of its manifestations. They do not easily learn by experience, yet they do not worry.

They ought to dress in vivid emerald green as much as possible, and wear their own emerald always.

Good days for the May-born throughout the year are the 4th, 22nd, and 28th. Good days for everyone are the 4th and 20th May. The 9th of June is very auspicious for May people; and they should marry partners born in May or June, though they marry confidently and successfully with partners born in any month in the year.

NOVEMBER

The November-born are reckless, extravagant, discontented, riotously happy or miserably depressed, fond of adventure, fond of spending as well as fond of giving, fond of luxury, fond of food and drink, and of the "high-life" generally. They are clever and far-seeing in worldly affairs, and are only unwise when they love.

They ought not to marry too early nor too "easily". The November-people are "great givers" both in love and friendship. When happily married, which is rare for the November-born, they make devoted wives and husbands, but may be over-strict as parents.

They should dress in yellow, with shades of golden brown, for these are the colours of their birthday stone, the glorious topaz. They ought to live on plain food. June is the best month for November people, and Friday is their best day. Lucky days for them in love matters are Wednesdays and Saturdays. Good days in November for those born in this month, are the 6th, 9th, 15th, and 23rd.

Since marriage either makes or mars the passionate November folks, their partners ought not to be much older or too much younger than they are; and they should, if possible, be people born in October or June.

OCTOBER

The October-born are equable, sensible, fond of knowledge, but always practical and willing to use what they know to their own advantage. Those born in the first half lack ambition, those born after the 22nd of October are more ambitious and are capable of more patient work.

They are unwise in money matters, and will 'spend a shilling to save a penny'. They are also careless about small debts. They dislike manual work, are averse from travelling, and they like to 'go easy'. They are constant in love and friendship, but over-apt to dominate those they love. October people are successful when working on the land, and will do well to acquire land of their own as they grow older. October folks also make good professionals.

The opal is the stone for October people. Unlucky for others, it is lucky for them, and its wearer may always count on keeping the love of those whose love they have won, so long as they wear this beautiful stone with confidence in its power.

January is a good month for the October people. 4th and 15th October are good days for everybody. Number 6 is lucky for the October-born, though number 5 is still more so for those born in the earlier half of the month. The October people always look well when dressed in greys and dark blues, which are the colours of their stone; but reds and red mauves and pinky reds will also induce a woman to feel happy, especially in the evening. Their life partners should preferably be born in February, March, July or August.

SEPTEMBER

Those born in September are full of nervous energy, talented, but not really practical, with a special gift for languages; serious, sympathetic, and warmly affectionate, but not especially devoted, for their weakness is laziness, and they are over-disposed to be easily 'sorry for themselves'. As middle age approaches, there may be a tendency towards gluttony.

July is lucky for them, especially for travelling. The numbers 5 and 6 will serve them well; the 4th, 7th, 9th, 17th, 28th, and 30th of September are good days for all. Those born in the first week in September ought to wear primrose; in the second week, violet; in the third and fourth weeks, pale greens. But September folks are generally happy when wearing blues, violets, and primrose yellows.

Their stone is the sapphire. They should marry people born either in March or January.

3.2 Saving a document

When saving a document for the first time, you should use the **Save As** command from the **File** menu (**Alt F A** *or* **F12** if you have this function key on the keyboard). This will give you an opportunity to save the document to a particular disk with a name (*filename*) chosen by you. Certain options allow Word for Windows to make automatic backups of files when you save them more than once.

If you save a document for a second time, or more, then you should use **Save** from the **File** menu instead (**Alt F S** *or* **Shift F12** if you have this function key on the keyboard) unless you wish to save the document using a different filename. Alternatively, use the **Save** button found in the Toolbar. The **Save** command re-saves a file using the previous disk and filename used before with **Save As**.

This guide assumes that you are using a floppy disk in drive A: (referred to in this text as the 'Samples Disk') to store your documents. If you are using a different disk to store data, make the necessary adjustments to the text.

Saving a document to a floppy disk

EXERCISE

1 Select **Save As** from the **File** menu (**Alt F A** *or* **F12**). A *Save As* dialogue box will be displayed.

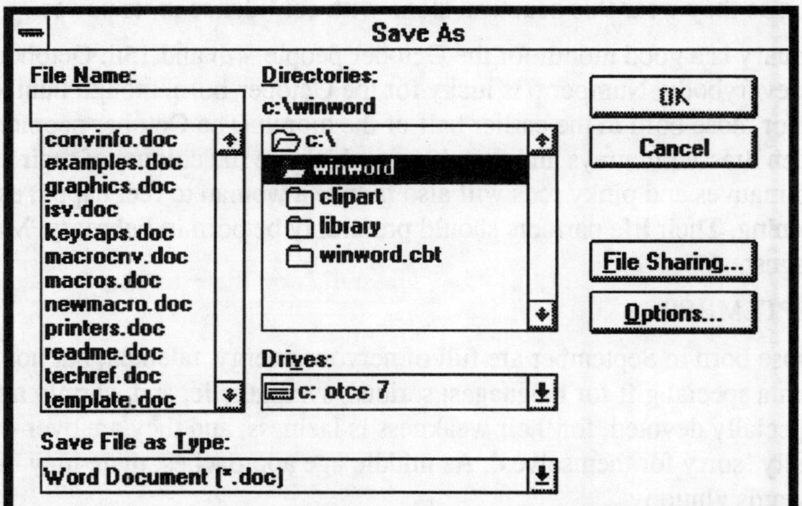

2 Select the **Options** command button (**Alt O**) and notice that the same dialogue box seen earlier on page 15, which was used for setting **Save** default values, is displayed. The values that you set at that stage will be shown.

If you save the same file at a later point for a second time with the **Always Create Backup Copy** option selected, a backup copy will be retained, i.e. you will have your first version retained as a backup (with .BAK – referred to as a *file extension* – added to the end of the document or file name) and the second, most recent version, will be stored on disk as a separate file (with a .DOC extension).

The purpose of the **Prompt for Summary** Info option will be explained below.

3 Cancel (point and click on the **Cancel** command button *or* press **Alt C**) to return to the *Save As* dialogue box.

4 Activate the **Drives** drop-down list by clicking on the appropriate **drop-down list** button (*or* press **Alt V**).

5 Click on **a:** in the *Drives:* area of the dialogue box (*or* use the cursor control keys to highlight it). This will redirect the file to disk drive A:. The disk drive letter (a:) will appear in the *File Name:* text box if using the keyboard or a:\ will appear under the *Directories:* area if using the mouse.

6 Point inside the *File Name:* text box and click (*or* press **Alt N**). A flashing cursor should appear.

7 Type **MONTHS** for the filename (upper or lower case letters).

8 Accept (point to **Ok** and click or press **Enter**).

9 A *Summary Info* dialogue box will appear. It is always good practice to enter some, or all of the details about a document for future reference (these will be explored in Chapter 6). These details will be stored along with the document when saved to disk. An example is shown below:

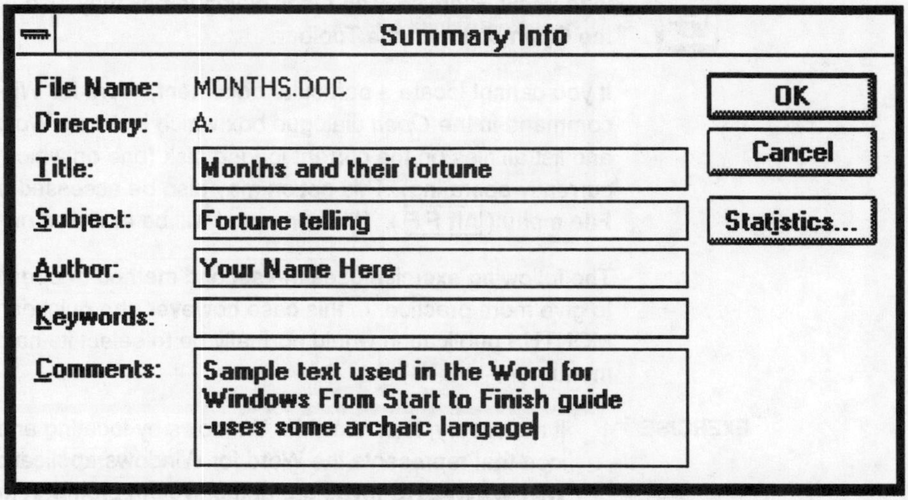

Note that the *Author: text* box should display your name which was set up on page 18 as a default value.

To enter any detail, point to the appropriate box and click (*or* press Alt followed by the underlined letter). The text cursor should appear.

10 Type in any details and repeat for any other information boxes. *Do not* press Enter until all the information boxes that you want to fill in have been completed, since this has the same effect as accepting.

11 Before completing the saving process, you may wish to view details about your document by selecting the **Statistics** command button (Alt I).

12 Accept (or accept twice if you are currently viewing the document statistics) to store the file MONTHS to the disk in drive A:.

13 **Exit** from Word for Windows (*see* pages 19-20).

3.3 Opening a document

Documents may be re-loaded into Word for Windows in one of two basic ways:

Word stores the details (filename and path, i.e. disk and directory) of the last four documents that have been saved. These are displayed when you select the **File** menu (Alt F). To load (**Open**) any one of these documents simply select the appropriate document name from the list (or press the corresponding number on the keyboard).

If the document that you wish to load does not appear in the **File** menu, then the **Open** option in the **File** menu (Ctrl F12) allows you to redirect Word for Windows to a different disk and directory using the *Open* dialogue box explained in the next Exercise. The *Open* dialogue box may also be displayed by selecting the **Open** button in the Toolbar.

If you cannot locate a particular document, Word for Windows offers a **Find** command in the *Open* dialogue box which instructs Word for Windows to locate and list all files on the current logged disk (one on which Word for Windows is currently operating). This option may also be accessed by selecting **Find** from the **File** menu (Alt F F). This command will be explored on pages 91-96.

The following exercise uses the second method of opening a publication in order to give more practice. In this case however, the quickest method of opening the MONTHS publication would normally be to select its name directly from the **File** menu.

EXERCISE

1 If necessary, load Word for Windows by locating and double-clicking on the icon that represents the Word for Windows application. Alternatively, type **WIN WINWORD** if you are at the system prompt (e.g. C>, A>) and press Enter.

2 Insert the Samples Disk in drive A: if necessary.

3 Select **Open** from the **File** menu (Ctrl F12 or select the **Open** button in the Toolbar). An *Open* dialogue box will be displayed similar to that shown below:

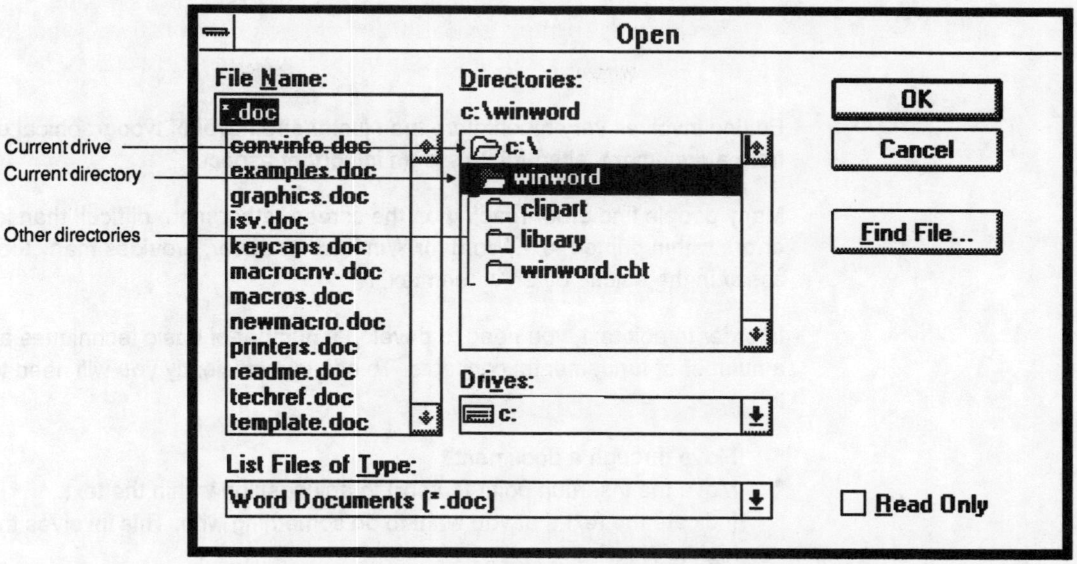

4 If necessary, activate the *Drives:* drop-down list and select **a:** in the list. This will direct Word for Windows to 'look at' the Samples Disk in drive A:.

5 A list of available documents on the disk in drive A: should appear in the *File Name:* area (note that Word for Windows automatically added .DOC to the end of the filename when you saved your document to disk). *Either* double-click on **MONTHS.DOC** in the *Files:* area *or* select **MONTHS.DOC** and accept. After a short pause, your text should appear inside the document window on the screen.

This method of opening a publication allows you to change the disk drive and directory that Word for Windows will search. The program will look for files that contain the three letter extension .DOC.

To demonstrate the ease of opening any document which is listed in the **File** menu:

6 Select the **MONTHS.DOC** document from the **File** menu. The document will be loaded immediately.

4 Editing a document

Editing involves very much more than just the removal of typographical errors from a document, although this is an important aspect.

Many people find proof-reading on the screen rather more difficult than identifying errors within printed text. Word for Windows however, provides many tools that assist in the editing of 'on-screen text'.

In order to edit text, you need to develop a number of basic techniques and grasp a number of fundamental concepts. To edit text efficiently you will need to be able to:

- Move through a document.
- Move the insertion point (cursor) to any position within the text.
- Indicate the text that you want to do something with. This involves the use of highlighting.
- Insert text.
- Delete text.
- Copy text.
- Move text.
- Search text.
- Find and replace text.
- Spell-check the text.
- Use the Thesaurus.
- Grammar-check the text.

All the above are explored in the exercises found within this chapter.

4.1 Moving around the text

Now that you have a reasonable length of text to work with, you will practice a variety of methods (using the mouse and keyboard) of moving around the document.

Moving with the Scroll bar

EXERCISE 1 Load the Word for Windows application program and **Open** the **MONTHS.DOC** document if necessary.

The insertion point (a vertical line cursor) should be flashing at the beginning (top-left) of the text.

2 Select **Page Layout** from the **View** menu (Alt V P). This will instruct Word for Windows to display the document as if each page of text was placed on its own sheet of 'paper' on the screen.

3 At the bottom end of the vertical Scroll bar are two **Page** icons (visible only in **Page Layout** document view), these allow for movement through the document by a page at a time. Click on the **Down Page** icon at the bottom of the Scroll bar. This will move you to the top of page 2.

4 Click on the **Up Page** icon to move you back to the top of page 1.

5 Use the Scroll bar itself to move backwards and forwards through the text (see page 6) using **Normal** and **Page Layout** document views.

Moving with the Goto command

EXERCISE 1 The number of pages and the current page number of the current insertion point position are displayed in the Status bar at the bottom of the screen. Select **Go To** from the **Edit** menu (Alt E G).

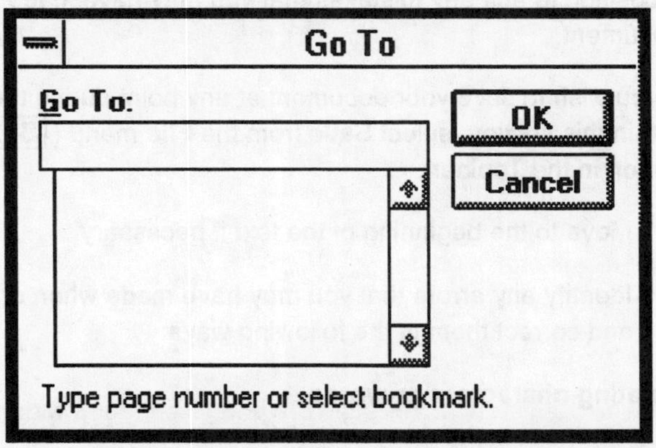

2 Type in a page number to go to (such as 3) and accept.

This function allows you to move directly to a specific page. This can be particularly useful for a long document.

3 Double-click anywhere on the Status bar at the bottom of the screen if you have a mouse. The same *Go To* dialogue box appears as before. Cancel the dialogue box.

4 Press F5 (the Go To key). You will be prompted for a page number in the Status bar. Type in a page number and accept.

5 Go to page 1 if necessary before continuing.

Moving with the keyboard

EXERCISE

1 Press and hold down the **Down** cursor control key on the keyboard. The insertion point will move down through the text which will begin to scroll upwards as your finger remains on the key. Releasing the key will stop the text from scrolling and the insertion point will remain at the current location.

2 Press the **PgUp** and **PgDn** keys to move a screen-full of text up or down respectively.

3 Use the **Up** cursor control key to return to the top of page 1.

4 Select the **Normal** document view from the **View** menu (**Alt V N**) if necessary, before continuing.

4.2 Editing the text

Having experimented with various methods of moving through the text, you are in a position to edit any mistakes that you may have made when originally typing the document.

If you wish to save your document at any point during the remaining exercises within this section, select **Save** from the **File** menu (**Shift F12** , *or* the **Save** button in the Toolbar).

EXERCISE

1 Move to the beginning of the text if necessary.

2 Identify any errors that you may have made when originally keying in the text and correct them in the following ways:

Deleting characters or words

Place the insertion point (the flashing, vertical line cursor) immediately to the right of the character/s that you wish to delete. This may be accomplished in one of two ways:

Method 1:
With the **mouse**, point at the position in the text where you would like the insertion point to be moved and click. This will re-position the insertion point. Use the **Backspace** key (found at the top-right of the main part of the keyboard) to delete the unwanted character(s).

Alternatively, place the insertion point immediately to the left of the characters to be deleted and use the **Del** key to delete characters to the right of the insertion point.

Method 2:

With the cursor control keys on the **keyboard**, use the **Up**, **Down**, **Left** and **Right** keys to re-position the insertion point to the right of the character(s) that you wish to erase and use the **Backspace** key to delete.

Alternatively, use the cursor control keys to position the insertion point to the left of the characters to be deleted and use the **Del** key to delete characters to the right of the insertion point.

Inserting characters or words

Move the insertion point as above to where you wish to insert text and type in the required text. The text entered will appear at the insertion point position and any text to the right of the insertion point will be moved automatically along the line (and onto the next line if necessary, the process being known as *wordwrap*).

Inserting a paragraph break

Move the insertion point as above to where you wish to start a new paragraph and press **Enter** to insert a paragraph break into the document at the current insertion point position.

Deleting a paragraph break

Position the insertion point at the beginning of the line/paragraph that you wish to move up and press **Backspace**. This will delete the paragraph break inserted into the document at the end of the line above.

3 Locate the text associated with the month in which you were born.

4 Add the following paragraph to the end of the section (you will need to insert a paragraph break in the appropriate position to start a new paragraph):

With perseverance, those people born in this month, are more likely to succeed with modern tecnology.

Note: please spell technology as above as this will be used for spell-checking purposes on page 43.

5 Select **Save** from the **File** menu (**Shift F12** or the **Save** button in the Toolbar) when complete.

4.3 Copying, moving and deleting text

The processes of copying, moving and deleting (normally large sections of text) revolve around the **Cut**, **Copy** and **Paste** commands found within the **Edit** menu.

Copying a file

In case you get into a muddle with the next exercises, you will take the precaution of making a second copy of the **MONTHS.DOC** document and store it to disk with the name **MONTHS2.DOC**.

EXERCISE 1 Place your Samples Disk in drive A: and open **MONTHS.DOC** if necessary.

2 Select **Save As** from the **File** menu (**Alt F A** *or* **F12**).

3 The *Save As* dialogue box which appears should indicate a *File Name:* of **MONTHS.DOC** and the cursor should already be in the *File Name:* text box. Type **MONTHS2** and accept. The document will be saved on drive A: under the name of MONTHS2.DOC (.DOC will be added automatically by Word for Windows).

This process has given you a copy of your document. You will be able to 'fall back' on this copy if the next, or subsequent exercises cause you problems.

4 Before continuing, select the original document **MONTHS.DOC** from the bottom of the **File** menu.

Moving and deleting text

You may have noticed that the sample text used in previous chapters is organised into alphabetical order, by month. The following exercise illustrates the use of the **Cut** and **Paste** commands, found in the **Edit** menu, in moving sections of text.

The text is to be re-organised into a more normal chronological order, starting with January.

When you **cut** text from a document, the text itself is not lost, but rather stored in a separate part of the Windows system called the *clipboard*. The clipboard only holds the last text (or illustration) to be cut. Anything held by the clipboard may be retrieved at any point by pasting back from the clipboard into the application (it does not necessarily mean the same application from which it was originally cut – in this case you could paste any text cut from Word for Windows into any other Windows application program).

In order to move, copy or delete sections of text, you must first instruct Word for Windows as to which part of the text you want to work with. To do this, highlight (select) the section of the document. This is seen on the screen as white text on a black background. The exercise that follows, demonstrates various methods of highlighting text.

EXERCISE 1 Load Word for Windows and the document **MONTHS.DOC** if necessary. Locate the paragraphs for January.

2 Highlight all the text associated with January as shown below using one of the methods that follow:

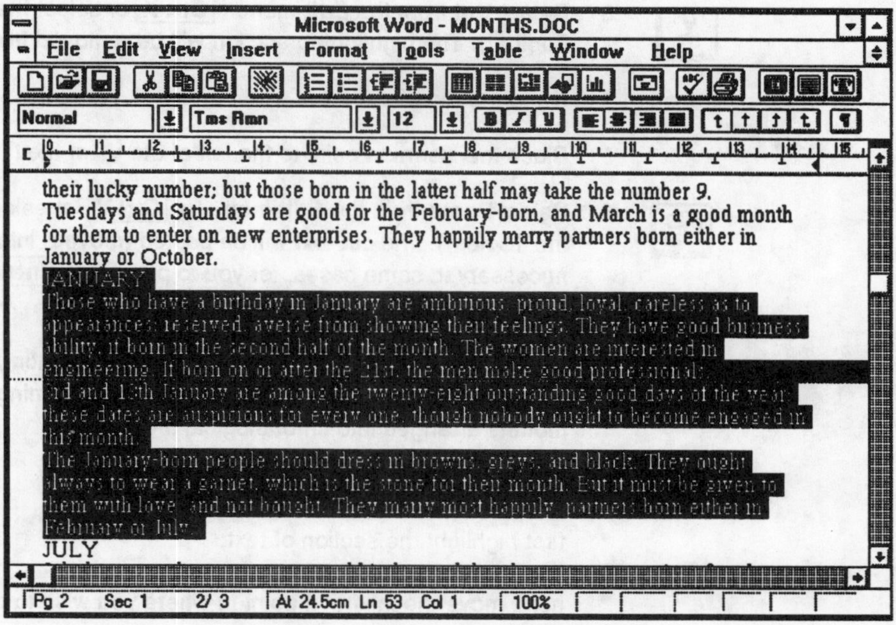

Highlighting text with a mouse

Method 1:

Point to the left of the 'J' in the title 'JANUARY'. Click and hold the mouse button in. Drag the mouse down and to the right (the text will become highlighted). Readjust the mouse position if necessary so that the entire text for January is highlighted. Release the mouse button – the text should remain highlighted.

Method 2:

Place the insertion point to the left of the 'J' in the title 'JANUARY'. Hold down the **Shift** key, point and click at the end of the text for January. The text should remain highlighted.

If you need to cancel the highlight produced using either of these two methods, click anywhere in the text (the highlight will be removed) and try again.

Highlighting text using the keyboard

Method 1:

Move the insertion point to the left of the 'J' in the title 'JANUARY'. Press the extend selection key, **F8**. Re-position the insertion point (with the cursor control keys) at the end of the January section. The text should remain highlighted.

Method 2:

Move the insertion point to the left of the 'J' in the title 'JANUARY'. Hold down the **Shift** key and re-position the insertion point at the end of the January section.

If you need to cancel the highlight produced using either of these two methods, move the insertion point to another position.

3 Select **Cut** from the **Edit** menu (Ctrl X *or* select the **Cut** button from the Toolbar). The highlighted section will be removed from the document.

4 Go to the top of page 1.

5 Place the insertion point to the left of the 'A' of the title 'APRIL'.

6 Select **Paste** from the **Edit** menu (*or* Ctrl V, or select the **Paste** button from the Toolbar). The cut text will be pasted (moved) into position. It may be necessary in some cases, for you to press the Enter key to move the heading (APRIL) onto a new line.

7 Experiment with the different methods of highlighting text and move all sections of text into appropriate positions, forming a document with the months arranged into chronological order.

Remember, *to move a section of text:*

- first highlight the section of text;
- then cut the text;
- next, move the insertion point to where you wish to place the text;
- finally, paste the text.

If you ever wish to simply delete a section of text, then you need only highlight it and cut it - you obviously do not paste it.

If you wish to start the process again from the beginning of this section, just select **MONTHS.DOC** from the **File** menu again.

8 If you are happy with the movement of the various sections of text, save the document using **Save** from the **File** menu or select the **Save** button from the Toolbar.

Moving with drag and drop

If you have a mouse attached to your system, any amount of text (from a single character upwards) may be moved more conveniently using the 'drag and drop' technique (this was activated as a default value on page 14). To move text using drag and drop:

- Highlight the text that you wish to move;
- Point at the highlighted text, click and hold down the mouse button;
- Drag the highlighted text to the required position;
- Release the mouse button to complete the text movement.

EXERCISE 1 Load the **MONTHS2.DOC** document.

2 Practice moving the sections of text associated with each month as before, using the drag and drop technique. Do this until you are happy with the process. You will find that the document area will scroll as you drag the highlighted text to a new position. Do not panic when this happens, just ensure that you do not release the mouse button until the drag and drop cursor is in the required position.

3 It is not necessary to save the document.

Copying text

The following exercise illustrates the use of the **Copy** command also found in the **Edit** menu.

Instead of cutting a section of text and pasting it somewhere else, the text is copied (the original section remaining in position) and this may be copied any number of times, wherever required.

EXERCISE

1 Highlight any section of text.

2 Select **Copy** from the **Edit** menu (*or* Ctrl C or select the **Copy** button from the Toolbar).

3 Move to the end of the document.

4 Press Enter if necessary, to place the insertion point on a new line (you cannot move the insertion point below the end of file/document marker).

5 Select **Paste** from the **Edit** menu (Ctrl V *or* select the **Paste** button from the Toolbar) as before to place a copy of the text that was copied to the clipboard.

6 Press Enter if necessary, to move down onto another blank line.

7 Paste another copy of the text. You should note that any number of copies may be taken of the text in the clipboard and these may be pasted anywhere inside the text.

8 Highlight the text that has been copied and pasted into position at the end of the document and delete it using **Cut** from the **Edit** menu (Ctrl X or select the **Cut** button from the Toolbar).

Should you wish to delete a section of text at any point and you do not want to send it to the clipboard, simply highlight the text and press Del. *Note:* Since a section of text deleted in this way will not been sent to the clipboard, it will be lost.

9 Since this exercise should not have altered MONTHS.DOC, you do not need to re-save it at this point.

4.4 Find & find and replace

Word for Windows offers Find & Find and Replace facilities which are useful during the editing stage of wordprocessing.

The Find function gives you the means of directing the program to locate words, parts of words, combinations of upper and lower case characters and text formatting (summarised in *Appendix D*), wherever they may appear in the document. This is particularly useful for longer documents.

Searching (finding) may take place either forwards or backwards through the document, starting from the current position of the insertion point.

Using the Find command

The **Find** facility is activated from the **Edit** menu.

In the next exercise, you will be searching for the word 'vexed' (this is often referred to as the 'search string') which appears somewhere in the document. Once located, the word will be replaced by another.

EXERCISE

1 Load **MONTHS.DOC** if necessary and move the insertion point to the beginning of the document.

2 Select **Find** from the **Edit** menu (Alt E F). A dialogue box similar to that shown below will be displayed:

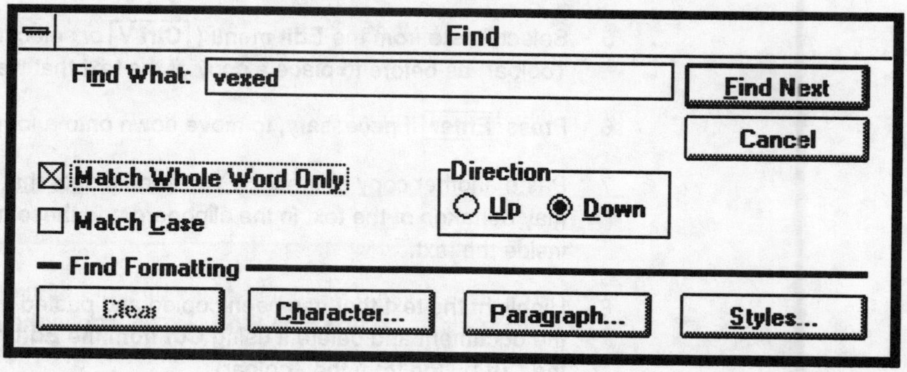

3 Type **vexed** into the *Find What:* text box and set the check boxes as shown above.

Word for Windows is instructed to locate this text character for character (**Match Whole Word Only**), starting from the current insertion point position (beginning of the document) and working downwards.

4 Select the **Find Next** command button when ready. The word 'vexed' will be located in the text and will be left highlighted on the screen.

5 Cancel (select the **Cancel** command button) to return to the document window. The found word should remain highlighted.

6 Press **Del** to delete the highlighted word.

7 Type the word **'provoked'** in the place of 'vexed' (the insertion point should already be in the appropriate position).

8 Since you have made a change to the document, it would be wise to re-save it at this point. Select **Save** from the **File** menu or the **Save** button in the Toolbar.

Searching for information

In the next exercises, the document will be searched to locate various items of information. The **Match Whole Word Only** checkbox in the *Find* dialogue box should be reset (no cross in the checkbox). The insertion point should be placed at the beginning of the document before each search.

EXERCISE Using the **Find** facility, find the answers to the following:

(a) Which month has the birthstone diamond?

Hint: Set up a search for 'diamond'. Once located, you may need to scroll the text upwards to find the name of the month.

(b) In which birth month are people described as being 'generous and big-hearted'?

(c) Which birth month has the lucky 'number 9'?

(d) In which month may people dress in 'deep yellow'?

Repeating a search

There may be occasions when there may be more than one occurrence of a *search string* within the text. The **Find Next** button in the *Find* dialogue box allows you to find the next occurrence of the search string. In addition, the use of **Shift F4** allows you to repeat the last search without the need to display the *Find* dialogue box again.

In which birth months may people wear the colour 'white'?

EXERCISE 1 Move to the beginning of the document and set up a search for the word 'white' in the normal way.

2 When the first occurrence of the word is found, note the month and then select the **Find Next** command button. The next occurrence of the search string will be found.

3 Note the month and select the **Find Next** command button again. When the end of the document has been reached, an information box will appear which gives you the opportunity of repeating the search from the beginning of the document (Yes) or to stop (No) as shown below:

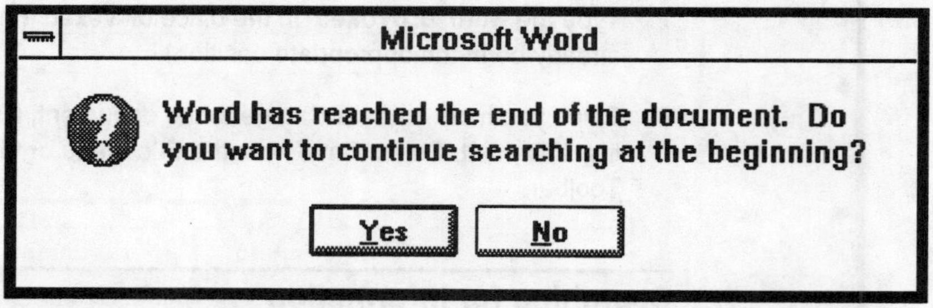

4 Select the **No** command button to end the search. Word for Windows will report that 'the search text is not found'. Accept to return to the working document.

5 Move the insertion point to the beginning of the document and press **Shift F4** (the repeat search keystroke). The same search string will be found. Word for Windows remembers the last search string used and **Shift F4** activates a search based upon this.

6 Press **Shift F4** twice more. Word for Windows will report that it has reached the end of the document as before. Return to your working document.

7 In the same way as above, find out how many months contain the colour 'blue' within the document.

The Replace command

The **Replace** function allows you to search for particular search strings within a document and to replace those located with different *text strings.*

As with the Find facility, the Replace function gives the option to match specific upper and lower case characters, whole or part words, and formatting. These are summarised in *Appendix D.*

In the following exercise, the word **'folks'** will be replaced with the word **'people'** throughout the document.

EXERCISE

1 Load **MONTHS.DOC** if necessary and move the insertion point to the beginning of the text.

2 Select **Replace** from the **Edit** menu (**Alt E E**). A *Replace* dialogue box similar to that shown on the next page will appear.

3 Type **'folks'** into the *Find What:* text box and **'people'** into the *Replace With:* text box as shown below.

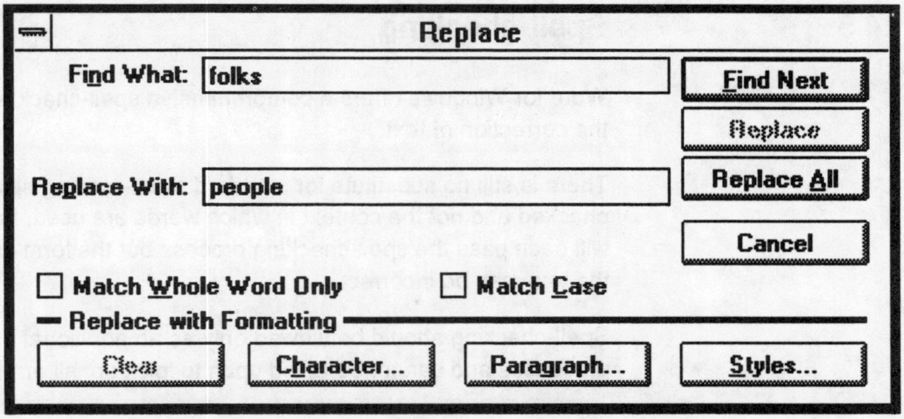

4 Select the **Find Next** command button. The first occurrence of the word will be located and highlighted on the screen. The previously greyed-out **Replace** command button will become available (black text).

5 Select the **Replace** command button to automatically replace the word 'folks' with the word 'people'. Note that there is a **Replace All** command button which, if selected, would replace all occurrences of the search string with the replacement text string in one operation. This may lead to unexpected changes to your text. It is suggested that, unless you are absolutely sure, you always replace a located search string with the **Replace** command button. This gives you an opportunity of bypassing a particular located search string (by finding the next occurrence with the **Find Next** button) that you do not wish to replace.

6 Select the **Find Next** command button again and replace the search string with the replacement text string as before. Repeat for all occurrences of the search string.

7 When there are no further search strings to be replaced, the program will display a message to that effect. Accept to return to the *Replace* dialogue box.

8 Cancel (select the **Cancel** command button) to return you to the working document.

9 Save the document using **Save** from the **File** menu or the **Save** button in the Toolbar.

4.5 Spell-checking

Word for Windows offers a comprehensive spell-checking facility which assists in the correction of text.

There is still no substitute for standard proof-reading since only spellings will be checked and not the context in which words are used. For example, 'of' and 'off' will each pass the spell-checking process but the form used within the context of the text may be incorrect.

Spell-checking should be viewed only as an additional aid to normal editing processes and cannot be relied upon to 'pick up' all errors.

Spell-checking the whole document

Spell-checking in Word for Windows takes place from the current insertion point position downwards through the document although, if you start in the middle, Word for Windows will ask whether you wish it to continue spell-checking at the top of the document once it has reached the end of the text.

Spell-checking is activated by selecting the **Spelling** command from the **Tools** menu or the **Spelling** button in the Toolbar.

EXERCISE

1 Position the insertion point at the beginning of the text.

2 Select **Spelling** from the **Tools** menu (**Alt O S**) *or* the **Spelling** button from the Toolbar. The spell-checking process will begin and if Word for Windows encounters a word which it does not recognise as being in its main dictionary or the supplemental user dictionary (CUSTOM.DIC which is used to store any words specific to you), it will stop and display the word in the *Not in Dictionary:* text box inside a *Spelling* dialogue box.

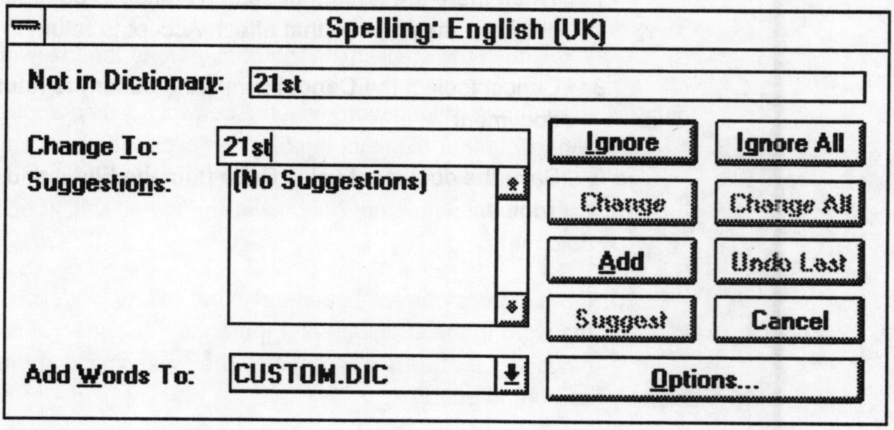

3 Select the **Options** command button. The *Options* dialogue box for the *Spelling:* default settings category encountered earlier, will be displayed. The **Always Suggest** option was set as a default value for the spell-checking

process on page 15. This instructs Word for Windows to display alternatives to any unrecognised words automatically inside the *Suggestions:* text box of the *Spelling* dialogue box. Note also that there is a *custom dictionary* with the name of CUSTOM.DIC where you may save your own, customised words which act as a supplement to the main dictionary. Other supplemental dictionaries may be added as required.

4 Cancel the *Options* dialogue box to return to the *Spelling* dialogue box.

5 If you wish to see a word in context within the text, the *Spelling* dialogue box may be moved to a different position on the screen, if necessary, by dragging the Title bar as you have done in a previous exercise.

6 A list of suggestions for any unrecognised word will be displayed in the *Suggestions:* text box. The example shown below, is based upon the deliberate mis-spelling of the word technology from page 33.

The most likely suggestion will be highlighted (white text on a black background). It may be necessary in some cases to scroll through the items in this window with a Scroll bar (*or* the **Down** cursor control key).

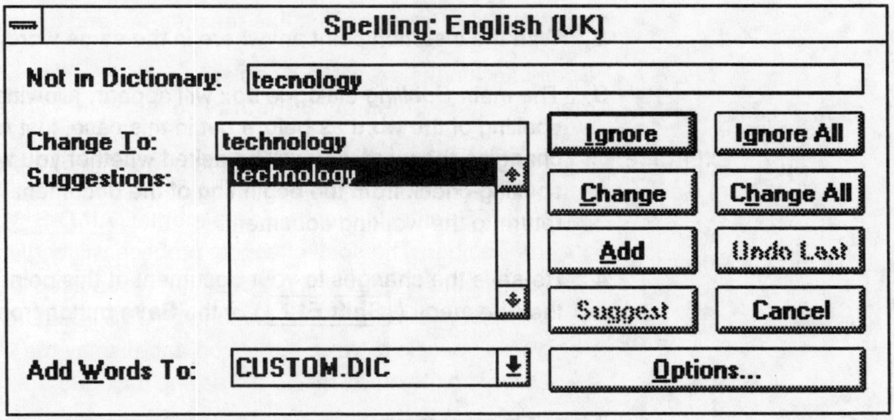

7 Check the spellings in the document in the following ways:

If an unrecognised word with the correct spelling appears in the *Suggestions:* window, either highlight it (point and click) and then select the **Change** command button to change the word in the text, *or* double-click on the correct spelling. The **Change All** command button will change all similar occurrences throughout the document.

If the word is correctly spelt but is not recognised, you have the option of saving the word in the supplemental (personal) dictionary. To add a word to this dictionary for future reference by the spell-checking program, select the **Add** command button.

If the word is correctly spelt but you do not wish to save it in the user dictionary (it might be a name of a person for example), then you may select the **Ignore** command button to bypass the word. Alternatively, you may select the **Ignore All** command button to ignore all similar occurrences throughout the document.

You may wish to change the spelling of a word manually by typing text into the *Change To:* text box.

Should you make an error at any point, you may select the **Undo Last** command button to undo the last operation.

You may exit from the spell-checking facility at any time by selecting the **Cancel** button.

Spell-checking individual words

Word for Windows provides a quick method of checking the spelling of an individual word, rather than the spellings throughout the document. The spelling key (F7) is used to activate this facility.

EXERCISE

1 Edit any word in the text so that it is incorrectly spelt.

2 With the insertion point anywhere in the same word, press F7.

3 The main *Spelling* dialogue box will appear, allowing you to change the spelling of the word as before but in this case, just for the one word. After changing the word, you will be asked whether you wish to continue the spelling-check from the beginning of the document. Cancel the prompt to return to the working document.

4 Re-save the changes to your document at this point by selecting **Save** from the **File** menu (Shift F12) *or* the **Save** button from the Toolbar.

4.6 The Thesaurus

The process of editing text may be further assisted by the use of the Thesaurus facility. This allows you to look up words which have a similar meaning (*synonyms*) to another word. In addition, word meanings, related words and *antonyms* (opposite meanings) may be easily found.

As with the *Spelling* dialogue box on page 42, the *Thesaurus* dialogue box may be moved around the screen if necessary by dragging the Title bar.

EXERCISE

1 Using the same document **MONTHS.DOC**, move to the beginning of the text for April.

2 Move the insertion point somewhere into the word 'headstrong' in the first line of the first paragraph for April.

3 Select **Thesaurus** from the **Tools** menu (Shift F7).

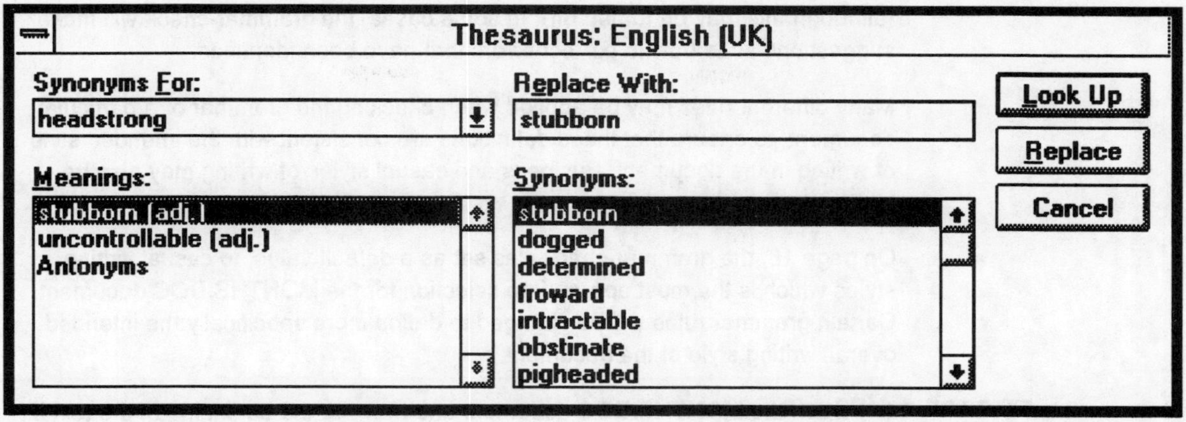

The *Synonyms:* box in the *Thesaurus* dialogue boxshows alternative words for headstrong which have a similar meaning.

Sometimes a word may have several meanings and these will all be displayed in the *Meanings:* box.

4 With 'stubborn' as an adjective highlighted in the *Meanings:* box, 'look up' the synonyms of 'stubborn' by either double-clicking on it, or by pointing and clicking on it and selecting the **Look Up** command button.

Note that 'Look Up' now displays the word stubborn and seven different definitions (use the Scroll bar if necessary) for the word appear.

5 Activate the *Synonyms For:* drop-down list and select **headstrong** in the list to return to the word headstrong.

6 Experiment with different synonyms.

7 If you find a word that you would prefer in the text rather than headstrong, select the word in the synonyms window and select the **Replace** command button.

You may exit from the *Thesaurus* dialogue box at any time by selecting the **Cancel** command button.

8 Experiment with the Thesaurus facility, using other words in the text.

9 If you have made any changes to the text, re-save the document by selecting **Save** from the **File** menu or the **Save** button in the Toolbar.

4.7 Checking grammar

Word for Windows contains a grammar-checking facility which examines sentences in a document for possible grammatical errors and weak writing styles. Spelling checks are made on the text at the same time as grammar checks (although this may be turned off). In some cases, the grammar-check will make suggestions as to how to correct errors that have been identified.

Many different rules may be applied when checking the grammar of a particular document, to ensure that these definitions are consistent with the intended style of writing in the document. Business and casual styles of writing may also be taken into account.

On page 16, the grammar-check was set as a default value, to casual writing styles which is the most appropriate selection for the MONTHS.DOC document. Certain grammar rules will be changed to define more specifically the intended overall writing style of the document.

EXERCISE

1 Open the **MONTHS.DOC** document and move to the beginning of the text if necessary.

2 Select **Grammar** from the **Tools** command (**Alt O G**) to activate the grammar-checking process. After a short pause, the *Grammar* dialogue box will be displayed with a possible grammar error indicated:

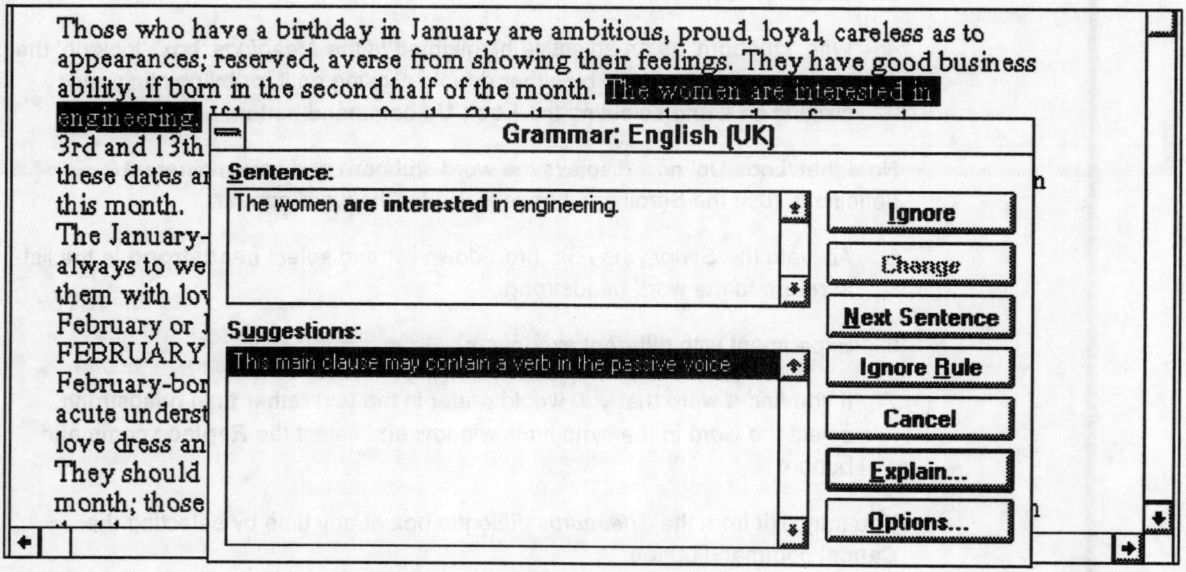

3 Select the **Explain** command button. An information box will be displayed, offering an explanation of the grammatical error:

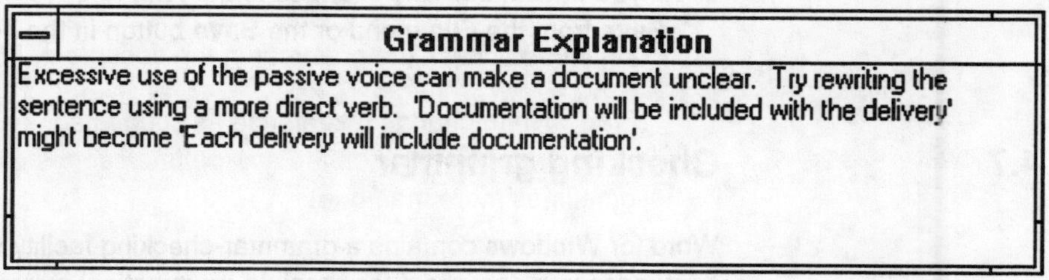

4 Close the information box by double-clicking on its **Control box**.

5 Select the **Options** command button. The *Options* dialogue box, *Category:* **Grammar** will be displayed as seen previously on page 16.

6 Select the **Customize Settings** command button. The following will be displayed:

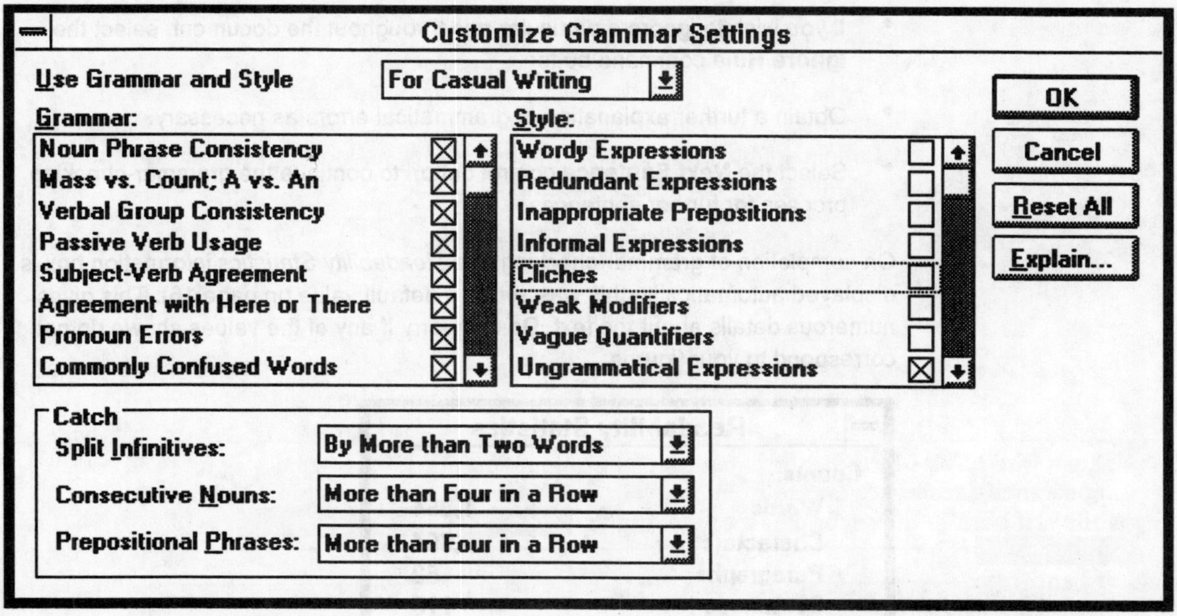

The *Customize Grammar Settings* dialogue box contains a large number of *Grammar:* and *Style:* rules that may be applied to the grammar-checking process. If a check box is selected (it contains a cross), then the appropriate rule will be applied to the text, otherwise it will not. An explanation for a selected rule is available by selecting the **Explain** command button. Other factors affecting sentence construction may also be set in the *Catch:* area of the dialogue box.

7 Examine the various rules that may be applied to the grammar-checking process and obtain explanations where appropriate.

8 De-select the **Spelling Errors** check box in the *Grammar:* area, since you have already carried out a spelling-check on the text.

9 Accept when ready, to return to the *Options* dialogue box and accept again to return to the *Grammar* dialogue box.

10 Continue to check the grammar in the document. For each sentence:

- If you wish to change a sentence as suggested, select the **Change** command button or double-click on the appropriate suggested change (there are sometimes more than one).

- If you wish to type a correction into the document: click inside the document window (Ctrl Tab); edit the text as required; select the **Start** command button that appears inside the *Grammar:* dialogue box *or* select **Grammar** from the **Tools** menu to restart the grammar-checking from the current insertion point position.

- If you wish to ignore the grammatical errors for the current sentence, select the **Ignore** command button.
- If you wish to ignore a particular rule throughout the document, select the **Ignore Rule** command button.
- Obtain a further explanation of grammatical errors as necessary.
- Select the **Next Sentence** control button to continue the grammar-checking process for further sentences.

On completion of grammar-checking, the *Readability Statistics* information box is displayed automatically (this was set as a default value on page 16). This gives numerous details about the text. Do not worry if any of the values shown do not correspond to your figures.

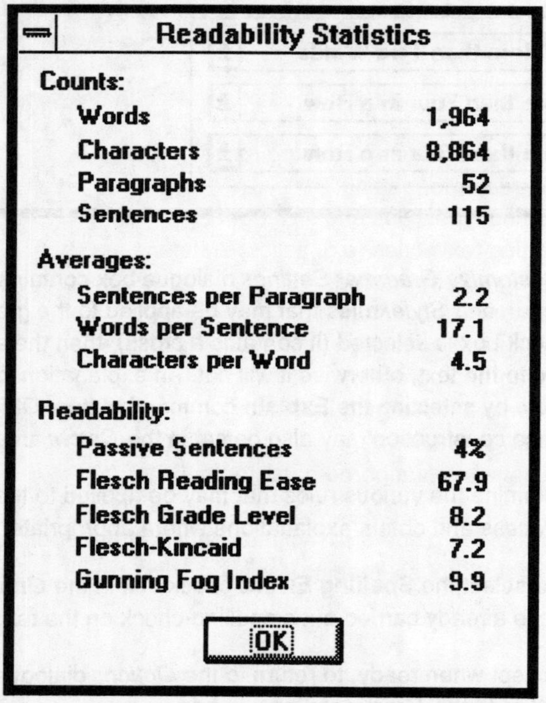

11 With the *Readability Statistics* information box displayed, press F1 to obtain an explanation of each displayed element from the Help system. Close the Help window when ready. Readability scales are also summarised in *Appendix E*.

12 Save the document when ready.

5 Formatting a document

Having now typed and edited the document, you are ready to consider the final and most powerful stage in the wordprocessing sequence, namely formatting.

The formatting process involves the use of a range of tools provided by the wordprocessor for altering the appearance, placement and alignment of text and graphics on the printed page. The formatting tools and functions provided by the Word for Windows program, go far beyond what it is possible to achieve using manual methods or manual and electronic typewriters. In addition, changes can be made easily and efficiently, without the necessity to start again.

In the remaining chapters of Part I of this guide, the basic document formatting facilities are practised, while more advanced formatting functions are encountered in Parts II and III (Intermediate and Advanced levels).

The basic formatting skills to be considered in this section include:

- Setting page size and margins;
- Character formatting;
- Setting typestyles and size (font);
- Setting text styles (e.g. italics, underline etc.);
- Paragraph formatting;
- Paragraph alignment;
- Paragraph spacing;
- Paragraph borders;
- Indents and hanging indents;
- Tabs and tables;
- Bullets and numbered paragraphs (lists);

This part of the guide also includes details of the printing process as well as certain basic 'house-keeping' tasks.

5.1 Setting page size and margins

In this section, you will be setting up the page layout by using the **Page Setup** command found in the **Format** menu (**Alt F U**). This command allows you to change the page size, its orientation (*landscape* or *portrait* as shown below) and the type of paper used in your printer (e.g. cut/single sheets, envelopes, fanfold – sometimes called continuous paper).

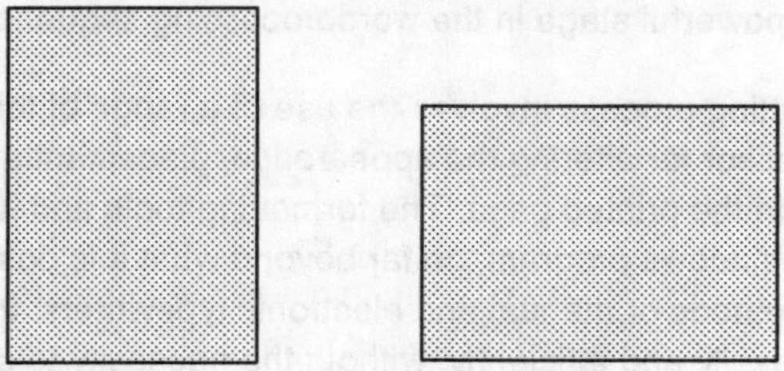

Portrait orientation   Landscape orientation

EXERCISE

1. Open the **MONTHS.DOC** document if necessary and select **Page Setup** from the **Format** menu (**Alt F U**).

   If the following dialogue box does not appear, select the **Margins** check box (*or* press **M**) in the *Select which Page Attributes to Modify* area found towards the top of the dialogue box.

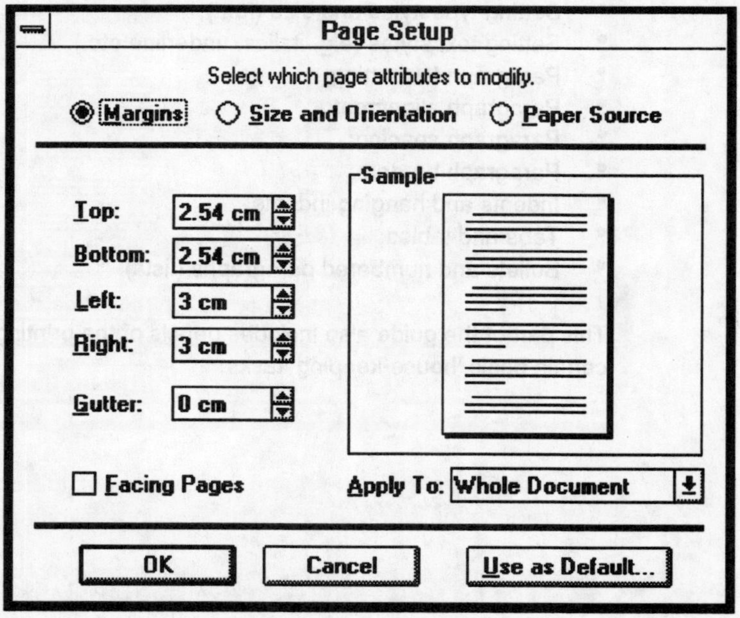

2. Set the values in the dialogue box that appears to those shown above for the *Top:*, *Bottom:*, *Inside:*, and *Outside:* margins. Do **not** press **Enter**.

An example of the page with the currently set margin values will be shown in the *Sample:* area as you alter any margin values.

- To change values with the **mouse**, point to the right of the number in the appropriate box and click to place the text cursor. Use the **Backspace** key to delete unwanted figures and key in the required values (using a full stop to represent a decimal point if necessary).
- Alternatively with the **keyboard**, press **Alt** followed by the underlined letter for the option as you have done before (the current value for the selected option will be highlighted). Type the new value (the centimetre units will be assumed, therefore there is no need to type 'cm' after the value).

This will set up a page with 2.54 cm (2.54cm is the equivalent of one inch) margins at the top and bottom and 3.00cm left and right margins on the page. Accept when ready.

The *Gutter:* margin represents additional space left towards the edge of a page near to where pages might be bound together.

3 Select the **Size and Orientation** check box found towards the top of the *Page Setup* dialogue box. The following options will be displayed:

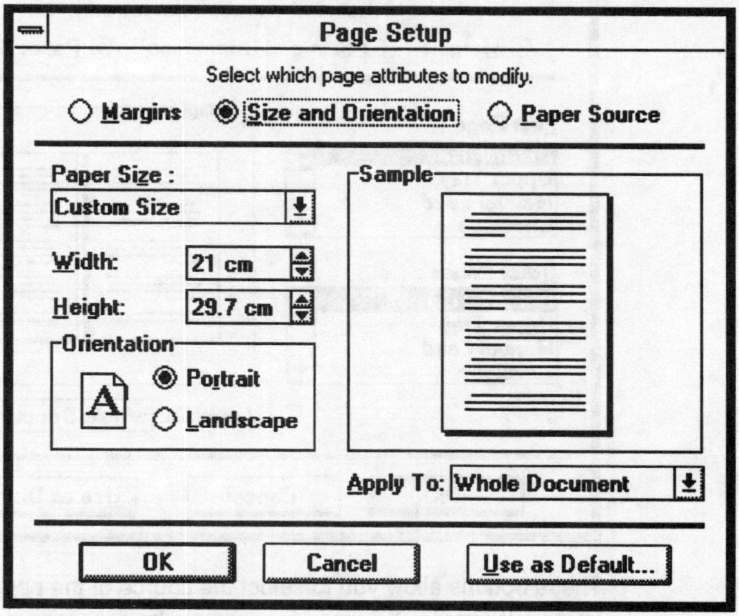

4 Set the *Paper Size:* to **A4** and the *Orientation:* to **Portrait** as shown above by activating the drop-down list for the option as you have done before.

If you are using continuous (fanfold) paper instead of A4 cut sheets, you will still be able to print out your documents sized to A4.

5 Select the **Use as Default** button. The information box shown on the next page will be displayed.

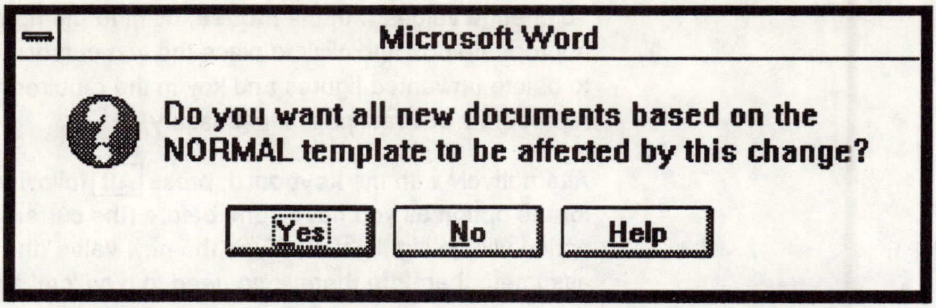

6 Select the **Yes** button (accept) to ensure that all subsequent documents are automatically sized to A4 as a default.

7 If necessary, re-display the *Page Setup* dialogue box and select the **Paper Source** checkbox found towards the top of the dialogue box. Similar options to the following will be displayed:

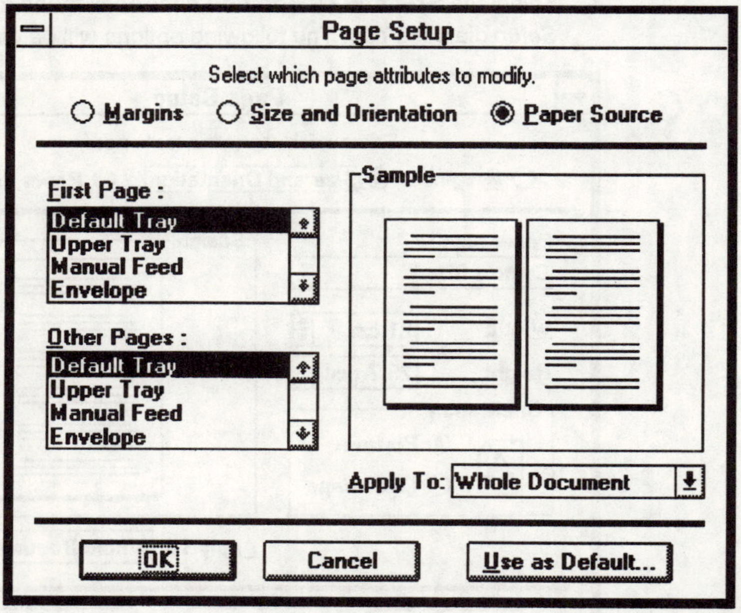

These options allow you to select the source of the paper to be used for printing from your printer. You may for example be preparing a multi-page document which requires letter-headed paper for the first page (from one paper tray) and plain paper for subsequent pages (from another paper tray).

8 Select the same *First Page:* and *Other Pages:* paper source for your printer. If in doubt, select **Default Tray** for both options if necessary.

9 Save the document using **Save** from the **File** menu or use the **Save** button in the Toolbar.

5.2 Printing

Even though little has been done to the document (in terms of formatting), it would be useful at this point to obtain a printout (hard-copy). This will be used for comparison purposes at a later stage.

Print Preview and printing

Before printing, it is useful to be able to have an idea of how the document will actually look. Word for Windows offers a **Printer Preview** function which allows you to see entire pages and their layout.

EXERCISE 1 Go to page 1 of the **MONTHS.DOC** document if necessary.

2 Select **Print Preview** from the **File** menu (**Alt F V**). A whole page view will be displayed as shown below, with the *Print Preview Icon bar* shown towards the top of the screen.

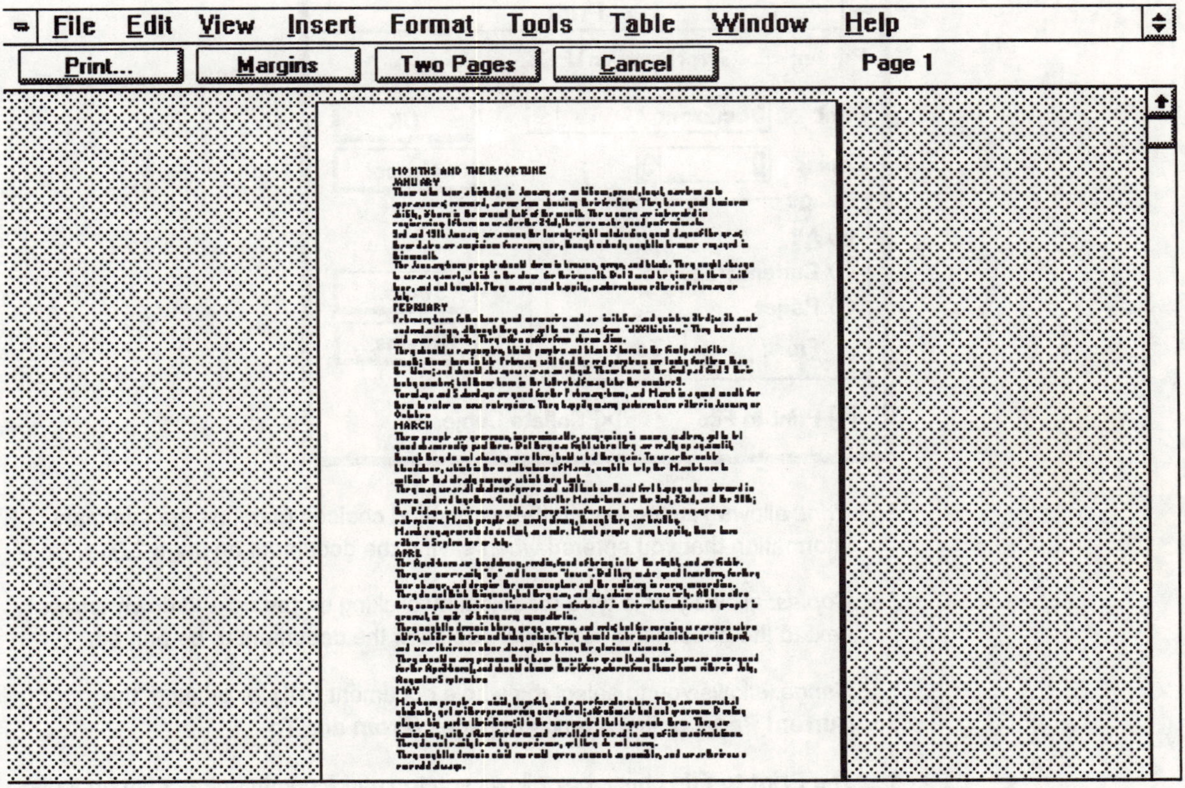

The **Margins** button (*or* press **M**) displays the margins set for the document.

The **Two Pages** button (*or* press **A**) displays two pages of the document at a time (left and right pages). The page number(s) currently on view will be indicated on the right of the Icon bar.

The **Cancel** button (*or* press [C]) will exit from *Print Preview*. Pressing [Esc] will have the same effect.

The **Print** button (*or* press [P]) will display a *Print dialogue* box which may also be accessed via the **Print** command found in the **File** menu.

3 Select the **Two Pages** button (*or* press [A]) to display two pages at a time. Note that the **Two Pages** button has now changed to a **One Page** button.

4 Use the vertical Scroll bar (*or* the [PgUp] and [PgDn] keys) to view the other pages in your document. At this stage, there are likely to be 4, or 5 pages.

5 Examine the options that are available from the 'pull-down' menus in the menu bar. Note that only a small number of options are available. These include commands for: Saving; Printing; returning to other page Views; Formatting the whole document and Repagination.

6 Select the **Print** button (*or* press [P]). A dialogue box will be displayed similar to that shown below:

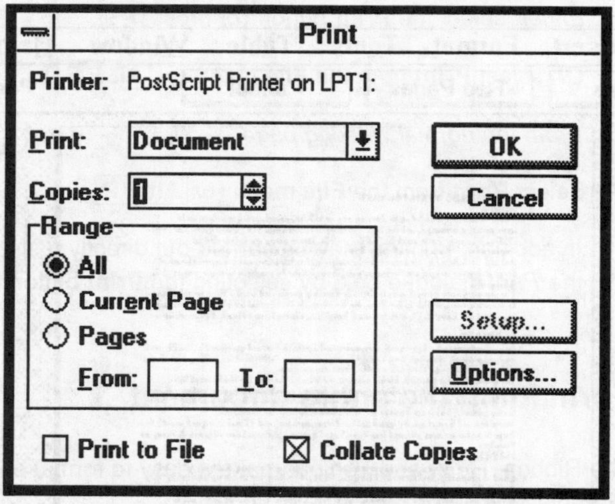

- *Print:* allows you to select different printing choices (e.g. just the summary information that you entered when saving the document on page 27).

- *Copies:* allows you to type (*or* select by clicking on the up and down arrows next to the option) the number of copies of the document to be printed.

- *Range:* allows you to select the whole document (**All**) for printing, the **Current Page,** or just a range of pages (**From** and **To**).

- The **Print to File** check box allows you to send a document to a file on a disk for later printing (or you may wish to transfer it to another program).

- The **Collate Copies** check box instructs the program to print automatically the pages of one copy of the document before printing the next copy.

- The **Options** command button gives the further printing facilities seen previously when setting default values (accessed by selecting the **Options** command from the **Tools** menu).

7 Set the options in the *Print* dialogue box as above and accept, to send the document to the printer.

8 When the printing process is finished you will be returned to **Print Preview** (this may take some time). Select the **Close** button (*or* press [C]) to return to the normal working page.

Printing from the File menu

The *Print* dialogue box may be displayed in the following ways:

- *From Print Preview* ([Alt F V])

  Either: select the **Print** button (*or* press [P]).

  Or: select **Print** from the **File** menu (*or* [Alt F P]).

- *From the normal working page:*

  Select **Print** from the **File** menu (*or* [Alt F P]).

- In addition, printing may be carried out directly, using the current settings in the *Print* dialogue box, by selecting the **Print** button found in the Toolbar:

5.3 Formatting the entire document

The Ribbon, Ruler and Toolbar make it easy to format sections of text. As examples:

- The size of text, measured in *points*, may be quickly changed using the Ribbon. The point is a traditional printers' unit of measurement where one point = 1/72 of an inch.

- The typestyle (**font**) may also be quickly selected for any section of text, again using the Ribbon.

The Ribbon is responsible for simple character formatting (setting the point size, typestyle, underlining etc.) as well as paragraph and tab alignements, while the Ruler is responsible for simple paragraph formatting including the setting of tabs, margins and indents.

Since printers vary enormously in the range of fonts and sizes that they may output, this guide will be restricted to **Tms Rmn** (Times-Roman) and **Helv**

(Helvetica) fonts. If the point sizes mentioned in the text are not available for your system, choose the nearest available value.

Highlighting the whole document

In order to format text, it first needs to be highlighted on the screen. The exercise that follows demonstrates how the font and point size for the whole MONTHS.DOC text may be applied in one operation.

EXERCISE 1 Go to page 1 of the **MONTHS.DOC** document if necessary. Hold down the Ctrl key and click anywhere in the *Selection bar* (*or* Ctrl 5 on the numeric keypad). The Selection bar is the area between the left document window border and the left text margin. The text in the whole document should be highlighted as a result of this operation.

The *Font:*, *Style:* and *Pts:* boxes, being empty in the Ribbon also indicate that the whole text has been selected (highlighted).

Setting character formatting for highlighted text

EXERCISE 1 With the text in the whole document highlighted, point to the arrow (a drop-down list icon) found on the right of the *Font:* text box and click (*or* press Ctrl F and use the up/down cursor control keys to select a font). A list of fonts available for your printer will be displayed. A Scroll bar may be present, as in the example below, depending upon the number of fonts installed in your Windows system.

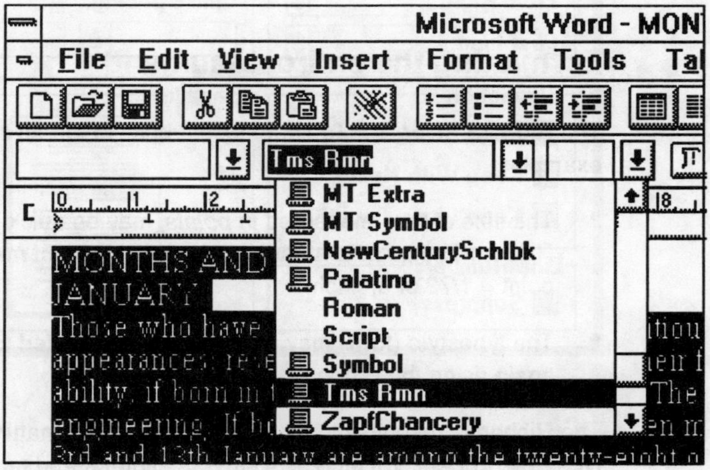

If an icon (depicting a printer) appears to the left of a font (typeface), then this indicates that the font is resident in your printer; otherwise it is an installed Windows system font.

2 Locate and select the **Tms Rmn** (Times-Roman) font, or other if appropriate. If this font had not been selected before, you will note that the text will have changed appearance on the screen (it should also still be highlighted).

3 Point to the arrow found on the right of the *Pts:* text box and click (*or* press **Ctrl P** and use the cursor control keys to scroll through the list). An empty list of font sizes will be displayed with a flashing cursor in the dialogue box.

4 Type **12** into the text box and press **Enter**. The text throughout the document should now be set at Times Roman 12pt.

Setting paragraph spacing for highlighted text

Paragraph spacing refers to the additional space (often referred to as '*white space*') which may be automatically added above or below paragraphs. Paragraph spacing has no effect on the white space between lines of text within paragraphs (known as *line spacing*).

EXERCISE 1 With the entire text still highlighted, select **Paragraph** from the **Format** menu (**Alt T P**). A *Paragraph* dialogue box similar to that shown below will be displayed:

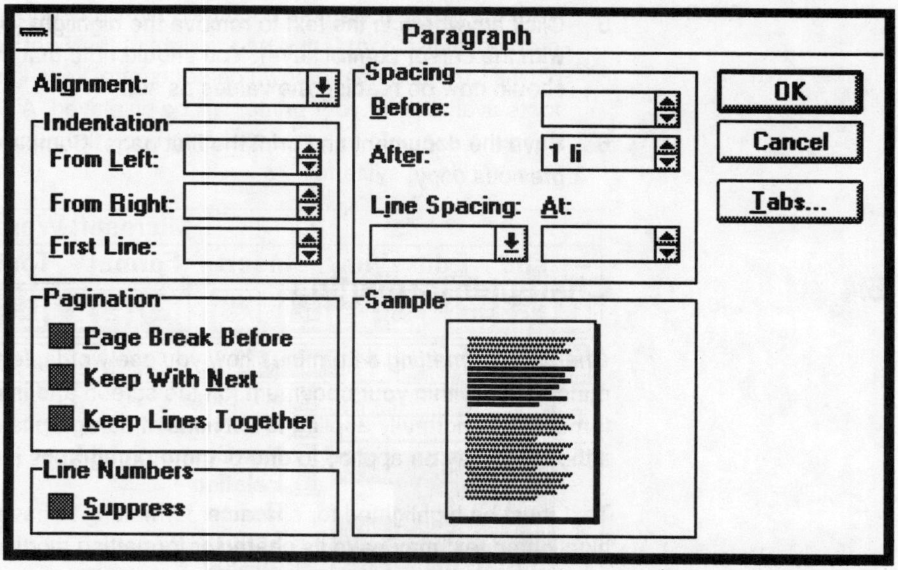

This dialogue box allows you to set: the alignment of paragraphs; line spacing; a range of pagination options; automatic line numbering; and paragraph spacing. For now, you will just consider paragraph spacing.

The *Before:* option refers to the automatic addition of white space above highlighted paragraphs.

The *After:* option refers to the automatic addition of white space below highlighted paragraphs.

In both cases, the amount of white space may be specified using a variety of different measurement units. This is explored later.

Line Spacing: allows you to specify the spacing between lines of text within a paragraph.

2 If using a **mouse**, click on the upwards pointing arrow found to the right of the *After:* text box until **1 li** (one line) appears

If using the **keyboard**, press **Alt E** to select the After: text box and use the **Up** cursor control key until **1 li** (one line) appears in the text box. Alternatively, type **1 li** into the text box.

3 In a similar fashion, set the *Line Spacing:* text box (**Alt I**) to read **Auto**. This sets the minimum height of each line of text to the height of the tallest character in the line.

4 Accept when ready. The highlighted text (the whole document in this case) will be reformatted to include an additional line of white space between (below) paragraphs.

5 Click anywhere in the text to remove the highlight (*or* move the insertion point with the cursor control keys). You should note that the *Font:* and *Pts:* boxes should now be reading the values as set.

6 Save the document and print the first page. Compare this printout with your previous copy.

5.4 Character formatting

Character formatting determines how you see words, letters, numbers and punctuation within your document, on the screen and in print. Character formatting is normally applied to sections of paragraphs (e.g. underlining a word) although it may be applied to one or more paragraphs if required.

Text must be highlighted for character formatting to have an effect. Any highlighted text may have its character formatting modified by setting one or more options from a broad range of possible values. These include the following:

- the font (typestyle);
- point size (height) of the font;
- colour of the font;
- bold, italic, underline, word underline, double underline etc.;
- spacing between characters in words;
- the case of the characters in words.

Character formatting may be applied to highlighted text by using the Ribbon, a menu command or the keyboard. The following exercises explore each of these methods in turn.

Character formatting using the Ribbon

Word for Windows provides a simple, convenient way of setting the most often used character formats of text by selecting appropriate buttons found in the Ribbon.

The various character formatting buttons found in the Ribbon are shown below:

Bold Italics Underline

In the following exercise, sections of paragraphs in the sample text will be reformatted using the buttons found in the Ribbon.

EXERCISE

1 Locate and highlight **'garnet'** in the third paragraph of text for 'January'.

2 Select the **Bold** button (Ctrl B) in the Ribbon, which will embolden the highlighted text. Note that the button in the Ribbon is highlighted, indicating that the highlighted text has been emboldened.

3 Highlight **'browns, greys and black'** in the same paragraph and select the **Italics** button (Ctrl I) from the Ribbon. This button will italicise the highlighted text.

4 Highlight the text **'3rd and 13th January'** in the paragraph above and select the **Underline** button (Ctrl U) in the Ribbon, which will underline the highlighted text. You will later see a **Word Underline** option which would underline any highlighted words as above, but would not include any spaces between words.

5 Select the **Page Layout** command from the **View** menu at this point so that you may more easily see the text arranged onto pages on the screen.

6 For each month on the first page, locate the birth stone and colours of clothing (ignore any special days at this point). Set the appropriate character formatting for each. An example is shown below.

Note: Any character formatting that has been set, may be removed by highlighting the text if necessary and selecting the appropriate button in the Ribbon for a second time. The character formatting buttons work as though they were switches, turning particular character formats on and off. An example is shown on the next page.

7 Save your document using **Save** from the **File** menu (Shift F12 *or* select the **Save** button found in the Toolbar) and print one page.

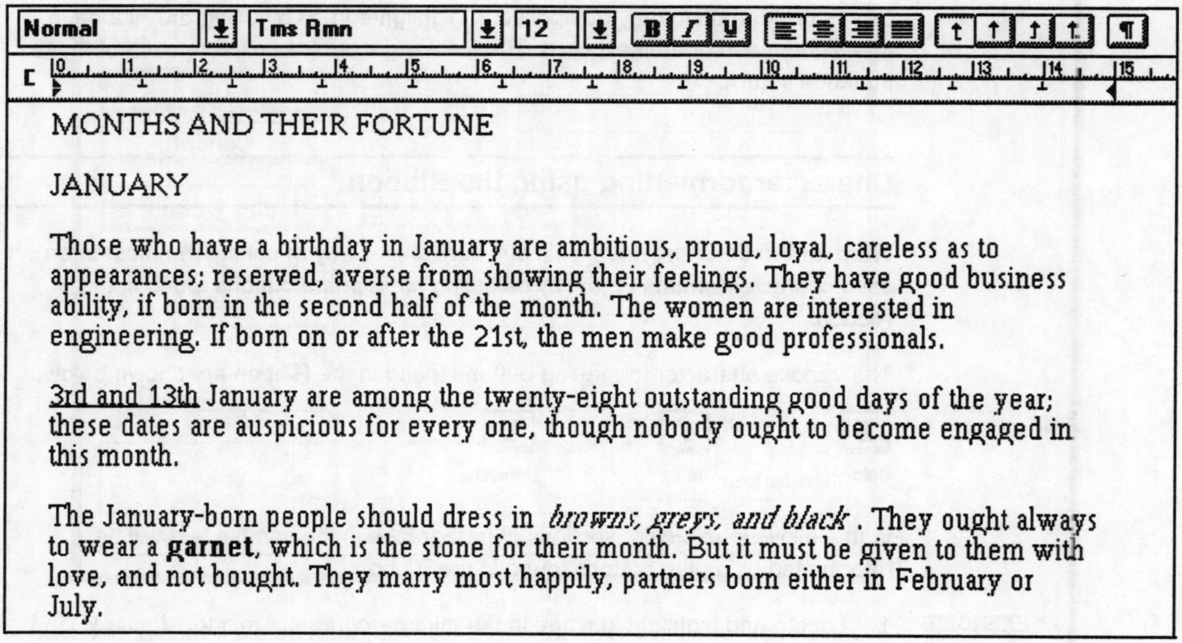

MONTHS AND THEIR FORTUNE

JANUARY

Those who have a birthday in January are ambitious, proud, loyal, careless as to appearances; reserved, averse from showing their feelings. They have good business ability, if born in the second half of the month. The women are interested in engineering. If born on or after the 21st, the men make good professionals.

3rd and 13th January are among the twenty-eight outstanding good days of the year; these dates are auspicious for every one, though nobody ought to become engaged in this month.

The January-born people should dress in *browns, greys, and black* . They ought always to wear a **garnet**, which is the stone for their month. But it must be given to them with love, and not bought. They marry most happily, partners born either in February or July.

8 Take a copy of MONTHS.DOC (using **Save As** from the **File** menu *or* Alt F A *or* F12) and save it on the Samples Disk under the name of **CFORMAT** (for character formatting). Add any comments that you feel are useful in the *Summary Info* dialogue box which appears immediately prior to saving the document on the disk.

Character formatting using a command

The **Character** command found in the **Format** menu (Alt T C) displays the *Character* dialogue box shown on the next page.

Using this dialogue box, it is possible to make numerous changes to the highlighted text at one time. It forms an alternative method (offering more extensive options) of character formatting other than using buttons in the Ribbon.

- The *Font:* text box allows you to select a different font (typestyle).
- The *Points:* text box allows you to set the size (in points) of the font.
- The *Colour:* text box allows you to set the colour for the text.
- The *Style:* area contains a number of check boxes allowing you to select options from a range of text styles.
- The *Underline:* text box allows you to select a style of underlining.
- The *Super/subscript:* text box allows you to set superscript (e.g. ^{super}script, x^2) and subscript text (e.g. $_{sub}$script, H_20).
- The *Spacing:* text box allows you to adjust the space between letters within words.
- The effect of any changes to the character formatting are reflected in an example of the text shown in the *Sample:* area.

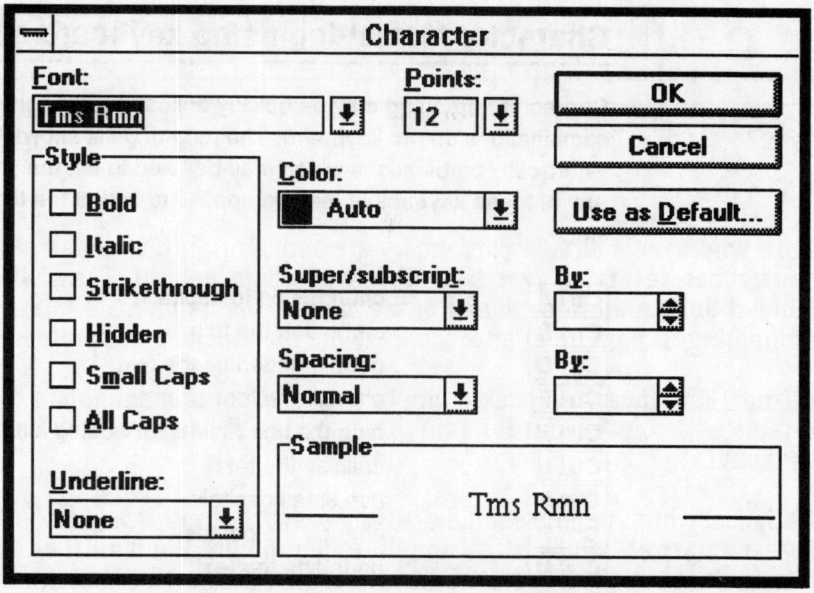

Note: Double clicking anywhere on the Ribbon (apart from a button or text box) will display the *Character* dialogue box.

EXERCISE

1 Highlight the paragraph (the title) at the beginning of the **CFORMAT.DOC** document.,

2 Select **Character** from the **Format** menu (Alt T C *or* double-click on any empty area in the Ribbon). The *Character* dialogue box described above will be displayed.

3 Using this dialogue box, set the text to:

Helv (Alt F and use the up and down cursor control keys to move through the list of available fonts); **14 pts** (Alt P and use the up and down cursor control keys); **Bold** (Alt B); **Double underlined** (Alt U and use the up and down cursor control keys).

Accept when ready.

4 Locate and highlight the underlined text '**3rd and 13th January**' in the section for January.

5 Display the *Character* dialogue box as before and set *Underline:* to be **Words Only**, to word underline the text (i.e. not including spaces between words).

6 Locate any further 'special dates' in the text on page 1 of the document and set **Words Only** for underlining as above.

7 Save the document before moving on using the **Save** command *or* the **Save** button found in the Toolbar.

Character formatting using keyboard quick keys

Character formatting may be quickly applied to highlighted text using key combinations on the keyboard. The following list shows the 'quick key' or 'short-cut' combinations which may be used to set the character formatting of text. Any of these keystrokes may be applied to text at the time of entering, or at a later stage.

Ctrl A	change text to capitals
Ctrl B	embolden the text
Ctrl D	double underline the text
Ctrl F	change the font
Ctrl H	hide the text (useful for adding hidden comments to the text)
Ctrl I	italicise the text
Ctrl K	use small capitals
Ctrl P	change the point size
Ctrl U	underline the text
Ctrl W	word underline the text
Ctrl =	set the text to subscript
Ctrl Shift =	set the text to superscript
Ctrl F2	increase the point size to the next available value
Ctrl Shift F2	decrease the point size to the next available value
Ctrl Spacebar	remove character formatting and reset to the default values
Shift F3	change the case of the characters

EXERCISE

1. Move to page 2 of the **CFORMAT.DOC** document.
2. Use the appropriate quick keys to embolden the birthstones in the text for each month on the page.
3. Italicise the colours of clothing within the text on the page using the appropriate quick keys.
4. Word underline any special dates in the same text using the appropriate quick keys.
5. For practice, set the formatting of similar sections of text in the remaining pages of the document, using any of the three methods of setting character formatting.
6. Save the document when ready (use **Save As** from the **File** menu , *or* Alt F A , *or* F12), under the new name of **PFORMAT** on the Samples Disk in drive A:.
7. Re-save this document (use **Save As** again) under the name of **EXPMNT** (for experiment) on drive A:.

5.5 Paragraph formatting

Paragraph formatting affects the appearance of whole paragraphs. A paragraph consists of one or more sentences (or lines). You instruct Word for Windows to end one paragraph and start a new one whenever you press the **Enter** key in your text.

The paragraph formatting facilities provided by the program include:

- aligning paragraphs of text (e.g. left, centre, right, justify);
- indenting paragraphs of text;
- setting tabs;
- setting line spacing within paragraphs as well as above and below paragraphs;
- setting borders around paragraphs;
- adding shading to paragraphs;
- automatically placing bullets before paragraphs (such as this paragraph);
- automatically numbering paragraphs.

For paragraph formatting to take effect, the insertion point should be placed anywhere inside the paragraph to be modified, or the paragraph (or group of paragraphs) should be highlighted.

As with character formatting, paragraph formatting may be activated by use of buttons found in the Ribbon, the **Paragraph** command found in the **Format** menu or by use of the keyboard. In addition, the Ruler and the Toolbar may be used for some paragraph formatting operations.

Paragraph alignment

Individual, or groups of paragraphs may be aligned in four basic ways:

- *Left aligned* – the text is aligned on the left margin, leaving a ragged right edge.

- *Centre aligned* – the text is centred between the left and right margins.

- *Right aligned* – the text is aligned on the right margin, leaving a ragged left edge.

- *Justified alignment* – both left and right edges are aligned on the left and right margins respectively.

The following exercise illustrates methods of setting paragraph alignment.

Paragraph alignment using the Ribbon

The buttons in the Ribbon provide a simple method of affecting paragraph alignment (and tabs). The functions of the Ribbon buttons affecting paragraph formatting are shown below:

Left alignment

Centre alignment

Right alignment

Justified alignment

Left tab

Centre tab

Right tab

Decimal tab

Display/hide hidden characters

EXERCISE

1 Load the **PFORMAT.DOC** document and move to the top of page 1 if necessary.

2 Highlight the heading **'Months and their Fortune'** at the top of the page.

3 Select the **Centre alignment** button (Ctrl E) to centre the text between the margins.

4 With the same paragraph highlighted, use the Ribbon to set the text to **Helv** (Ctrl F) **18 pts** (Ctrl P) and **bold** (Ctrl B). Move the insertion point to remove the highlight in order to see the effect on the text.

MONTHS AND THEIR FORTUNE

JANUARY

Those who have a birthday in January are ambitious, proud, loyal, careless as to appearances; reserved, averse from showing their feelings. They have good business ability, if born in the second half of the month. The men are interested in engineering. If born on or after the 21st, the women make good professionals.

<u>3rd</u> and <u>13th</u> <u>January</u> are among the twenty-eight outstanding good days of the year; these dates are auspicious for every one, though nobody ought to become engaged in this month.

The January-born people should dress in *browns, greys, and black* . They ought always to wear a **garnet**, which is the stone for their month. But it must be given to them with love,

5 Highlight the sub-heading '**January**' on the line below the main heading.

6 Select the **Right alignment** button (**Ctrl R**) on the Ribbon to right justify the text.

7 With the same paragraph highlighted, use the Ribbon and the *Paragraph* dialogue box to set the text to **Helv 14 pts** and **double underlined** (**Ctrl D**).

8 Move the insertion point anywhere within the first paragraph of text under the heading for January.

9 Select the **Justified alignment** button (**Ctrl J**). The whole paragraph should be justified (compare the right edge with other similar paragraphs which are left aligned).

Note: Paragraph alignment may be set when the paragraph is highlighted or if the insertion point is somewhere within it. However, character formatting may be accomplished only when the text is highlighted.

Paragraph alignment using a command

EXERCISE

1 Locate and highlight the heading '**February**' in the **PFORMAT.DOC** text.

2 Select **Paragraph** from the **Format** menu (**Alt T P**). The *Paragraph* dialogue box seen previously on page 57 will be displayed.

3 You will return to this dialogue box in later exercises, but for now, select **Right** in the *Alignment:* text box (**Alt G**) and accept. The highlighted text should now be right aligned. This is an alternative (offering more extensive options) method to using the buttons in the Ribbon.

Note: double-clicking anywhere on the upper half of the Ruler (where the units are found) will display the *Paragraph* dialogue box.

Paragraph alignment using quick keys

The following quick keys may be used to set the alignment of paragraphs:

Ctrl L	Left alignment
Ctrl E	Centre alignment
Ctrl R	Right alignment
Ctrl J	Justified alignment

Paragraph spacing

As with paragraph alignment, paragraph spacing may be accomplished as seen on page 57 by using the *Paragraph* dialogue box (**Paragraph** from the **Format** menu *or* **Alt T P**, *or* double-click on the upper half of the Ruler). The **Spacing** area within this dialogue box allows you to change the automatic spacing *Before:* (above) and *After:* (below) selected paragraphs and allows the spacing (*Line Spacing:* which is often called *leading*) between lines of text within a paragraph.

Values may be entered into the *Spacing* text boxes using any of the following units: **li** (lines); **pt** (points); **cm** (centimetres); **in** (inches).

The spacing below paragraphs was set for the whole document on page 58. The following exercise gives further practice with the additional options available for paragraph and line spacing.

EXERCISE

1 Open the **EXPMNT.DOC** document if necessary.

2 Move the insertion point anywhere inside a paragraph of text (do not choose a heading).

3 Display the *Paragraph* dialogue box.

4 Select **1.5** Lines from the *Line Spacing:* drop-down list (**Alt I**). Note that the *Sample* area in the dialogue box reflects this change.

5 Accept when ready to return to the working document. Note that the lines of text within the paragraph containing the insertion point are now more widely spaced.

6 Select **Double** from the *Line Spacing:* drop down list in the *Paragraph* dialogue box and accept. Note that the lines of text within the paragraph are more widely spaced.

7 In the same fashion, select **Single** from the *Line Spacing:* drop-down list in the *Paragraph* dialogue box and accept. Note that the text has now returned to normal, single spacing.

8 Display the *Paragraph* dialogue box as before.
If using a **mouse**, click on the up and down arrows found to the right of the *At:* text box until **4 li** (four lines) appears.
If using the **keyboard**, activate the *At:* text box (**Alt A**) and *either* use the **Up** and **Down** cursor control keys until **4 li** (four lines) appears, *or* type the value.

Note that the contents of the *Line Spacing:* text box changes to read **At Least**.

9 Accept, to return to the document. The line spacing for the paragraph will be set at four lines.

If you require line spacing in excess of two lines (**Double**), then you may enter the required value in the *At:* text box as above.

The *Line Spacing:* options may be summarised as follows:

Auto: the line spacing is automatically adjusted for the largest font (or graphic) in a line.

Single, 1.5 Lines and **Double:** sets the appropriate line spacing, but the program will increase this if necessary to adjust for the largest font (or graphic) within a line.

At Least: sets a minimum line spacing as displayed in the *At:* text box which the program may increase if necessary to adjust for the largest font (or graphic) in a line.

Exactly: sets a specific line spacing which is not adjusted by the program. The use of a larger font within a particular line will result in this case, with the tops of some characters not being displayed.

The units of li (lines) is assumed, but if you wish to use alternative units of measurement, then simply enter the value into the *At:* text box with the chosen units (e.g. 1.5 cm would give a line spacing for the paragraph of one and a half centimetres). This principle also applies to *Before:* and *After:* paragraph spacing.

EXERCISE

1 Load the **EXPMNT.DOC** document if necessary and move the insertion point into any paragraph (not including the main or sub-headings).

2 Set the following spacing using the *Paragraph* dialogue box.

Before: **1.2 cm**
After: **15 pt**
Line Spacing: **.4 in** (0.4 inches)
Accept when ready.

10 Experiment with paragraph spacing using other sections of text. *Remember:*

You may apply paragraph spacing to a single paragraph by moving the insertion point to any position within it.

You may apply paragraph spacing (and formatting) to more than one paragraph at a time – including the whole document – by first highlighting them.

Paragraph borders and shading

Using the **Border** command found in the **Format** menu (Alt T B), it is possible to:

- set sections of text which are outlined automatically with boxes around (with or without a shadow effect), or with lines above, below or to either side;
- set the line style to be used (thin to thick, single and double lines);
- set the colour to be used to display any paragraph border;
- set the background shading pattern and colour of a paragraph.

Box borders

EXERCISE

1. Using the **EXPMNT.DOC** text, locate the section for February.
2. Set the paragraph line spacing to be **Auto**, with **1li** space *After:* each paragraph if necessary.
3. Highlight the paragraphs in this section, not including the heading.
4. Select **Border** from the **Format** menu (Alt T B). The following dialogue box will be displayed:

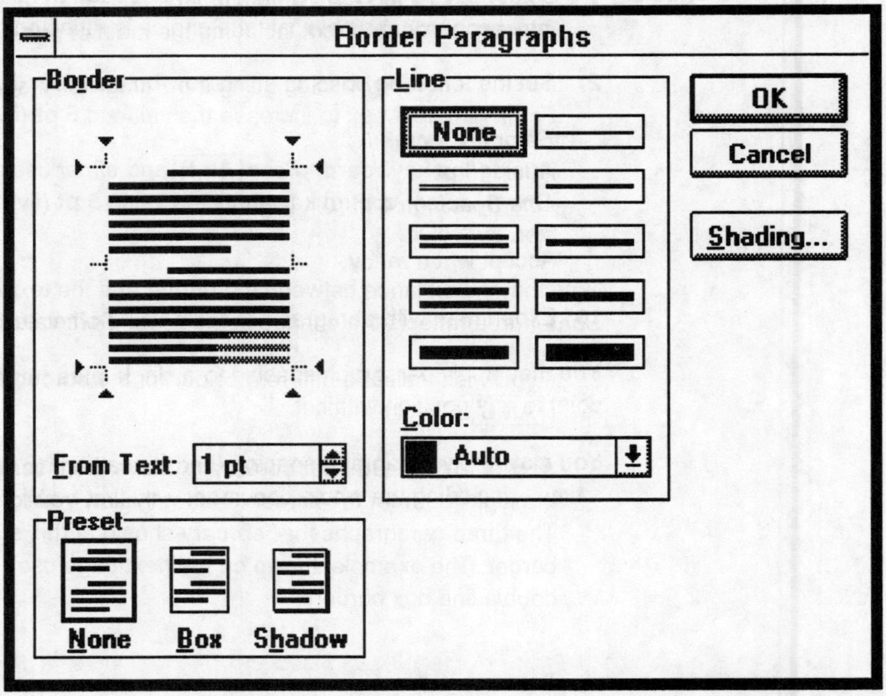

The *Border Paragraphs* dialogue box allows you to effect one or more of five different borders surrounding paragraphs of text: left; right; top; bottom; and between paragraphs (if more than one paragraph is currently highlighted).

The *Line* area (Alt L) allows you to select from a range of single and double line styles of different thicknesses for borders (the **None** option turning a border off). The colour of the border may also be chosen within the *Color:* text box.

The *Preset* area allows you to quickly set a **Box** border (Alt B) or a box border with a **Shadow** effect (Alt S) around highlighted paragraphs with the chosen *Line* style, in one operation. Alternatively, one or more of the five different border positions may be applied to highlighted paragraphs, each with its own *Line* style, using the **None** option (Alt N) in conjunction with the *Border* area.

The *Border* area allows you to select one or more of the five border positions that you require around the highlighted paragraphs. In addition, the distance from the border to the text in the paragraphs (white space) may be set, by altering values inside the *From Text:* text box.

The **Shading** command button displays a *Shading* dialogue box which allows you to set the background shading of the selected text.

5 Select **Box** (Alt B) in the *Preset* area of the *Border Paragraphs* dialogue box. Note that the four borders surrounding the sample paragraphs in the *Sample* area are displayed with a default single, thin *Line* style.

6 Select any other *Line* style (Alt L and use the cursor control keys if using the keyboard) and note that the choice is reflected in the *Border* area.

7 If using a **mouse**, click on the arrow buttons found on the right of the *From Text:* text box to increase the value to **5 pt** (five points).

If using the **keyboard**, press Alt F and *either* use the Up and Down cursor control keys until the value **5 pt** (five points) is displayed, *or* type the value.

Note that the distance between the border and the text in the illustration in the *Border* area reflects the change in the *From Text:* value.

8 If you wish, select a different colour for the border from the *Color:* text box (Alt C).

9 Accept to return to your document. Move the insertion point in order to remove the highlight from the screen. This will allow you to see your text more easily. The three paragraphs for February should at this stage be outlined with a box border. The example shown on the next page uses a medium thickness, double line box border.

FEBRUARY

February-born folks have good memories and are imitative and quick-witted; with acute understandings, although they are apt to run away from "stiff thinking". They love dress and crave authority. They often suffer from rheumatism.

They should wear *purples, bluish purples* and *black* if born in the first part of the month; those born in late February will find the *red purples* more lucky for them than the blues; and should always wear an **amethyst**. Those born in the first part find 3 their lucky number; but those born in the latter half may take the number 9.

Tuesdays and Saturdays are good for the February-born, and March is a good month for them to enter on new enterprises. They happily marry partners born either in January or October.

10 Highlight the same three paragraphs of text for February as before and select **Border** from the **Format** menu to display the *Border Paragraphs* dialogue box again.

11 Select the **Shadow** *Preset* option (Alt S) and note that a shadow border is displayed in the *Border* area for the bottom and right-hand borders.

12 Select an appropriate *Line* style and *Color.* Alter the *From Text:* value and accept to return to view the changes in your document.

13 With the same three paragraphs highlighted, select *Preset* **None** in the *Border Paragraphs* dialogue box. The *Line* style will default to **None**.

The simplest method of removing borders around paragraphs is to highlight the required paragraphs and select the **None** option from the *Preset* area of the *Border Paragraphs* dialogue box. Any borders that have been set, will be removed when you accept.

14 Accept to remove the borders that were previously set.

Selecting borders

You may not want a box or shadowed box completely surrounding one or more paragraphs. The *Border* area of the *Border Paragraphs* dialogue box however, allows you to select one or more of the five possible border positions which you may wish to apply to selected text. This is accomplished by using *either* the **None** *or* **Box** *Preset* option found in the *Border Paragraphs* dialogue box.

The *Border* area of the dialogue box with the **None** *Preset* option set, appears as shown on the next page.

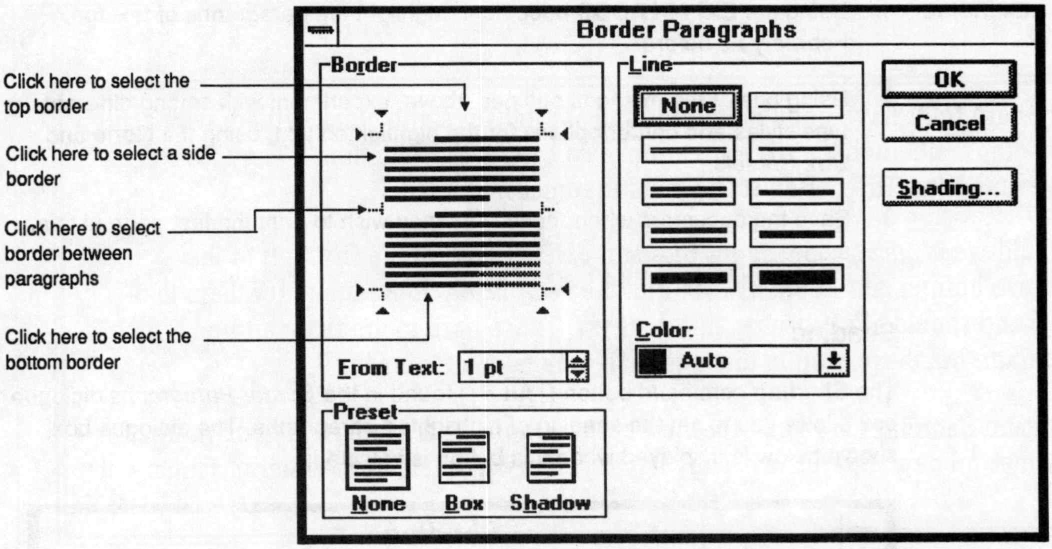

The border markers are used to indicate the currently selected border positions.

Using a **mouse** to set custom borders

- Highlight the required paragraphs.
- Select **Borders** from the **Format** menu.
- Select either **None** *or* **Box** *Preset.*
- Point to the required border in the *Border* area and click.
- Select the appropriate *Line* style.
- Select other borders and *Line* styles as required.
- Accept to complete the operation.

Note: If you wish to set a number of borders with the same *Line* style, you may hold down the **Shift** key while selecting the required borders. Borders between paragraphs in the highlighted text may be selected by pointing at the blank line between the two sample paragraphs in the *Border* area.

Using the **keyboard** to set custom borders

- Highlight the required paragraphs.
- Press **Alt T B** to select **Borders** from the **Format** menu.
- Select either **None** (**Alt N**) *or* **Box** (**Alt B**) *Preset.*
- Press **Alt R** to activate the *Border* area.
- Use the **Up** and **Down** cursor control keys to highlight each border position in turn until the required position is selected.
- Press **Alt L** to activate the *Line* area.
- Use the cursor control keys to make the appropriate *Line* style selection.
- Select other borders and *Line* styles as required.
- Accept to complete the operation and return to the document to view the effect of the changes.

EXERCISE 1 Using the **EXPMNT.DOC** document, highlight the paragraphs of text for February as before.

2 Using one of the methods outlined above, experiment with setting different *Line* styles and border options for the highlighted text, using the **None** and **Box** *Presets*.

3 Save the document when ready. You may wish to print the first page at this stage.

Shading

The **Shading** command button (Alt S) found in the *Border Paragraphs* dialogue box allows you to set the shading of highlighted paragraphs. The dialogue box shown below is displayed when this button is selected:

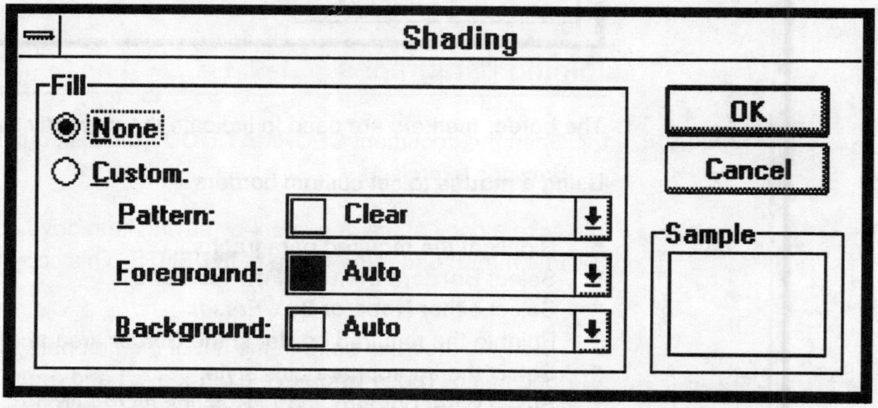

The *Pattern:* (Alt P) text box allows you to select from a wide range of shading intensities (5% to 90%) and shading patterns.

The *Foreground:* (Alt F) and *Background:* (Alt B) text boxes allow you to select from a range of 16 colours. Combining the two colours together allows you to create some special effects.

A sample of the chosen *Shading* selections is displayed in the *Sample* area of the dialogue box.

EXERCISE 1 Using the **EXPMNT.DOC** document, experiment with different *Border* and *Shading* options for different sections of text.

2 Save the document when ready. You may wish to print a sample, or the whole of the document at this stage.

5.6 Paragraph indents

An *indent* affects the spacing between paragraphs, and the left and right margins. In effect, this controls the width (or line lengths) of selected paragraphs.

- A *first line indent* refers to the amount of additional indentation automatically added to the first line of each selected paragraph.
- A *hanging indent* (often called an *outdent*) refers to the first line of selected paragraphs having less of an indent than the remaining lines of text within the paragraphs. This is useful for side headings.

There are four methods of controlling indents and these will be practiced in the following exercises. Which method you ultimately adopt is a matter of personal preference.

Joining paragraphs

EXERCISE

1 Open the document **CFORMAT.DOC** from disk drive A:, which you saved in a previous exercise.

2 Take a copy of the document by saving it on drive A: (use **Save As** from the **File** menu) under the name of **INDENTS**. This copy is to be used in this exercise.

3 Place the insertion point to the left of the first paragraph of text for JANUARY (beginning 'Those who have a birthday..') and press the **Backspace** key to remove the paragraph break (this was inserted in the text when you pressed **Enter** to start a new paragraph). The two paragraphs should join to form one.

If your computer gives a warning beep and will not allow you to delete the paragraph break, then it indicates that you have inadvertently changed the paragraph formatting of either of the two paragraphs that you are intending to join together. The beep essentially warns you that the formatting of the two paragraphs is different in some way. In this case, position the insertion point immediately to the right of the sub-heading 'JANUARY' and press the **Del** key to delete the paragraph break which is found immediately to the right of the insertion point (hidden from view).

4 Insert a space (with the **Spacebar**) between the two joined sections.

Setting indents

Setting indents with the Ruler and keyboard

EXERCISE

1 Highlight the three paragraphs of text for JANUARY in the **INDENTS.DOC** document.

2 Activate the Ruler by pressing **Ctrl Shift F10**. A marker will appear to the left end of the Ruler.

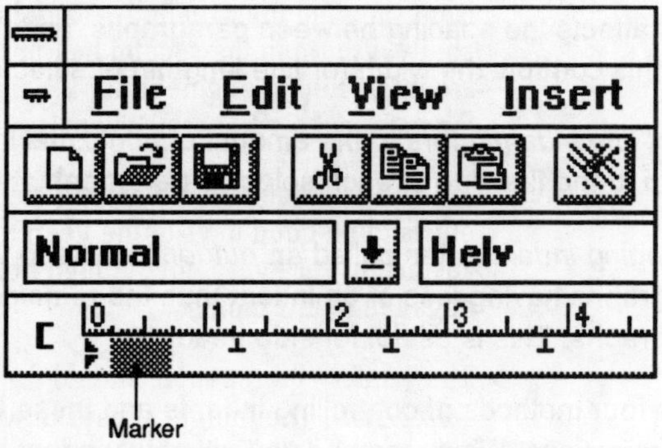

3 Press the right cursor control key until the marker is positioned upon the **3 cm** mark on the Ruler.

4 Press **L** (for left indent). The highlighted paragraphs will be indented from the left by **3 cm**.

5 Press the right cursor control key until the marker on the Ruler lies upon the **14 cm** mark.

6 Press **R** (for right indent). The highlighted paragraphs will be indented from the right by 1cm.

7 Press the left cursor control key until the marker on the Ruler lies upon the **4 cm** mark.

8 Press **F** (for first line indent). The highlighted paragraphs will have their first lines indented by an additional 1cm.

9 Move the marker back to the **3 cm** mark and press **F** again to reset the first line indent to the same value as the left indent. Accept the values by pressing **Enter**. This will also de-activate the Ruler.

10 Remove the highlight by positioning the insertion point anywhere within the first paragraph of text for JANUARY.

11 Activate the Ruler once more (**Ctrl Shift F10**).

12 Set the first line indent for this paragraph to be at **0 cm**, press **F** and then **Enter**. The first line of this paragraph should now be lined up against the left margin.

13 In order to line up the text after the heading 'JANUARY' with the rest of the lines in the paragraph: move the insertion point to the left of the '**T**' in the text beginning 'Those who have a birthday..' and press the **Tab** key. The text to the right of the insertion point will be lined up with the rest of the paragraph, leaving 'JANUARY' as a side heading.

JANUARY Those who have a birthday in January are ambitious, proud, loyal, careless as to appearances; reserved, averse from showing their feelings. They have good business ability, if born in the second half of the month. The women are interested in engineering. If born on or after the 21st, the men make good professionals.

3rd and 13th January are among the twenty-eight outstanding good days of the year; these dates are auspicious for every one, though nobody ought to become engaged in this month.

The January-born people should dress in *browns, greys, and black* . They ought always to wear a **garnet**, which is the stone for their month. But it must be given to them with love, and not bought. They marry most happily, partners born either in February or in July.

14 Highlight the same three paragraphs once more and set the left indent to **0 cm**; right indent to **15 cm**; and first line indent to **0 cm.** This will reset the indents to their original values. Keep the tab character between the heading (January) and the rest of the text that you inserted earlier on pages 21-25.

Setting indents with a command

EXERCISE 1 Highlight the paragraphs for 'JANUARY' in the **INDENTS.DOC** document as before.

2 Select **Paragraph** from the **Format** menu (**Alt T P**). The *Paragraph* dialogue box will be displayed. This will allow you to change left, right and first line indents in one operation.

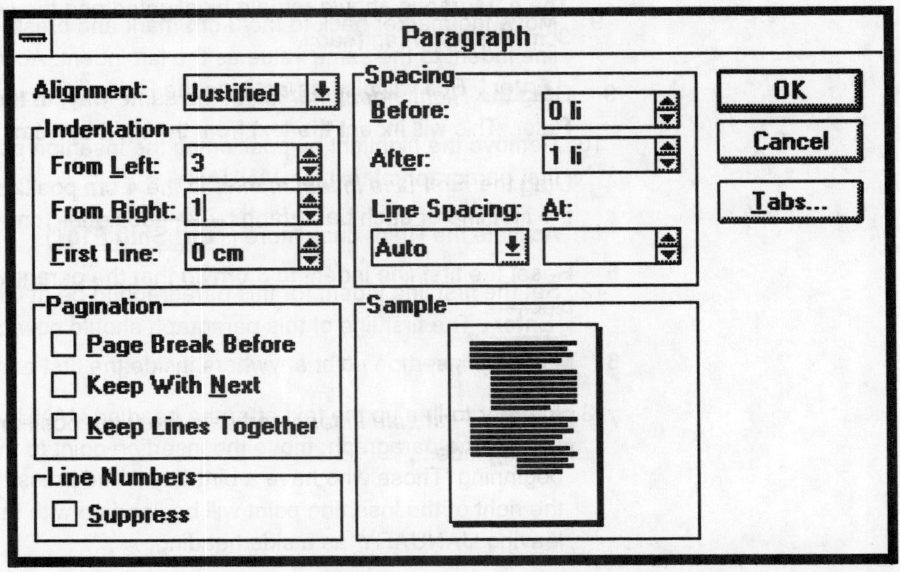

3 Set the *Indentation* values to those shown (the units will default to cm) and accept.

4 Move the insertion point into the first paragraph and select **Paragraph** from the **Format** menu as before.

5 Set the *First Line:* indent to **–3 cm** (minus three) and accept. The selected paragraph should appear with a hanging indent as before.

6 Highlight the three paragraphs as before and reset the indents (using the **Paragraph** command) to their original values (*From Left:* **0cm**; *From Right:* **0cm**; *First Line:* **0cm**).

Setting indents with the Ruler and mouse

If you do not have a mouse attached to your system, move on to the next exercise.

The Ruler contains three markers used for setting indent values:

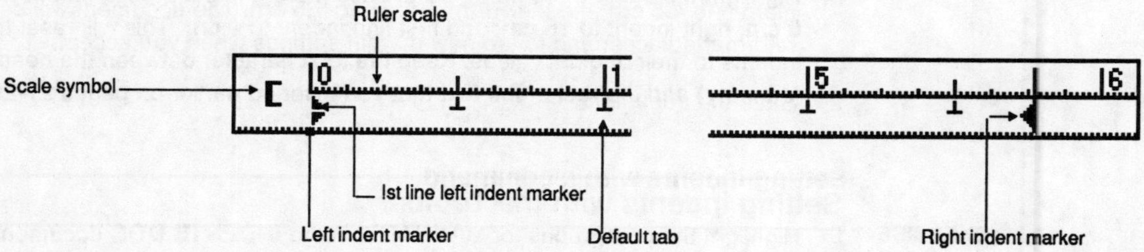

EXERCISE 1 Highlight the same three paragraphs of text for January.

2 Drag (point, click and hold the mouse button in) the *Left indent marker* found to the left of the Ruler, to the **3 cm** position and release the mouse button. The paragraphs should remain highlighted and they should be indented by 3cm. Accept when ready.

3 Drag the *Right indent marker*, in the same way, to the **14 cm** position on the Ruler. This will indent the text from the right by 1cm.

4 Drag the *First Line indent marker* to the **4 cm** position on the Ruler to indent the first line of each paragraph by an additional 1cm.

5 Reset the first line indent to **3 cm** so that the paragraphs are once again blocked.

6 Move the insertion point anywhere inside the first paragraph.

7 Drag the *First Line indent marker* to the **0 cm** position on the Ruler to set a hanging indent.

8 Highlight the three paragraphs as before and reset the indents (using the **Paragraph** command) to their original values (*From Left:* **0cm**; *From Right:* **0cm**; *First Line:* **0cm**).

Setting margins

In the following exercise, you will change the margins for the document. The line length across the page will be longer than the screen can display at one time.

If you are using a mouse and you do not have the horizontal Scroll bar (used for moving left and right across the page) displayed above the Status bar for any reason, select **Options** from the **Tools** menu and set the option to be on.

If you are using the keyboard, the screen will automatically scroll left and right as you move across the page using the cursor control keys.

EXERCISE

1 Select **Page Setup** from the **Format** menu (**Alt T U**) and set the **Left** margin to **4.5 cm** and the **Right** margin to **1.5 cm**. The document will be reformatted according to the new margin settings when you accept.

2 Save the document.

Setting indents with the Toolbar

The Toolbar contains two buttons which allow you to affect the indentation of highlighted text:

- The **Indent** button indents highlighted paragraphs to the next default tab position to the right.

- The **Unindent** button moves highlighted paragraphs so that they are indented to the next tab position to the left. Tabs are explained on page 80.

If you do not have a mouse attached to your system, move on to the next section.

EXERCISE

1 Load the **EXPMNT.DOC** document.

2 Either place the insertion point inside any one paragraph, or highlight a number of paragraphs.

3 Select the **Indent** button and note that the paragraph/s are indented.

4 With the same paragraph(s) selected, use the **Unindent** button to remove the indent.

5 Experiment with these two buttons as you wish.

6 Do not save the document.

Formatting practice

The document produced in the following exercise will be used in subsequent exercises.

EXERCISE

1 Ensure that you have the **Page Layout** view selected from the **View** menu.

2 Highlight the heading 'MONTHS AND THEIR FORTUNE' at the beginning of the INDENTS.DOC document. Set the character formatting to **Helv 18 pt, bold** and **Word Only** underlined using the **Character** command from the **Format** menu.

3 Select **Paragraph** from the **Format** menu (**Alt T P**). Set the line *Spacing After:* the paragraph to **3 li** (3 lines). This will give 3 additional lines of space underneath the heading. Accept when ready.

4 Place the insertion point somewhere inside the first paragraph for January (not the sub-heading).

5 Using your preferred method, set the *First Line Indent* to **–3 cm** (minus 3).

6 For the same paragraph, set the *Right Indent* to the **10 cm** mark on the Ruler.

7 Highlight the sub-heading, 'JANUARY' and set the character formatting to **Helv 12 pt, bold.**

8 Move the insertion point into the second paragraph for January and set the **Left** Indent to **4.5 cm.**

9 Move the insertion point into the third paragraph for January and set the **Left** Indent to **2 cm** and the **Right** Indent to **13 cm.** The text will appear as shown below:

<u>MONTHS</u> <u>AND</u> <u>THEIR</u> <u>FORTUNE</u>

JANUARY Those who have a birthday in January are ambitious, proud, loyal, careless as to appearances; reserved, averse from showing their feelings. They have good business ability, if born in the second half of the month. The women are interested in engineering. If born on or after the 21st, the men make good professionals.

<u>3rd and 13th January</u> are among the twenty-eight out good days of the year; these dates are auspicious for one, though nobody ought to become engaged in this

The January-born people should dress in *browns, greys, and black* . They ought always to wear a **garnet**, which is the stone for their month. But it must be given to them with love, and not bought. They marry most happily, partners born either in February or July.

10 Save the document and print the first page if required.

5.7 Zoom

Using a **Page Layout** or **Normal** view of a document on the screen, it is possible to zoom in for a closer view of part of your document, or zoom out to display more of a page. Zooming in or out does not affect the way in which your document prints and is for your convenience as you edit a document.

The current INDENTS.DOC has a line length which is too long to be displayed on the screen at one time using the current **Page Layout** view. This is because the Word for Windows program uses a default magnification (zoom) level of 100%. The program however, provides two methods of changing the zoom level.

Changing the zoom level with a command

When you select **Zoom** from the **View** menu (**Alt V Z**) the following dialogue box is displayed:

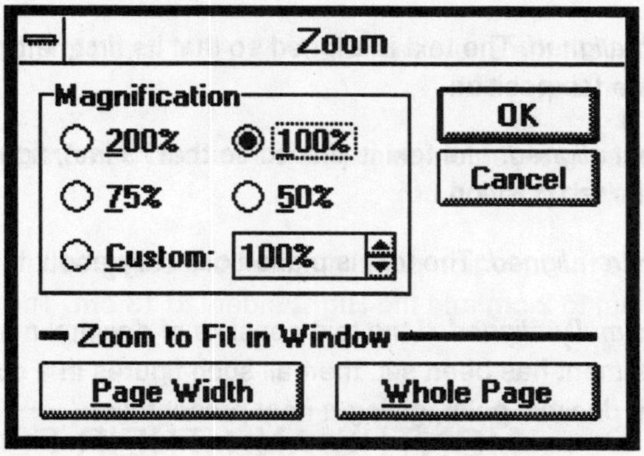

Zoom levels of 200%, 100%, 75% and 50% may be selected conveniently by setting the appropriate check box. Alternatively, the *Custom:* option allows you to set any zoom value of between 25% and 200%.

The **Page Width** command button allows you to view the full width of the document while the **Whole Page** command button allows you to view an entire page on the screen.

Changing the zoom level with the Toolbar

The Toolbar offers three buttons which affect the zoom level of a document. These are shown on the next page.

Zoom whole page Zoom 100% Zoom page width

EXERCISE 1 Using the **INDENTS.DOC** document, experiment with using different **Zoom** levels. Use either of the two methods described above.

5.8 Paragraph tabs

A *tab stop* is used to place and align text across the page. Tab stops are particularly useful for the alignment of individual items of text into columns, forming a table. Word for Windows has a much more advanced facility which may be used for the production of tables. This will be explored in Part III (Advanced) of this guide.

When Word for Windows starts, certain default tabs are set on the Ruler (as indicated by the ┳ sign). You may use these as set, or may change the position and nature of any, or all of them.

The text aligned to a tab stop may be:

- *Left aligned:* The text is aligned so that its first, left-most character is placed at the tab position.
- *Right aligned:* The text is placed so that its last, right-most character is placed at the tab position.
- *Centre aligned:* The text is placed centrally about the tab position.
- *Decimally aligned:* If the text consists of decimal numbers and decimal alignment has been set, then all such figures in a column will be lined up by their decimal point, giving a neat presentation.

Leaders: are characters such as dots, dashes and lines which may be automatically inserted between the end of the text at one Tab position and the beginning of the text at the next tab position. This inclusion in tables may often allow the reader to read across a table more easily since the eye is drawn across the page rather than down.

Text is moved to a tab position using the Tab key which is often marked as ⭾ on the keyboard. When you press this key, a tab character is inserted within the text at that point. This is normally hidden. However, the **Tabs** option, given by selecting **Options** from the **Tools** menu and selecting the *Category:* **View**, will allow you to see where tabs have been placed in the text. Each tab character with this option set will be displayed as an arrow (→).

Setting tabs with the Ruler and keyboard

As with Indents, there are three basic methods of controlling tab stops, which will be explored in the following exercises. Once again, it is very much up to personal preference as to which method/s you adopt.

EXERCISE

1 Open a new document by selecting **New** from the **File** menu (Alt F N).

Accept all the values in the dialogue box which appears. The insertion point should be located at the top-left of the document window.

2 Select **Options** from the **Tools** menu and set **Tabs** and **Paragraph Marks** (in the *Nonprinting Character* area) to be on in the **View** *Category:*. A cross should be present in the appropriate checkboxes. This will allow you to see more easily where you have pressed the Tab and Enter keys (shown on screen as → and ¶ respectively).

Note: Alternatively you may select the **Nonprinting Character** button found on the extreme right of the Ribbon. This will display all the non-printing characters (not usually shown on the screen) in one operation. Selecting the same button again will turn this option off, thus hiding the non-printing characters again as usual.

3 Activate the Ruler by pressing Ctrl Shift F10. The *Rule Cursor* should appear towards the left of the Ruler.

4 Move the *Rule Cursor* to the **4 cm** position on the Ruler by using the Right cursor control key.

5 The tab alignment may be selected by pressing: **1** for left align; **2** for centre align; **3** for right align; and **4** for decimal align. Press **1** for left aligned tab.

6 Press Ins to place the left aligned tab at the Ruler Cursor position (**4 cm**). If you make a mistake in positioning the tab, move the Rule Cursor onto a tab that you wish to delete and press the Del key. This will remove the tab.

7 Place another left aligned tab at **11cm** (use Ins).

8 Press Enter to accept when ready.

9 Set the text to be **Helv 10 pt**. When you enter some text, it will have these attributes.

10 Type in the following text using the tabs as set. Press the Tab key once to move to the next column (tab stop). Press Enter at the end of each line in order to move down to the next line.

Month	Colours	Birth Stone
January	brown, grey, black	Garnet
February	purple, blue-purple, black	Amethyst
March	green, green and red	Bloodstone
April	blue, grey, green, red, white	Diamond
May	emerald green	Emerald
June	red, yellow, white	Agate
July	all colours of the roses	Ruby
August	grey, tomato red, deep yellow	Sardonyx
September	primrose, violet, pale green	Sapphire
October	grey, dark blue, red, red-mauve, pink-red	Opal
November	yellow, gold-brown	Topaz
December	light blue, pink	Turquoise

11 Highlight the first line of the text containing the column headings.

12 Set the text to **Helv 12 pt, bold.**

13 With the same line highlighted, select the **Border** command from the **Format** menu and set a medium thickness *Line:* style below the paragraph (*Preset* should be **None** and the bottom *Border* should be selected). Accept when ready.

14 With the same line highlighted, change the **Right** indent to **13.5 cm**. This will reduce the length of the line under the paragraph.

15 Move the insertion point into the second line.

16 Select the **Paragraph** command from the **Format** menu and set the *Spacing Before:* to **1 li** (one line above the paragraph). Accept.

17 Move the insertion point into the last line of text.

18 Select the **Border** command from the **Format** menu and set a thin *Line:* style below the paragraph (*Preset* should be **None** and the bottom *Border* should be selected). Accept when ready.

19 Change the **Right** indent of this last line to **13.5 cm**. The table should appear as shown on the next page.

20 To avoid confusion in the next exercise, hide the **Tabs** and **Paragraph Marks** by de-selecting them by using the **Options** command from the **Tools** menu. Alternatively, select the **Non-printing Character** button found in the Ribbon.

21 Save the document by selecting **Save As** from the **File** menu (**Alt F A** *or* **F12**). Save the document on the Samples disk in drive A: (as you have done before) using the name **TABS1**. Print the document if required.

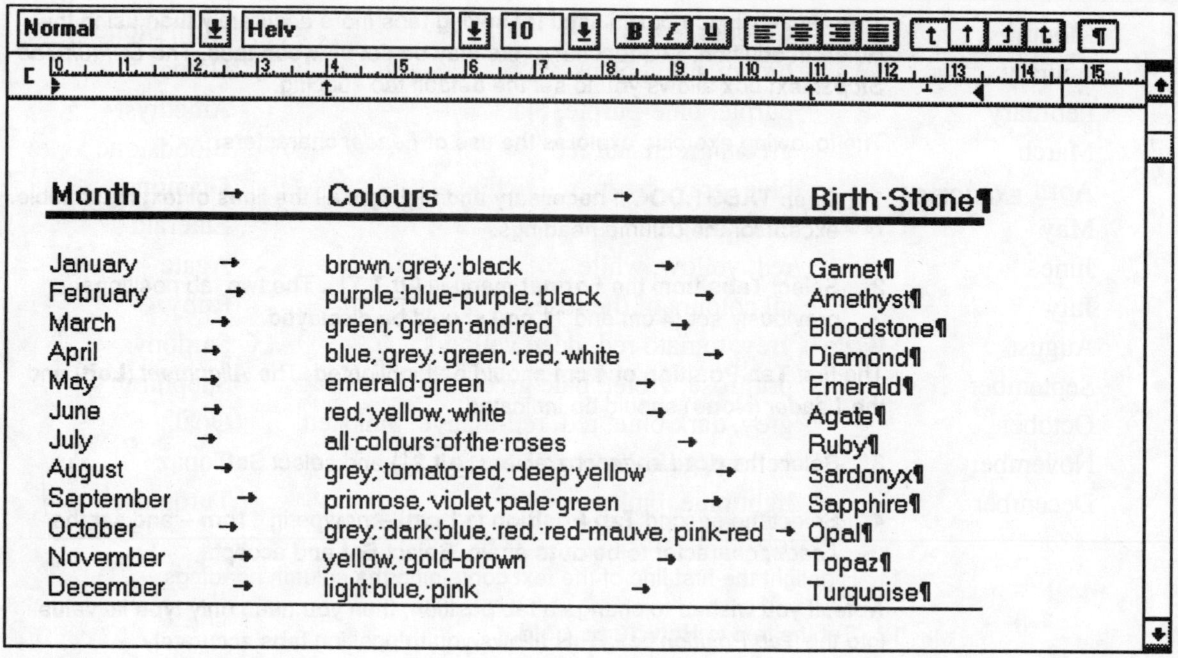

Month	Colours	Birth Stone
January	brown, grey, black	Garnet
February	purple, blue-purple, black	Amethyst
March	green, green and red	Bloodstone
April	blue, grey, green, red, white	Diamond
May	emerald green	Emerald
June	red, yellow, white	Agate
July	all colours of the roses	Ruby
August	grey, tomato red, deep yellow	Sardonyx
September	primrose, violet, pale green	Sapphire
October	grey, dark blue, red, red-mauve, pink-red	Opal
November	yellow, gold-brown	Topaz
December	light blue, pink	Turquoise

Setting tabs with a command

There are two ways of displaying the *Tabs* dialogue box shown below.

Method 1: select **Tabs** from the **Format** menu (**Alt T T**).

Method 2: select **Paragraph** from the **Format** menu (**Alt T P**) and then select the **Tabs** command button (**Alt T**). This will allow you to set up paragraph formatting and tabs in one operation.

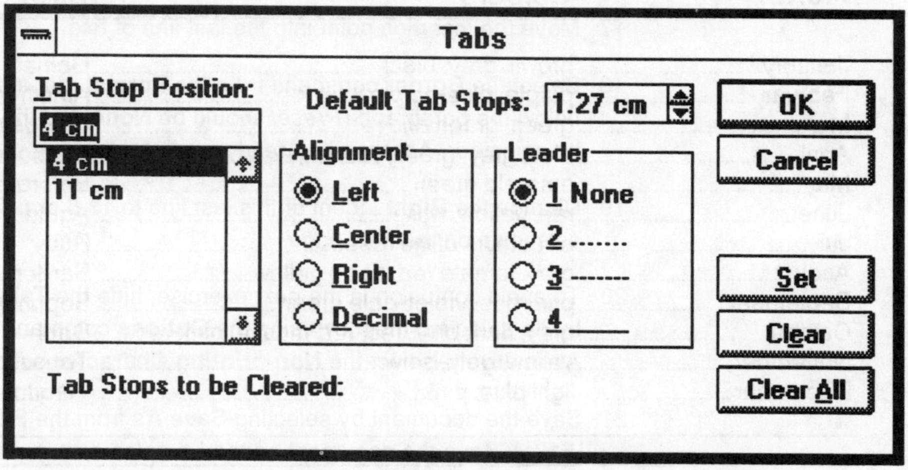

The *Tabs* dialogue box is used for setting tabs more accurately than using the Ruler. In addition, *Leader* characters may be set between tabs. The *Default Tab Stops:* text box allows you to set the default tab spacing.

The following exercise explores the use of *Leader* characters.

EXERCISE 1 Open **TABS1.DOC** if necessary and highlight all the lines of text in the table, except for the column headings.

2 Select **Tabs** from the **Format** menu (**Alt T T**). The two tab positions previously set (4 cm and 11 cm) should be displayed.

The first **Tab Position** of **4 cm** should be highlighted. The *Alignment* (**Left**) and the *Leader* (**None**) should be indicated.

3 Select the **dot** *Leader* character (**Alt 2**) and select **Set**.

4 Select the second **Tab Position** (**11 cm**) – *or* type in **11cm** – and set the *Leader* character to be **dots** again. Select **Set** and accept.

Note: if you wished to change a tab position, then you need only type its value into the *Tab Position* box. This allows you to position tabs accurately.

With Leaders between columns, the single ruled line at the bottom of the table looks unbalanced.

5 Move the insertion point to the end of the last line of text (for December).

6 Select **Border** from the **Format** menu and change the value in the *From Text:* text box to **12 pt**. Accept when ready. This will move the line drawn underneath the paragraph down by 12 points.

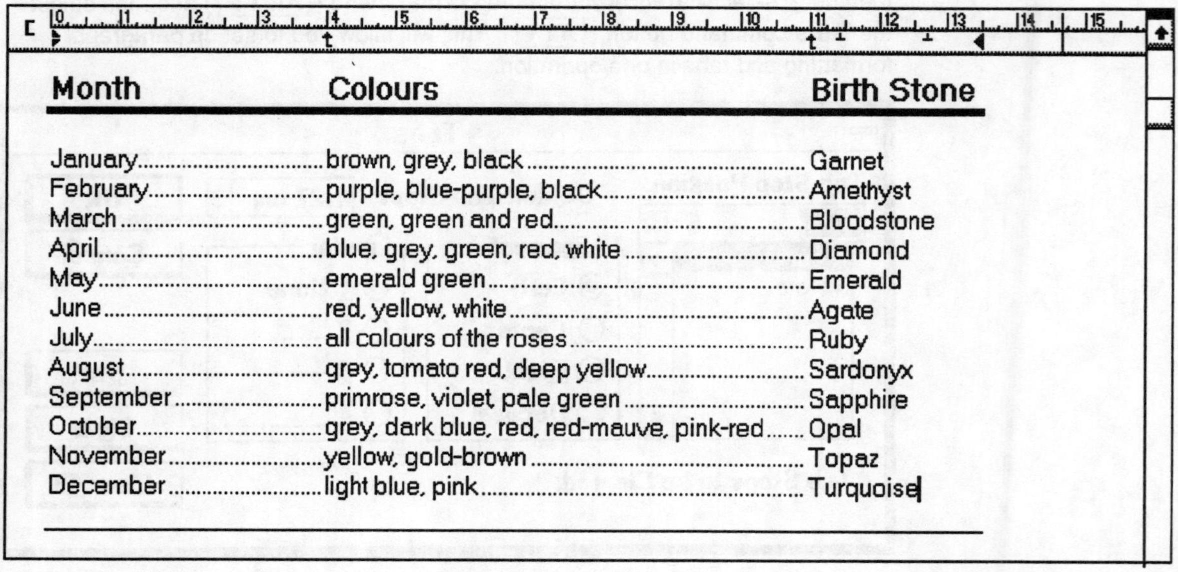

Month	Colours	Birth Stone
January........	brown, grey, black........	Garnet
February........	purple, blue-purple, black........	Amethyst
March........	green, green and red........	Bloodstone
April........	blue, grey, green, red, white........	Diamond
May........	emerald green........	Emerald
June........	red, yellow, white........	Agate
July........	all colours of the roses........	Ruby
August........	grey, tomato red, deep yellow........	Sardonyx
September........	primrose, violet, pale green........	Sapphire
October........	grey, dark blue, red, red-mauve, pink-red........	Opal
November........	yellow, gold-brown........	Topaz
December........	light blue, pink........	Turquoise

7 Save the document on the Samples disk in drive A: using the name of **TABS2** (**Save As** from the **File** menu). Print the document if required.

Setting tabs with the Ruler, Ribbon and mouse

For most applications, the mouse provides the simplest and most efficient way of setting tabs using the Ruler and the Ribbon. However, remember that precise tab measurements and leaders need to be set using a command as on pages 83-84.

- To *move a tab:* drag the tab to be moved to its new position on the Ruler. Release the mouse button to set the new position.

- To *remove a tab:* drag the tab to be removed either above or below the Ruler. Release the mouse button to complete the operation.

- To select a *Tab alignment:* select one of the four alignment buttons found to the right-hand side of the Ribbon.

Left tab Centre tab Right tab Decimal tab

- To *add a tab:* point to the position on the ruler where a new tab is required and click to set the tab in that position.

EXERCISE

1 Open **TABS2.DOC** if necessary and highlight the whole text (including the heading).

2 Drag (point, click and hold the mouse button in) the **Left align** tab icon found on the Ruler at the **4 cm** position to the **3 cm** mark and release the button. The text in column 2 will automatically re-align to the new position.

3 Select the **Centre align** tab button and point at the **10.5 cm** mark on the Ruler. This has placed a centre aligned tab at 10.5 cm. Because this is before the original left aligned tab set at 11 cm, this is now seen as the second tab position while that at 11cm is the third.

The text in column three should now be centred around the tab at 10.5 cm. Note also, that the leaders between columns 2 and 3 have been lost, since this new tab has not had leaders set.

4 Remove the **Centre aligned** tab by dragging the tab icon at **10.5 cm** either upwards or downwards, away from the Ruler.

5 In the same way as above, remove the tab set at **3 cm**. Do not worry if it appears that you have lost some text at this point.

6 Select the **Right align** tab button and place a new tab at the **9 cm** mark on the Ruler (point and click). The text in column 2 will now be right aligned on the tab set at 9 cm.

7 Highlight the lines of text for January to December.

8 Remove the **Left aligned** tab at **11 cm** and place a **Centre aligned** tab at **12 cm.**

9 Set **Leaders** between the columns (the **Tab** command from the **Format** menu). The table should look similar to that shown below.

10 Save the document (using **Save As** from the **File** menu) on the Samples Disk in drive A: using the name of **TABS3**. Print a copy of the document if required.

Month	**Colours**	**Birth Stone**
January	brown, grey, black	Garnet
February	purple, blue-purple, black	Amethyst
March	green, green and red	Bloodstone
April	blue, grey, green, red, white	Diamond
May	emerald green	Emerald
June	red, yellow, white	Agate
July	all colours of the roses	Ruby
August	grey, tomato red, deep yellow	Sardonyx
September	primrose, violet, pale green	Sapphire
October	grey, dark blue, red, red-mauve, pink-red	Opal
November	yellow, gold-brown	Topaz
December	light blue, pink	Turquoise

5.9 Bullets and numbered lists

A *bullet* is a symbol (often called a *dingbat*) placed automatically at the beginning of a paragraph. Its purpose is to draw the reader's attention to a particular section of text. A *numbered list* refers to the automatic numbering of paragraphs or lines within the text. In both cases, it is usual to have either the bullet or number (in the numbered list) organised as a hanging indent.

Word for Windows provides facilities for easily setting bullets or numbered lists using *either* appropriate buttons in the Toolbar *or* using the **Bullets and Numbering** command found in the **Tools** menu.

Setting bullets

EXERCISE 1 Load the **CFORMAT.DOC** document and save it (using the **Save As** command) on the Samples Disk under the name of **BULLETS**.

2 Highlight the main paragraphs for any one of the months.

3 Select the **Bullets and Numbering** command from the **Tools** menu (**Alt O B**). The dialogue box shown below will be displayed.

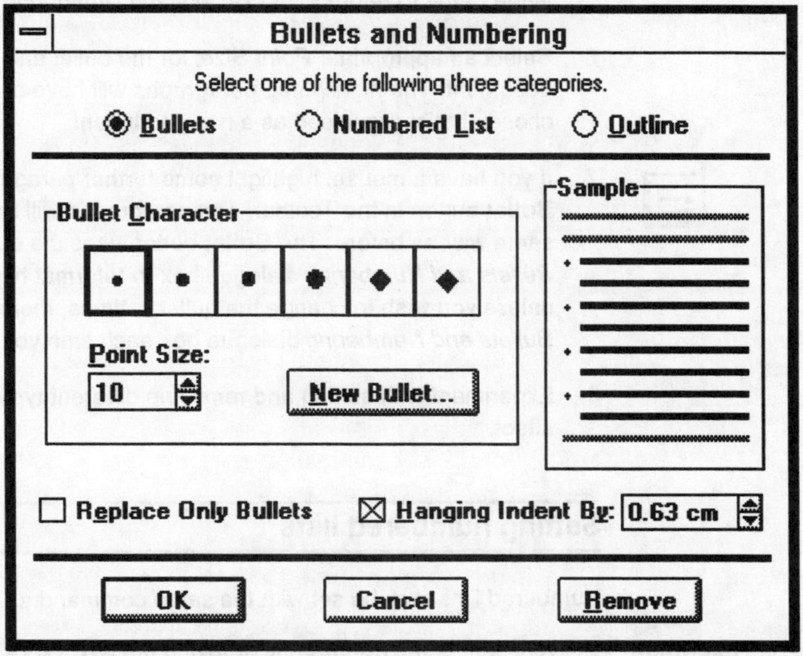

With the **Bullets** check box selected towards the top of the dialogue box, the *Bullet Character* area allows you to select an appropriate symbol for a bullet and its point size. If the required symbol is not displayed, then the **New Bullet** command button will allow you to choose an alternative symbol.

The *Sample* area displays the result of the current selections.

The amount of indentation for the main body of the paragraphs may be altered by changing the value in the *Hanging Indent By:* text box.

The **Remove** command button allows you to remove any bullets from highlighted paragraphs.

4 Select the **New Bullet** command button. The following will be displayed:

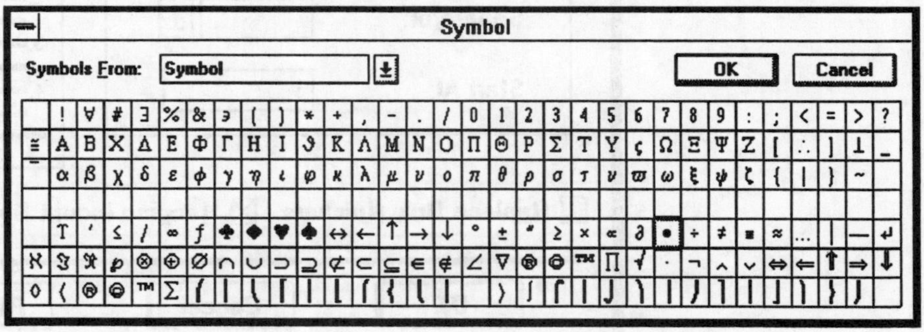

This *Symbol* dialogue box allows you to select alternative bullet symbols from a range of fonts selected in the *Symbols From:* text box.

5 Select an appropriate bullet symbol from the **Symbol** or other font. Accept when ready to return to the *Bullets and Numbering* dialogue box.

6 Select an appropriate *Point Size:* for the bullet and accept to return to the document. The highlighted paragraphs will have been formatted with the chosen bullet organised as a hanging indent.

7 If you have a mouse, highlight some further paragraphs of text and select the **Bullet** button in the Toolbar. The paragraphs will be formatted in exactly the same way as before. The **Bullet** button uses the current settings in the *Bullets and Numbering* dialogue box to reformat highlighted text. Therefore, unless you wish to change the bullet settings, there is no need to return to the *Bullets and Numbering* dialogue box each time you wish to set similar bullets.

8 Experiment with setting and removing different types of bullet to see their effect.

Setting numbered lists

Numbered lists may be set with the same command as bullets.

EXERCISE

1 Highlight some paragraphs of text in the **BULLETS.DOC** document and select the **Bullets and Numbering** command from the **Tools** menu as before.

2 Select the **Numbered List** check box. The dialogue box will change. This is shown below:

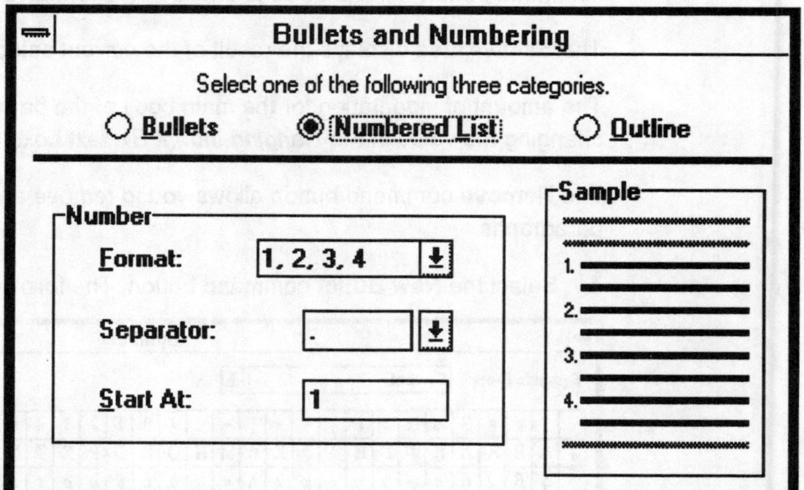

The *Number* area allows you to change the style of numbering (*Format:*).

The *Separator:* (which may be a comma, bracket, full stop or nothing), may also be chosen. This is placed after the automatically generated number with the selected *Format:*.

The starting number for the paragraphs of highlighted text, may be chosen using the *Start At:* text box.

3 Select an appropriate *Format:*, *Separator:* and *Hanging Indent By:* value and accept to see the effect on the document.

4 If you have a mouse, highlight some further paragraphs of text and select the **Numbered List** button in the Toolbar. The paragraphs will be formatted in exactly the same way as before. The **Numbered List** button uses the current settings in the *Bullets and Numbering* dialogue box to reformat highlighted text. Therefore, unless you wish to change the numbered list settings, there is no need to return to the *Bullets and Numbering* dialogue box each time you wish to set similar numbered lists.

5 Experiment with setting and removing different types of numbered list to see their effect.

6 Save the document and print any sections that you wish.

6 'House-keeping'

As you use the Word for Windows program over a period of time, you are likely to create a large number of different types of document. Each document may have undergone a number of revisions.

Locating a particular stored document (or a certain section within a document) that you wish to re-use, copy or delete can be time-consuming. This is particularly the case if you do not keep careful records of the filename, contents, the date the document was prepared, the name of the operator etc., since you will only have the maximum of eight characters for a filename to go on. The filename alone will often not give sufficient information for you to be able to locate a file quickly. Word for Windows however, provides a very flexible facility accessed by selecting **File Find** command found in the **File** menu (**Alt F F**) which allows you to:

- Locate specific documents;
- Search for specific or related documents, including text within documents;
- Delete documents that are no longer required;
- Copy documents to a different disk (and/or directory);
- Preview a document before loading it, so that you may view its contents;
- View and/or edit the summary information (saved with the file) for a document;
- Print a document without loading it;
- Open a document that has been located.

6.1 Summary information

In addition to the **File Find** command, the Word for Windows program provides a **Summary Info** command, also found in the **File** menu (**Alt F I**), which allows you to view (and modify) the summary information of any document which has been loaded. Remember that on page 15, a default value was set (**Prompt for Summary Info** in the **Save** *Category:* accessed by selecting **Options** from the **Tools** menu). This automatically prompts you to enter some summary information about a document prior to saving it for the first time. This information includes the title, subject, author, keywords and any comments associated with the document. Any details entered into the *Summary Info* dialogue box, seen before saving a document, may be used to locate the document at a later point .

In the exercise that follows, the summary information for a particular document will be viewed and modified to include a different comment. This comment will be used to demonstrate file searching facilities in subsequent exercises.

EXERCISE 1 Open the **MONTHS.DOC** document from the Samples Disk.

2 Select **Summary Info** from the **File** menu (**Alt F I**). The *Summary Info* dialogue box will be displayed and it will contain any information that you entered when you first saved the document.

3 Move to the *Keywords:* text box and enter the new keywords of **Original text**. Accept when ready. This text will be used to demonstrate document searching facilities on page 93.

4 Save the document. The new summary information will be saved with the document.

6.2 Sorting files

Sorting filenames (names of documents) into different orders, can often make it easier to locate an individual or group of related files. Word for Windows provides a facility which allows you to change quickly the way in which a list of files stored on a disk is displayed.

When you select **Find File** from the **File** menu, the *Find File* dialogue box shown on the next page, is displayed.

Paths Searched: indicates the disk (and directory) which the program is currently searching. This may be changed to any disk available to your system, using the **Search** command button.

Sorted By: indicates the order in which the names of the files stored on the disk (as shown by *Paths Searched:*) are displayed in the *File Name:* area. The sorting order may be changed by selecting the **Options** command button.

The *File Name:* area contains a list of all the document files on a disk (those with a .DOC file extension as a default), with the first item highlighted. The *Content:* area displays a preview (or other information about the document) of the highlighted file in the *File Name:* area, making it easy to see the contents of the file without needing to load it.

The **Print** command button displays the familiar *Print* dialogue box, allowing you to print any document without needing to first load it.

The **Open** command button allows you to open a document, once it has been located, directly from this dialogue box.

The **Delete** command button allows you to erase a file (which is highlighted in the *File Name:* area) from a disk.

The **Copy** command button allows you to copy a file from one disk or directory, to another.

The **Summary** command button displays the *Summary Info* dialogue box for the currently highlighted document in the *File Name:* area.

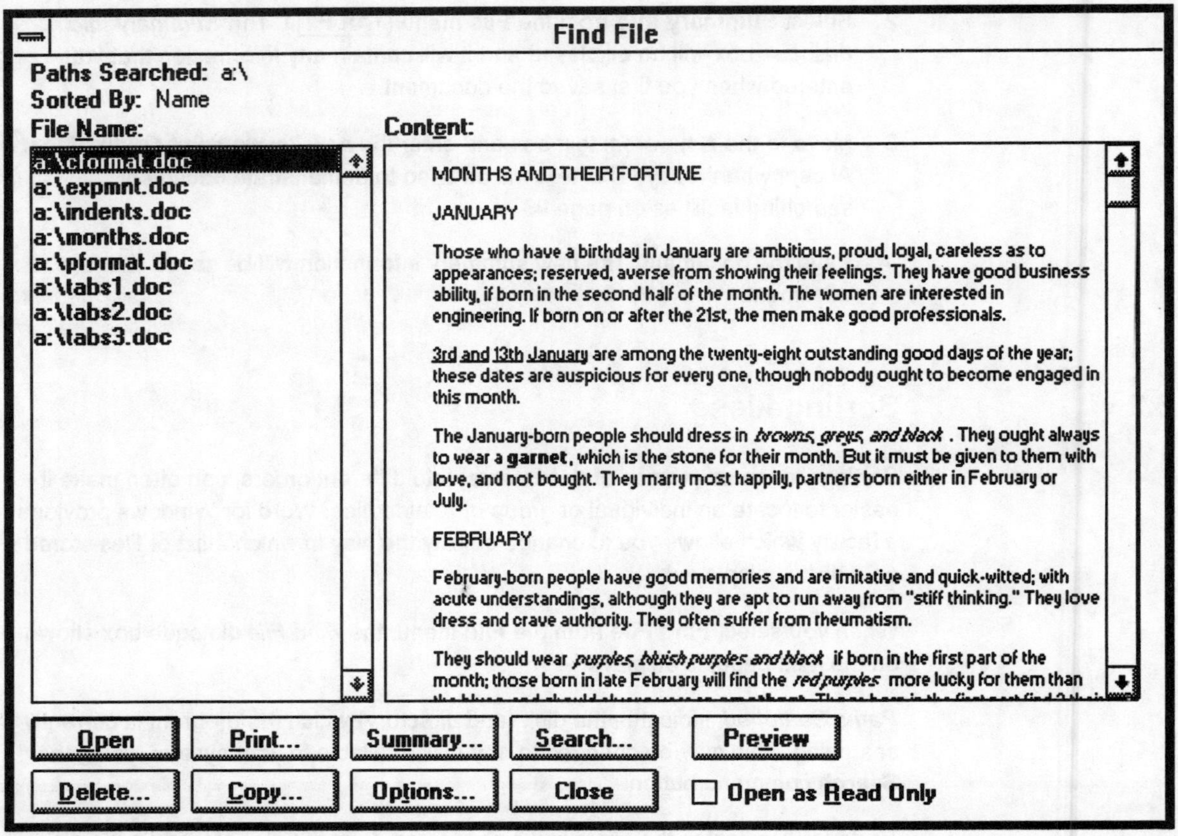

In the following exercise, the sort order (*Sorted By:*) of the files displayed inside the *File Name:* area of the *Find File* dialogue box will be explored.

EXERCISE

1. Select **Find File** from the **File** menu (Alt F F). The *Find File* dialogue box shown above, will be displayed.
2. Select the **Options** command button (Alt T). The following *Options* dialogue box will be displayed:

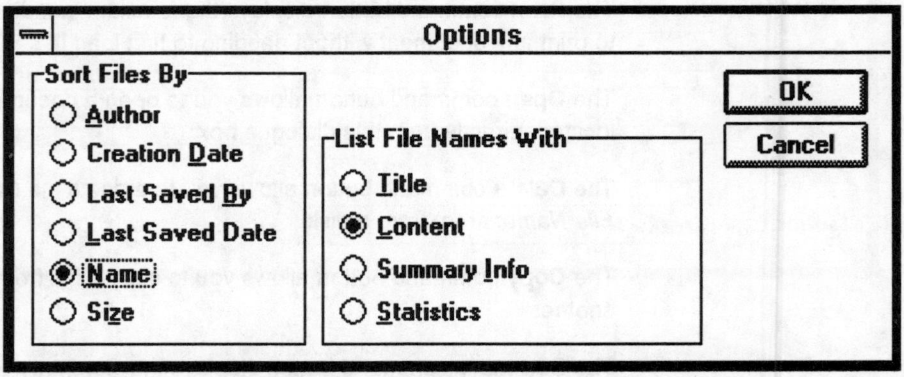

The *Sort Files By* area allows you to change the order by which the names of files are sorted and displayed inside the *File Name:* area of the *Find File* dialogue box.

The *List File Names With* area allows you to select the type of information that is displayed inside the area currently labelled *Content:*, inside the *Find File* dialogue box. As you select a different option, the area inside the *Find File* dialogue box is re-labelled to correspond to the *List File Names With* option.

3 Experiment with different *Sort Files By* and *List File Names With* options from the *Options* dialogue box and see their effect on the *Find File* dialogue box. With different options, the list of files in the *File Name:* area will change their order.

6.3 Searching for documents

The new summary information entered during the exercise on page 91 will be used to locate the MONTHS.DOC document on the Samples Disk.

EXERCISE 1 If necessary, display the *Find File* dialogue box by selecting the **Find File** command from the **File** menu as before.

2 Select the **Search** command button (Alt S). The following *Search* dialogue box will be displayed:

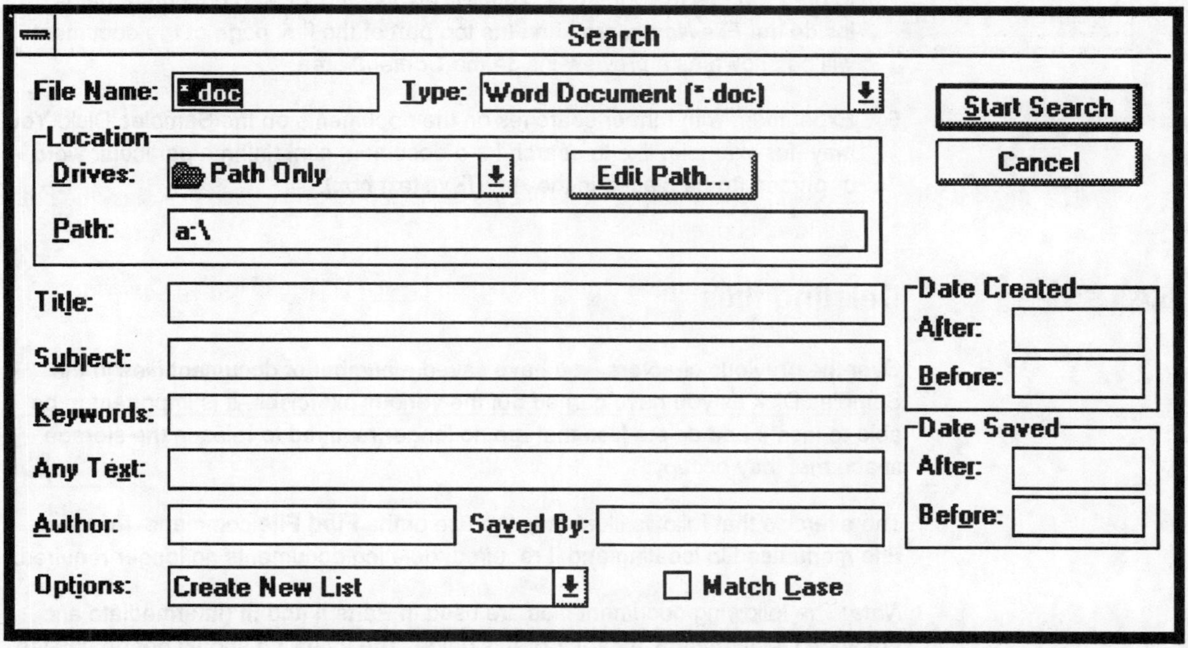

If you know any details about the file or group of files for which you wish to search, appropriate details may be typed into the *Title:*; *Subject:*; *Keywords:*; or

Author: text boxes. In addition, any text within documents for which you wish to search, may be entered into the *Any Text:* text box.

Searching may also be carried out according to the dates on which documents were first created or last saved by entering appropriate dates into the *Date Created* and *Date Saved* areas of the dialogue box.

If you know the filename for which you wish to search, this may be entered into the *File Name:* text box. In addition, the type of file (document, graphic, backup copy etc.) may be selected in the *Type:* text box.

The disk and path (disk and directory) to be searched may be altered inside the *Location* area of the dialogue box.

3 Move to the *Keywords:* text box and type **Original text** (the keywords entered in the *Summary Info* dialogue box in the previous exercise for the MONTHS.DOC document).

4 Ensure that the *Path:* text box reads **a:** (directing the search to the Samples Disk in drive A:). If it does not, *either* type **a:** into the *Path:* text box *or* activate the *Drives:* drop-down list and select **a:** from the list that appears.

5 Select the **Start Search** command button (**Alt S**). The Samples Disk will be searched for any documents that have the keywords 'Original text' in their summary information. After the disk has been searched, you will be returned to the *Find File* dialogue box. This will display the located document name inside the *File Name:* area and the top part of the first page of the document will be shown as a preview inside the *Content:* area.

6 Experiment with further searches on the documents on the Samples Disk. You may, for example, like to search for a document containing a particular word or phrase (to be placed in the *Any Text:* text box).

6.4 Deleting files

Over the previous chapters, you have saved a number of document files to the Samples Disk as you have carried out the various exercises. It is important to be able to locate and delete files that are no longer required to release the storage space that they occupy.

The exercise that follows illustrates the use of the **Find File** command from the **File** menu used in locating and if required, deleting documents no longer required.

Note: The following document files are used in Parts II and III (Intermediate and Advanced levels) and Chapter 7 of this guide. The following should not be deleted if you intend to work through the above.

MONTHS.DOC	CFORMAT.DOC	PFORMAT.DOC
TABS1.DOC	TABS2.DOC	

EXERCISE

1 With the Samples Disk in drive A:, select **Find File** from the **File** menu if necessary.

2 Highlight **TABS3.DOC** in the *File Name:* area.

3 If required, further information may be available by selecting the **Summary** button and, from the *Summary* dialogue box that appears, the **Statistics** button. Return to the *Find File* dialogue box if necessary.

4 Select the **Delete** button (**Alt D**). A message will appear as a double-check before deleting the highlighted file.

5 Select the **Yes** button to delete TABS1.DOC from the Samples Disk (the **No** button would cancel the operation).

6 In the same way as above, delete any other unwanted files from your Samples Disk.

7 Select the **Close** button when ready, to return to the document window.

6.5 Copying files

In Chapter 4, at 4.3, you took the precaution of making a copy of the MONTHS.DOC document and saving it for a second time under the name of MONTHS2.DOC. The **Find File** command however, provides a more convenient method of copying files from one disk (or directory) to another.

To copy a file using the **Find File** command:

- Select **Find File** from the **File** menu.
- Highlight the file in the *File Name:* area that you wish to copy.
- Select the **Copy** command button (**Alt C**) in the *Find File* dialogue box. The *Copy* dialogue box will be displayed as shown on the next page.
- Select the appropriate disk to copy the file to from the *Drives:* drop-down list and select the appropriate directory in the *Directories:* area if necessary. Alternatively type the disk and directory information inside the *Path:* text box.
- Accept to copy the file.

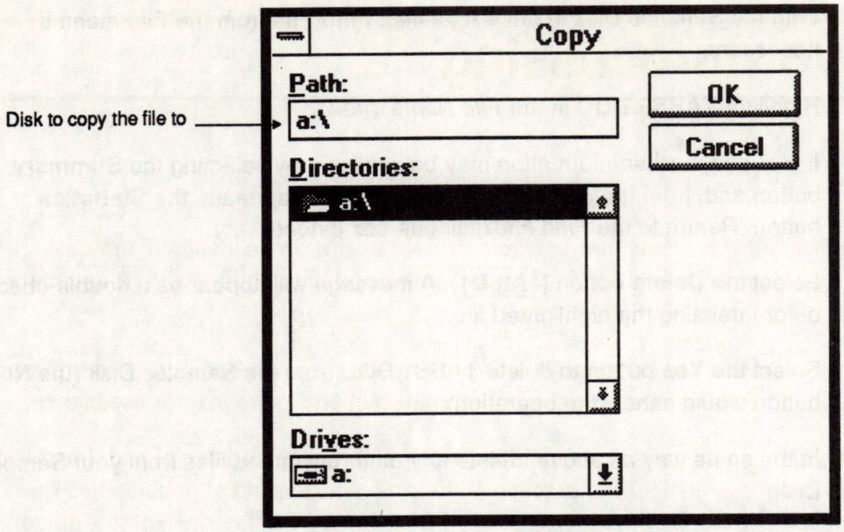
Copy
Path:
a:\
OK
Cancel
Directories:
a:\
Drives:
a:
Disk to copy the file to

7 Wordprocessing

This chapter contains three exercises used for the consolidation of the basic wordprocessing skills and techniques developed throughout Part I (Elementary Level) of this guide.

The exercises are deliberately less prescriptive than has been previously the case. If necessary, refer to the appropriate sections in the text for assistance.

The first two exercises give practice in the entering and editing of text. In addition, the exercises give further practice in the simple formatting of documents. The documents that result, will be used in Part II (Intermediate Level) of this guide.

7.1 Document 1: Memo

The document is to be formatted as shown in the example below:

Memorandum

To: James Tolley
From: Charles Black
Copies: Susan Maye, John Gaunt
Date: (enter today's date)
Subject: Availability of spare parts

Mr. Timpson has agreed to keep a reasonable stock of spare parts at his garage for the majority of makes of car owned by members of the Flying Wheels Motoring Club. He has guaranteed to obtain any spares needed that are out of stock, at two weeks notice.

I would like to discuss this fantastic offer with you. We need to decide how to recompense Mr. Timpson for all his help, without offending him.

Please let me know when you are available, so that we can arrange a meeting as soon as possible.

EXERCISE

1. Open a **New** document and set the page size to **A4** (21cm by 29.7cm) with **3.0 cm** margins all around.

2. Set a **Left** tab at the **2.5 cm** position on the Ruler and set one line (**1 li**) space before the paragraph.

3. Type the following text (inserting a tab character where appropriate) using **Helv** (Helvetica) **12 pt** with a **justified** right-hand margin:

> Memo
>
> To: James Tolley
> From: Charles Black
> Copies: Susan Maye, John Gaunt
> Date: (enter today's date)
> Subject Availability of spare parts
>
> Mr. Timpson has agreed to keep a reasonable stock of spare parts at his garage for the majority of makes of car owned by our members. He has verbally guaranteed to obtain any spares needed that are not in stock, at two weeks notice.
>
> I would like to discuss this fantastic offer with you. We need to decide how to recompense Mr. Timpson for all his help, without offending him.
>
> Please let me know when you are available, so that we can arrange a meeting.

4. Proof-read the text and edit where necessary. Use the Spell-checking facility to help you.

5. Save your document under the name of **MEMO** on your Samples Disk.

6. Load your printer with paper, set to the top of form, check the printer is on-line and print the document.

7. Continue to work with your MEMO document and set the paragraphs beginning with **Memo** to **Subject** so that there is no line space before them **(0 li)**.

8. Indent the last three paragraphs (beginning 'Mr. Timpson..') by **2.5 cm** from the left.

9. Amend the text in the first paragraph to read **'Memorandum'**.

10. Add **'as soon as possible'** to the end of the last paragraph.

11. Locate and delete the word **'verbally'**.

12. Locate and delete the word **'our'**. Add the following to the end of the same sentence (after the word 'members'): **'of the Flying Wheels Motoring Club'**

13. Replace **'not in stock'** with **'out of stock'**

14 Embolden **To:**, **From:**, **Copies:**, **Date:** and **Subject:**.

15 Set the first paragraph to **Tms Rmn 36 pt, bold** and **Italic.**

Draw a double line border (rule) below the same paragraph.

16 Set the line spacing below the paragraph beginning **'Subject:'** to **2** lines.

Draw a single line rule (border) below the same paragraph.

17 Save your amended file and print one copy.

7.2 Document 2: Membership analysis

The document is to be formatted as shown in the example below:

The Flying Wheels Motoring Club

Membership Analysis up to 31st December 1995

	Type of Membership:			
Make of car	**Full**	**Family**	**Junior**	**TOTAL**
Austin `Ruby'	17	6	2	25
Austin 7 `Chummy'	9	3	0	12
Morris Minor Traveller	35	5	0	40
Morris Minor Saloon	99	20	5	124
Morris 8	4	4	2	10
Riley 1.5	16	7	0	23
Jowett Javelin	6	2	0	8
Ford 8	9	4	2	15
Rover 14	10	6	1	17
Social Members				15
New Members	41	6	3	50
Total End 1995	**246**	**57**	**15**	**339**

The annual subscription was increased by 7% over last year, and the Club gained a total income of £14,750 from subscriptions alone. More detailed analysis can be found in the *Accounts* section.

EXERCISE 1 Open a **New** document and set the page size to **A4** (21cm by 29.7cm) with **3.0 cm** margins all around.

2 Set the following **Decimal** tabs on the Ruler: **5.5 cm; 7.5 cm; 9.5 cm; 11.75 cm.**

3 Type the following text (inserting a tab character where appropriate) using **Tms Rmn 10 pt**, with **Left** aligned paragraphs and **single line** spacing:

The Flying Wheels Motoring Club
Membership Analysis up to 31st December 1995
Type of Membership

Make of car	Full	Family	Junior	TOTAL
Austin 'Ruby'	17	6	2	25
Austin 7 'Chummy'	9	3	0	12
Morris Minor Traveller	35	5	0	40
Morris Minor Saloon	100	20	5	125
Morris 8	4	4	2	10
Riley 1.5	16	7	0	23
Jowett Javelin	6	2	0	8
Ford 8	9	4	2	15
Rover	14	10	6	117
Social Members			15	
New Members	41	6	3	50
Total End 1995	247	57	15	340

The annual subscription was increased by 7% over last year, and the Club gained a total income of £14,750 from subscriptions alone. More detailed analysis can be found in the Accounts section.

4 Proof-read the text and edit where necessary. Use the Spell-checking facility to help you.

5 Save your document under the name of **MEMBERS.**

6 Load your printer with paper, set to the top of form, check the printer is on-line and print the document.

7 Set the first paragraph formatting to be centred, spacing after to **3** lines and a shadow box border all the way round.
Set the character formatting of the same paragraph to be **Tms Rmn 24 pt, bold** and **italic**.

8 Set the character formatting of the second paragraph (line) to be **Tms Rmn 14 pt, bold.**

9 Increase the line spacing above paragraph **3** by one line.

10 Set the text in paragraphs (lines) **3** and **4** to be **bold**. **Underline** the text in paragraph **3**.

11 Alter the tab stops in paragraphs **3** and **4** to the following **Left** tab values: **5.0 cm; 7.0 cm; 9.0 cm; 11.0 cm.**

12 Draw a single-line rule below paragraph **4** and set the right indent for this paragraph to **12.5 cm**.

13 Draw a single-line rule below the paragraph (line) beginning 'Rover 14..' and set the right indent for this paragraph to **12.5 cm**.

14 Increase the line spacing above the paragraph for the paragraphs beginning 'Social Members' and 'Total End 1995' by **1** line.

15 Draw a double-line rule above the paragraph beginning 'Total End 1995'.

16 Increase the line spacing above the last paragraph by **2** lines. Set the character formatting for the same paragraph to **Tms Rmn 12pt.**

17 Save your document, using the name of **MEMBERS2**, on the Samples Disk.

18 Print a copy of your document.

19 Change the number of Full memberships for Morris Minor Saloons from 100 to **99**. Edit all the appropriate totals to reflect this change.

20 **Italicise** 'Accounts' in the last paragraph.

21 Save your document, using the same name as before.

22 Print a final copy of the document and close all open documents.

7.3 Document 3: Columns

The following exercise provides further character and paragraph formatting practice. The document produced, will be used in Part II (Intermediate level) of this guide.

EXERCISE

1 Open **INDENTS.DOC** saved previously on the Samples Disk in drive A: and save a new copy called **COLUMNS** (using **Save As** from the **File** menu).

2 Highlight the entire document and set the text to **Tms Rmn 10pt.**

3 Set the heading on page 1 of the document to **Helv 20pt** (or nearest value). Set the *Line Spacing After* the paragraph to **4 li** (4 lines).

4 Set the character formatting of the hanging indent 'JANUARY' to **Helv 10pt, bold.**

5 Set up a search for the text that you added to the document in Chapter 4 beginning **'With perseverance, those people..'**. Once located, delete the whole paragraph.

6 For each month other than January:

Close up the month heading with the first paragraph for the month, to create one paragraph (see page 73).

Insert a **Tab** between the month heading and the rest of the text in this, now joined, paragraph (see page 74).

Outdent (produce a hanging indent for) the same paragraph by **–3 cm** (minus 3).

Set the character formatting of the hanging indent to **Helv 10pt, bold.**

7 Save the document (using **Save** from the **File** menu).

Part II

Intermediate level

Introduction

The processes involved in editing have been practiced in Part I (Elementary level) of this guide. In addition, basic character and paragraph formatting have been explored.

The purpose of Part II (Intermediate level) is to introduce further formatting facilities, consistent with examination syllabuses at Intermediate level, offered by the Word for Windows program.

The new formatting techniques included in Part II are as follows:

- Formatting text into columns.
- Section, column, line, paragraph and page breaks.
- Headers and footers.
- The use of field codes.
- Paragraph styles, stylesheets and templates.
- Drawing, positioning, sizing and cropping graphics.

In order to complete the exercises found throughout Part II, the following documents need to be present on the Samples Disk:

CFORMAT.DOC (produced on page 60).
TABS2.DOC (produced on page 85).
COLUMNS.DOC (produced on page 101).
MEMBERS2.DOC (produced on page 101).

In addition, the following graphics files should be available in a subdirectory called \GRAPHICS:

WINGS.BMP
CAR1.BMP
CAR2.BMP

8 Working in columns

The COLUMNS.DOC document developed on page 101 of Part I of this guide, is to form the basis for the development of additional wordprocessing skills and concepts. Your Samples Disk should contain this file.

If you have not worked through Part I, then it is suggested that you spend a little time examining, and becoming familiar with the document before proceeding.

The formatting of the text for January on page one of COLUMNS.DOC is to remain intact, while the sections for February and March will be divided up into two and three columns respectively. Any text remaining on page 1 for April, will be moved to page 2.

Although this would not normally be a sensible columnar format for the page, this chapter will demonstrate the importance of *section*, *column* and *page breaks* in the formatting of text.

In order to change the number of columns on a page, the text has to be divided up into s*ections* using *section breaks*. These allow individual *sections* to be formatted entirely differently from others, even on the same page.

Breaks are accessed via the **Break** command found in the **Insert** menu (**Alt I B**).

8.1 Dividing text into sections

In order for you to understand more easily the instructions found in the following exercises, it is sensible to display the paragraph marks (where you have pressed the **Enter** key) on the screen. In addition, you may find that a **Page Layout** document view zoomed to display a **Full Page Width** will allow you to work more conveniently on your document. As a reminder, these operations may be accomplished as follows:

EXERCISE

1 Load **COLUMNS.DOC** from the Samples Disk.

2 Display the **Paragraph Marks** by selecting this option from the*:* **View** *Category* accessed via the **Options** command found in the **Tools** menu (**Alt O O**). Alternatively, select the **Non-printing character** button found on the right-hand side of the *Ribbon.*

3 Select **Page Layout** from the **View** menu if necessary.

4 *Either* select **Zoom** from the **View** menu and select the **Page Width** command button, *or* select the **Zoom Page Width** button in the *Toolbar.*

Inserting section breaks

EXERCISE 1 Move the insertion point to the beginning (left) of the hanging indent paragraph starting with the sub-heading 'FEBRUARY'.

2 Select **Break** from the **Insert** menu (**Alt I B**). The *Break* dialogue box will appear as below:

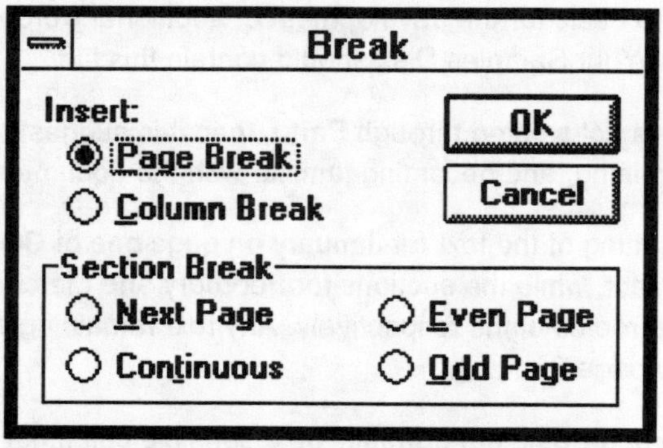

3 Select the *Section Break* to be **Continuous** (**Alt T**). This will allow this new section of text to remain on the same page as other sections.

Note that the Status bar now displays *Sec 2* (for section 2) and that a double, grey (dotted) line appears in the text. This line (which is non-printing) indicates the position of the section break – any text before the section break is in one section, while any text after the section break is in another.

4 With the insertion point still at the beginning of the text for February, insert another **Continuous** *Section Break* as above. The Status bar should now indicate *Sec 3* and another double, grey line will appear in the document.

Note: If a break has been placed into the wrong position by mistake, it may be deleted just like any other character using the **Backspace** key. In some instances, it may be necessary to position the insertion point to the left of the *Section Break* insertion and press the **Del** key which will delete to the right of the insertion point.

5 Move the insertion point to the beginning of the hanging indent for March and in the same way as above, insert two more *Section Breaks* (sections 4 and 5).

Inserting a page break

EXERCISE 1 Move the insertion point to the left of the hanging indent, 'APRIL' and insert a **Next Page** *Section Break* (section 6). This will move any text below the section break to the top of the next page.

Page 1 of the document has now been divided up into 5 different sections and the text for April has been moved to the top of page 2 as section 6.

2 Move the insertion point into section 2 (the blank line immediately above February). Set a **Double** *Line:* style border **above** the paragraph (use the **Border** command from the **Format** menu). If no borders appear, press the **Spacebar** to insert a space character into the paragraph. A double line border should now be drawn between the text for the two months.

Note: Borders are not drawn for empty paragraphs, hence the insertion of a space character, making the paragraph contain at least one character (non-visible in this case).

3 Adjust the **First Line Indent** for this ruled paragraph, re-positioning to the **0cm** mark on the *Ruler.* This will shorten the double ruled line.

4 Move into the first paragraph of text for February and reset the line spacing *Above* this paragraph using the **Paragraph** command found in the **Format** menu so that it has a value of **0 li** (zero lines). This will remove any extra line spacing above the paragraph and will help to balance the text when it is formatted into columns later.

5 Repeat steps 2 to 4 for section 4 (between February and March).

6 Save the document at this point.

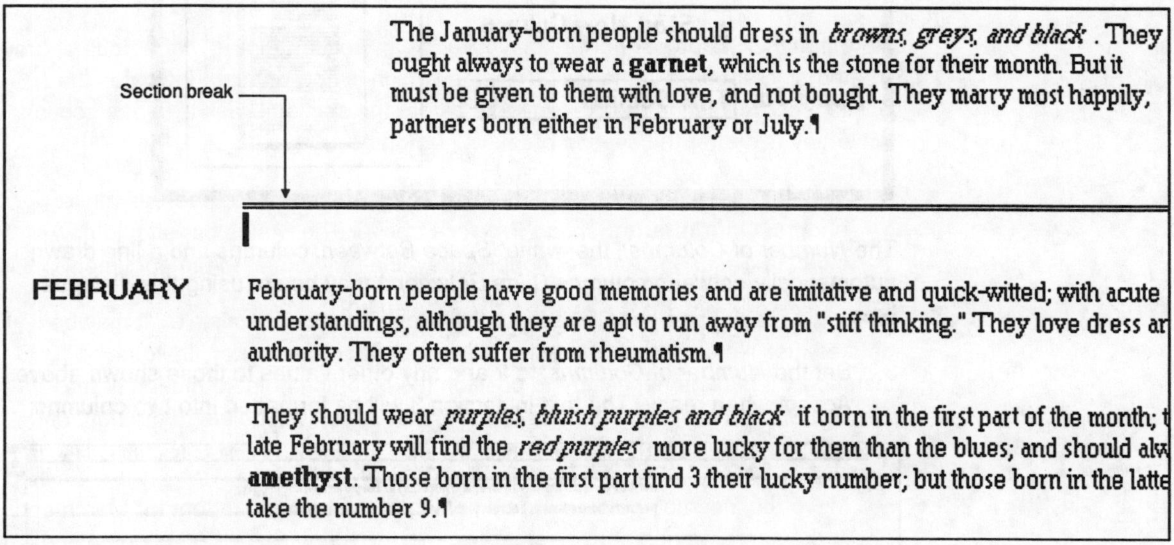

The January-born people should dress in *browns, greys, and black* . They ought always to wear a **garnet**, which is the stone for their month. But it must be given to them with love, and not bought. They marry most happily, partners born either in February or July.¶

FEBRUARY

February-born people have good memories and are imitative and quick-witted; with acute understandings, although they are apt to run away from "stiff thinking." They love dress ar authority. They often suffer from rheumatism.¶

They should wear *purples, bluish purples and black* if born in the first part of the month; t late February will find the *red purples* more lucky for them than the blues; and should alw **amethyst**. Those born in the first part find 3 their lucky number; but those born in the latte take the number 9.¶

8.2 Setting columns

Once the text has been divided up into sections, any section may be formatted differently from another. You may for example, have each section on a page formatted into different numbers of columns if you wish.

Text may be formatted in up to 100 columns across the page. The space between the columns may be adjusted and an optional vertical line may be automatically placed within this space.

Setting the number of columns with a command

In the following exercise, section 3 in the COLUMNS.DOC document is to be formatted into 2 columns using the **Columns** command found in the **Format** menu (**Alt T O**). This command provides the most flexible method of setting columns.

EXERCISE 1 Using the **COLUMNS.DOC** document, move the insertion point into *Section* 3 (the text for February).

2 Select **Columns** from the **Format** menu (**Alt T S**). The *Columns* dialogue box will be displayed as shown below:

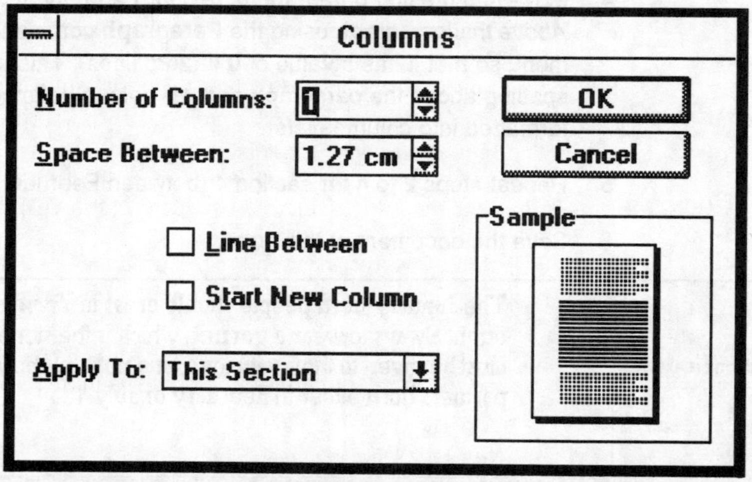

The *Number of Columns:*, the 'white' *Space Between:* columns and a line drawn automatically between columns (*Line Between:*) may be set using this dialogue box.

3 Set the *Number of Columns:* to **2** and any other values to those shown above. Accept when ready. The text in section 3 will be formatted into two columns:

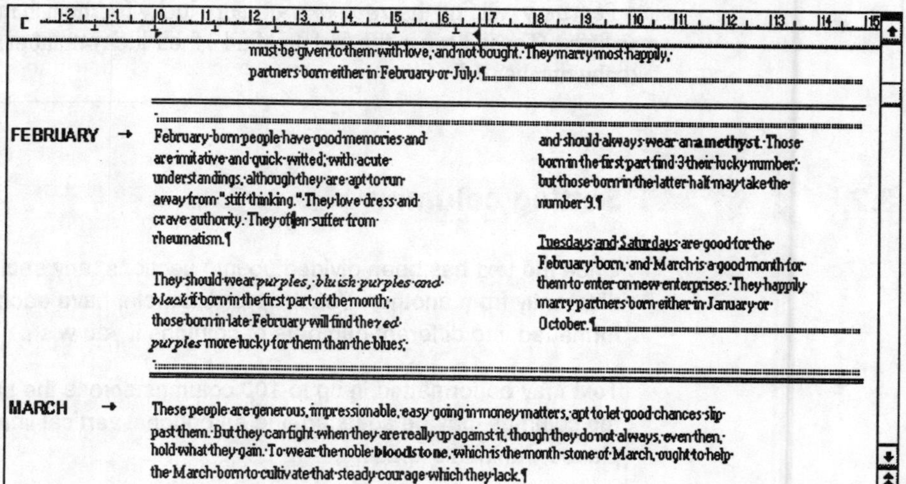

Note that the Ruler indicates the width of each column in the usual way with Left, Right and First Line Indent markers for each column.

4 With the insertion point inside the same section of text for February, display the *Columns* dialogue box once more and change the value for the *Space Between:*. Accept to return to your document and note that the distance (white space) between the two columns changes to reflect the value for *Space Between:* that you set.

Setting the number of columns with the Toolbar

Word for Windows provides a fast method of setting text in up to four columns using the **Columns** button found on the Toolbar.

If you do not have a mouse attached to your system, use the **Columns** command instead of the **Columns** button found on the Toolbar to set three columns as explained in the following exercise.

EXERCISE

1 Move the insertion point into section **5** of the **COLUMNS.DOC** document.

2 Select the **Columns** button in the Toolbar. A pull-down graphic appears which allows you to set up to four columns for the current section.

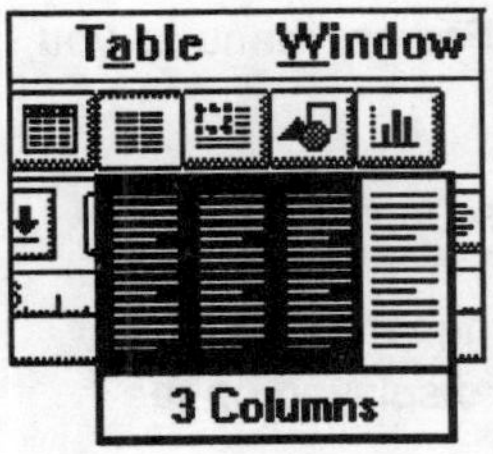

3 *Either* drag from left to right across the first three columns as shown and release the mouse button, *or* point at the third column from the left and click. This will set three columns with default *Space Between:* for the section of text for March.

When you return to your document, do not be surprised if the formatting of the text into three columns gives an unexpected result. This is explained in the next section.

Inserting column breaks

Because section 6 has been moved to the next page, the text in section 5 has flowed down to the bottom margin in the first (left-hand) column and then down the central column. By using *column breaks*, you will force the text to flow and balance across the three columns.

EXERCISE

1 Move the insertion point to the right-hand end of the line in column 1 in the text for March, which reads 'month-stone of March,'.

2 Insert a **Column Break** using the **Break** command from the **Insert** menu. The text will flow from the *column break* position, directly into column 2. A single, grey (dotted) line will indicate the position of the column break in the text.

3 Move the insertion point into an appropriate position within the text in column **2** and insert another *column break*. The text should now be arranged neatly into three balanced columns as shown on the next page.

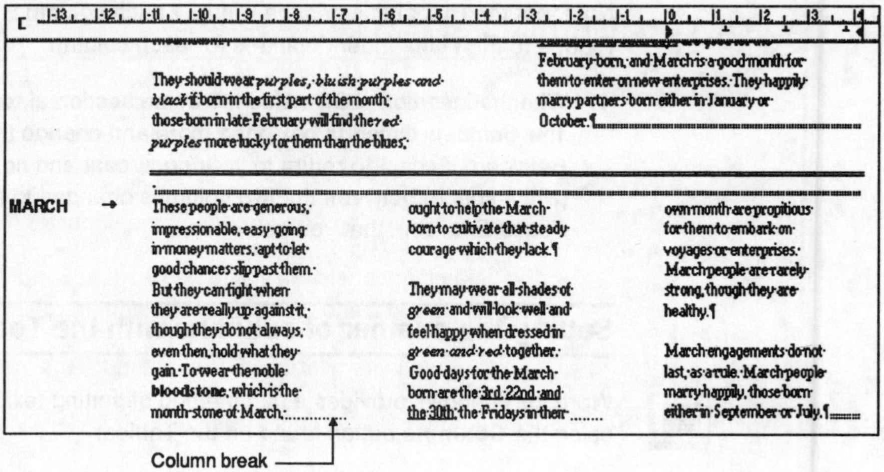

Drawing lines between columns

Vertical lines may be drawn automatically between columns of text. The **Columns** command used previously allows this to be set.

EXERCISE

1. With the insertion point inside section 5 (the text for March) in the **COLUMNS.DOC** document, select **Columns** from the **Format** menu as you have done previously.
2. Turn **Line Between** to on (cross in its check box) and accept.

Although you have instructed the program to automatically generate lines between the columns in this section of text, they will not be displayed on the screen.

3. Save the document (**Save** from the **File** menu or use the **Save** button in the Toolbar) before continuing.

Using Print Preview to display vertical rules

EXERCISE

1. Select **Print Preview** from the **File** menu (**Alt F V**) and examine page 1 of the COLUMNS.DOC document. The vertical rules between the columns in section 5 of the text should now be visible.

The vertical rules drawn automatically between columns are only visible on the screen when displaying the **Print Preview**.

2. Select the **Print** command button (**Alt P**) in the *Print Preview* **Icon bar** and print the first page of the document.

Formatting remaining pages

EXERCISE

1 Open **COLUMNS.DOC** if necessary and save a copy of it (**Save As** from the **File** menu) on the Samples Disk in drive A: under the name of **FORTUNE** which will be used in this and subsequent exercises.

2 Format the remaining three pages of the document.

Either: maintain consistency with page 1 (i.e. 3 months to a page, with text arranged with 1, 2 and 3 columns with double rules between months)

Or: experiment with alternative formatting for the various sections of text.

3 Save and print the full document.

9 Merging documents

A tabular document stored on the Samples Disk on page 85 will be joined together (*merged*) with the text in the FORTUNE.DOC document (saved on page 111), in order to create one document.

Although not necessary, it is suggested (for clarity) that before starting the next exercise you:

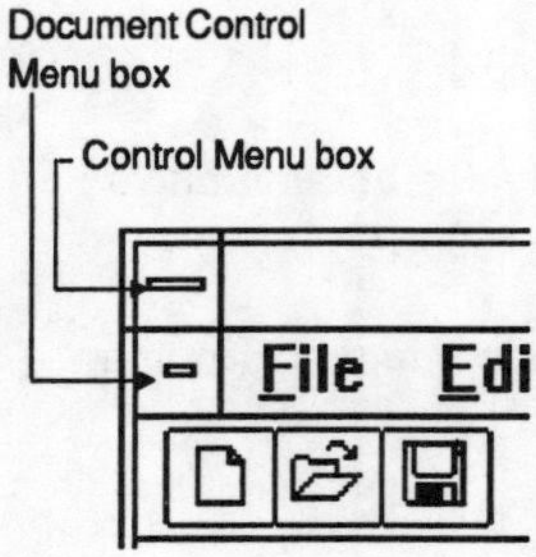

Either: exit from the Word for Windows program and re-load the program (to close all open documents)

Or: close each open document in turn by selecting **Close** from the **File** menu

Or: double-click on the **Document Control Menu box** (found at the top-left of the document window, directly under the Window **Control Menu box**) for each document in turn.

All documents will be closed when the only commands available in the *Menu bar* are **File** and **Help**.

9.1 Merging open documents

EXERCISE

1 Open the **FORTUNE.DOC** document.

2 Open the **TABS2.DOC** document.

3 Highlight all the text in **TABS2.DOC** document.

4 Select **Copy** from the **Edit** menu (Ctrl C *or* select the **Copy** button in the *Toolbar*) to copy the text to the *Clipboard.*

5 Select the **Window** pull-down menu (Alt W). This displays a list of currently opened documents. TABS2 is the current selection.

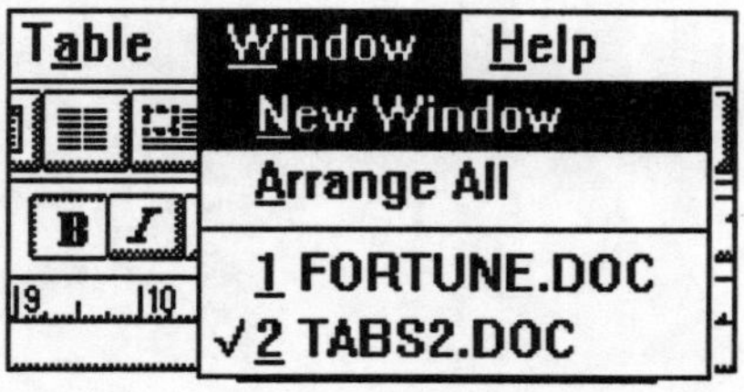

6 Select **FORTUNE.DOC.**

7 Move the insertion point to the end of the formatted document. Press Enter if necessary to move the insertion point onto a new line.

8 Insert a *Page Break*.

9 Select **Paste** from the **Edit** menu (Ctrl V *or* select the **Paste** button in the Toolbar) menu to place a copy of the text stored in the *clipboard* to the current insertion point position.

Although there are numerous ways of achieving this merging process, this is the simplest way of copying sections of text from one document to another.

10 Create a new line above the table and type a suitable heading. Format this heading (character and paragraph formatting) to suit you.

11 Save the document.

9.2 Merging documents with a command

The **File** command found in the **Insert** menu (Alt I L) provides an alternative method of merging complete documents. The process is as follows:

- Move the insertion point to where you wish to insert the contents of another document.
- Select the **File** command from the **Insert** menu.
- Select the appropriate file that you wish to merge with the current document from the dialogue box which appears.
- Accept to merge the file into the current document at the insertion point position.

10 Headers, footers and field codes

10.1 Draft document view

Until now, you have been using the **Normal** or **Page Layout** document views, where all formatting has been displayed on the screen. These document views should exactly match the printed document.

Word for Windows is able to display and print enormously complex documents which may include detailed graphics. With highly elaborate documents, printing and screen display may be slow. For this reason, a **Draft** document view is available both on screen and for printing. In this document view, most of the character formatting is not displayed (it is simply underlined to indicate some character formatting has been set) and columns of text are not shown side-by-side. Section breaks are indicated in this view by a double grey line across the page and a column break is shown as a single grey line.

Draft view is also useful when setting headers and footers as will be seen in the following exercises.

EXERCISE

1 Open **FORTUNE.DOC** if necessary and select **Draft** from the **View** menu (Alt V D). The **Draft** document view will be displayed as shown below:

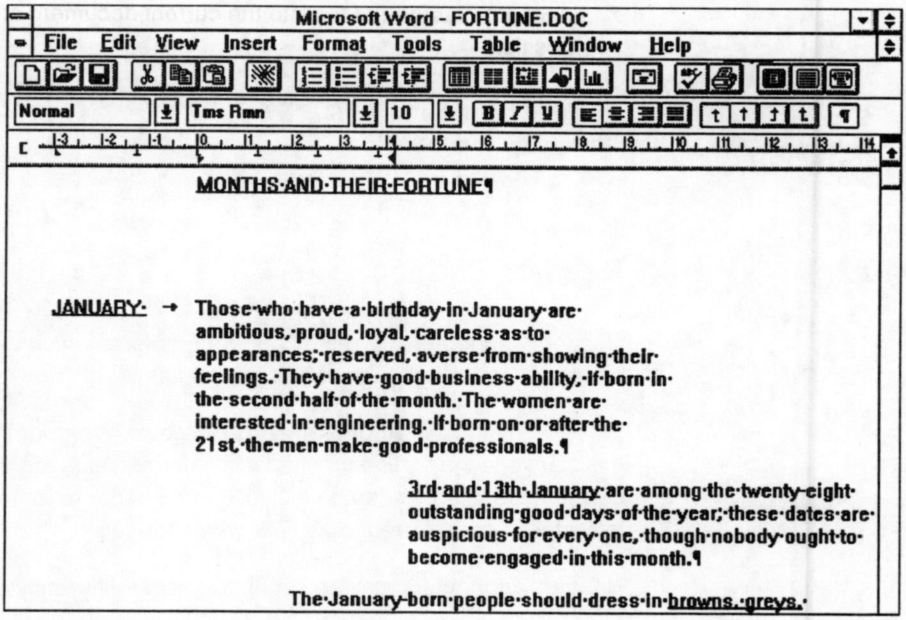

2 Move down through the document and notice:

- *Paragraph formatting* (including indents) is displayed as normal.

- *Character formatting* is displayed as underlined text only. The *Ribbon* displays the details for the section of text containing the insertion point.

- *Columns of text* are not displayed side-by-side, but as a single column of text. *Column breaks* are indicated by a single grey line drawn across the page.

- *Section breaks* are displayed as a double grey line drawn across the page.

Note also that the document is no longer divided into pages, but the Status bar indicates the current position of the insertion point (page number, section number etc.).

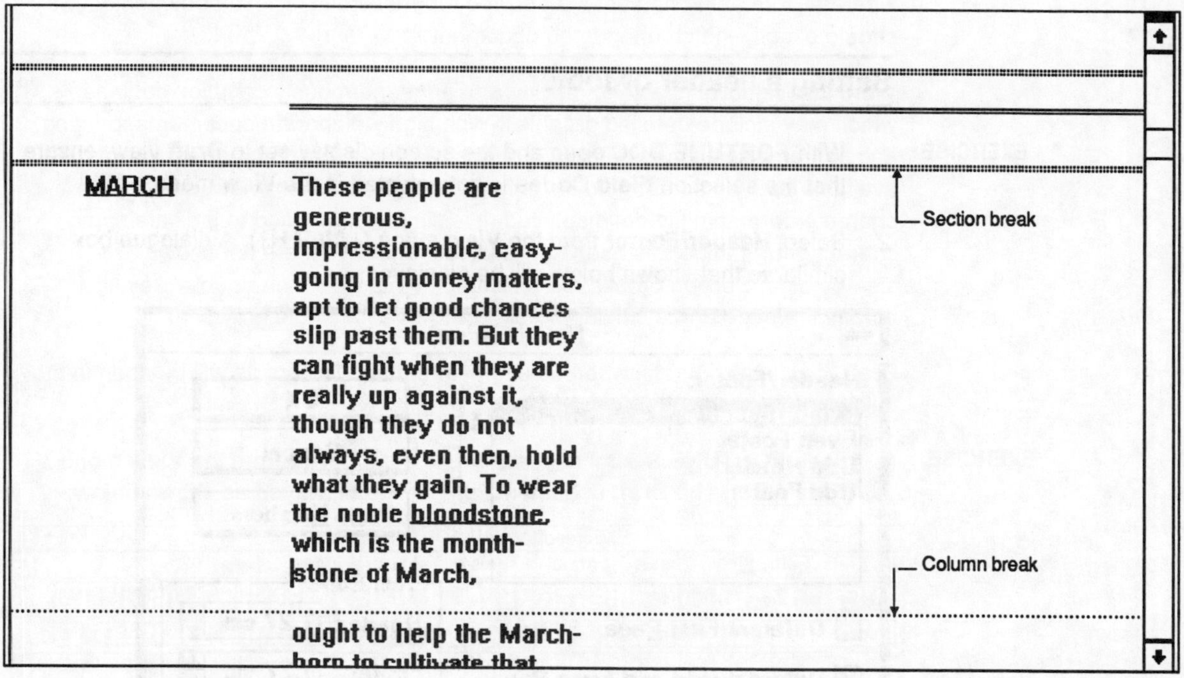

10.2 Headers and footers

Headers and footers consist of text (or graphics) which appear at the top (header) or bottom (footer) of each page of a document.

When working in **Draft** or **Normal** page views, Word for Windows gives additional assistance in the setting up of special information (such as page numbers, the current date, time etc.) to be included in a header or footer. These special items of information are referred to as *field codes* (or *fields*).

Headers and footers may be set up to appear differently on odd (right) and even (left) pages.

Since the first page of a document is normally treated differently (it may already contain headings used in subsequent headers or footers), you may choose not to display a header or footer on this page. Alternatively, you may set up a different header or footer for the first page of a document.

The exercises on pages 116 and 119 use the *Draft* view header and footer facilities to set a different footer for odd and even pages in the FORTUNE.DOC document. On page 119 you are introduced to the concept of field codes. Setting a header or footer in **Normal** page view would be carried out in the same way.

The exercise on pages 119-121 uses **Page Layout** view to set the footer on page 1 of the document. This demonstrates a different method of setting footers and gives more of an insight into *field codes.*

Setting a header or footer

EXERCISE

1 With **FORTUNE.DOC** open and the screen display set to **Draft** view, ensure that the selection **Field Codes** is not selected in the **View** menu.

2 Select **Header/Footer** from the **View** menu (**Alt V H**). A dialogue box similar to that shown below will be displayed.

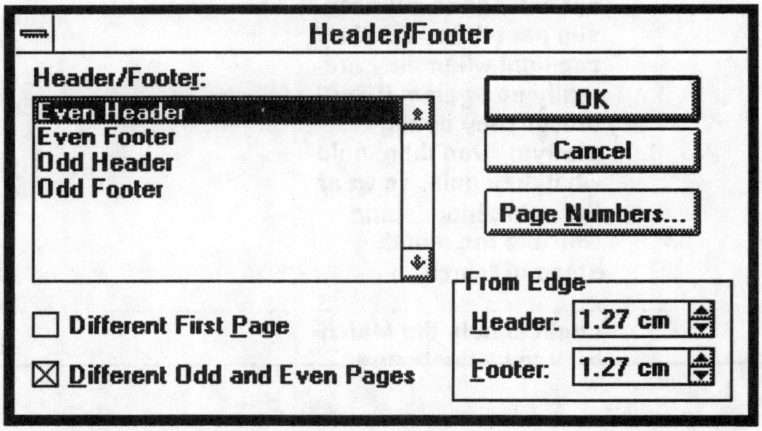

3 Set **Different First Page** (**Alt P**) and **Different Odd and Even Pages** (**Alt D**) to be on if necessary. This will allow a different header or footer on page 1 of the document and different headers and footers for subsequent even (left-hand) and odd (right-hand) pages in the rest of the document.

The *Header/Footer:* area allows you to set up one or more of the options shown for Headers and Footers.

The *From Edge* area allows you to specify the distance from the top or bottom margins at which the header or footer will be placed.

The **Page Numbers** command button allows you to select from a range of page number formats.

4 Select the **Page Numbers** command button (**Alt N**). The *Page Number Format:* dialogue box will appear as below:

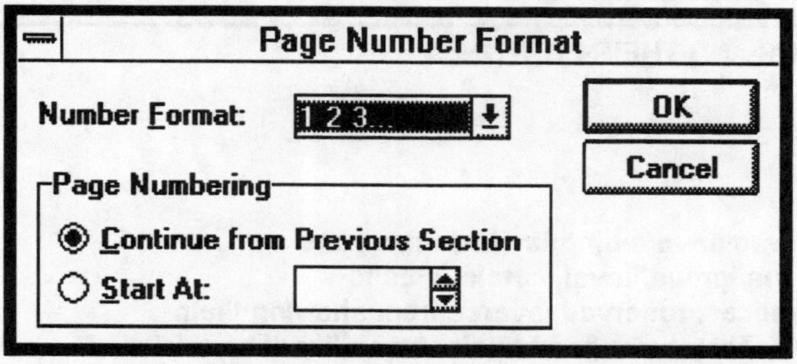

The *Page Numbering* area allows you to enter the number for the first page of the document using the *Start At:* text box, or set automatic numbering carrying on from any previous section (*Continue from Previous Section*), if it exists.

Number Format: allows you to select from a range of standard numbering systems.

5 If necessary, activate the *Number Format:* text box and choose the **1 2 3...** format.

6 Accept to return to the *Header/Footer* dialogue box.

Setting an even footer

EXERCISE 1 Select **Even Footer** in the *Header/Footer:* area of the *Header/Footer* dialogue box and accept (or double-click on **Even Footer**). The document window will split into two areas called *Panes* (*Window Panes*). The top Pane contains the document, the lower Pane contains an *Icon bar* and space for entry of the footer text. A line-shaped cursor, lined up with the left margin, will be flashing in this Footer Pane. Note also, that the Ruler contains a centre tab, set between the margins and a right tab is set just inside the right margin, automatically. These may be altered if required, in the same ways as you have practiced in previous exercises.

The Icon bar contains buttons which allows you to insert the page number, date or time into the footer (or header). This is shown on the next page.

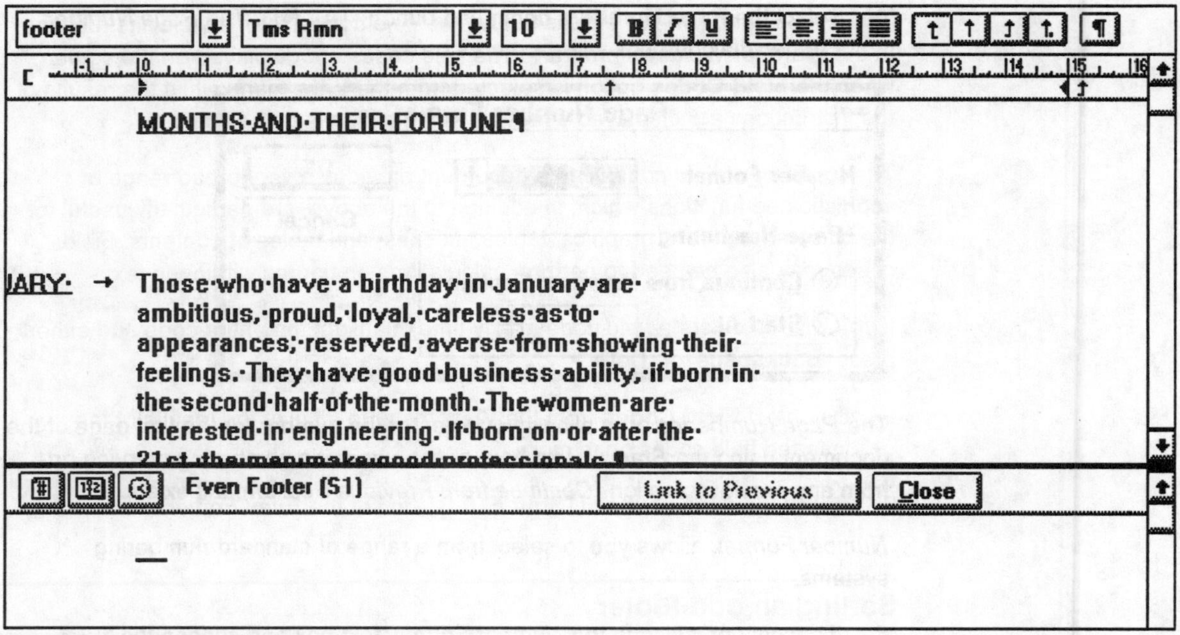

2 On the left of the text line in the *Footer Pane*, type: **Months and their fortune**

3 Press the **Tab** key to move to the centre of the line and type: **Page :**

4 Press the **Spacebar** to insert a space after the colon and select the **Page Number** button (**Shift F10 P**) to insert a page number.

5 Press **Tab** to move to the right margin and select the **Date** button (**Shift F10 D**) to insert the current system date. The *Footer Pane* should appear as shown below (with a different system date):

Field codes

EXERCISE 1 Select **Field Codes** from the **View** menu (**Alt V C**). The *Footer Pane* should change to display the following:

The {PAGE} and {DATE} entries (known as *field codes*) form special instructions to the Word for Windows program. The field codes are displayed on the screen when the **Field Codes** option is selected from the **View** menu while the results of the instructions are displayed when the same option is de-selected.

The insertion of field codes into a document provides a very broad range of sophisticated functions which, in addition to the above, are particularly useful for the placement of text, graphics, tables, indexes, and tables of contents. Field codes may also be used to perform calculations on figures within the text.

If you wish to delete a field code at any time, highlight the entire code and either press **Backspace** or **Del**.

2 De-select **Field Codes** from the **View** menu to display the results of the inserted field codes once more.

3 Select the **Close** button (**Shift F10 C**) to set the *Even Footer*.

Setting an odd footer

EXERCISE 1 Select **Header/Footer** from the **View** menu and select **Odd Footer** in the dialogue box which appears.

2 Set the following *Odd Footer* using the appropriate field codes where required:

3 **Close** the *Odd Footer Pane* when ready to set the footer.

4 De-select **Draft** from the **View** menu. This will switch the screen display to **Normal.**

5 Select **Page Layout** from the **View** menu and move to the bottom of page 2. The *Even Footer* will be displayed with the correct page number.

6 Move to the bottom of page 3. The odd footer will be displayed.

The appropriate odd or even footer will be displayed at the bottom of all pages, with the exception of page 1.

7 You may wish to save and print the document at this stage.

Setting a first page footer

EXERCISE 1 Move to the first page of the **FORTUNE.DOC** document if necessary. The document should be displayed in **Page Layout** view.

2 Select **Header/Footer** from the **View** menu and select **Footer** from the dialogue box which appears. The insertion point will move to the left of the footer line in the document.

3 Type **Number of words :**
Add a space at the end of the text.

4 Select **Field** from the **Insert** menu (**Alt I D**). A *Field* dialogue box will be displayed as shown below:

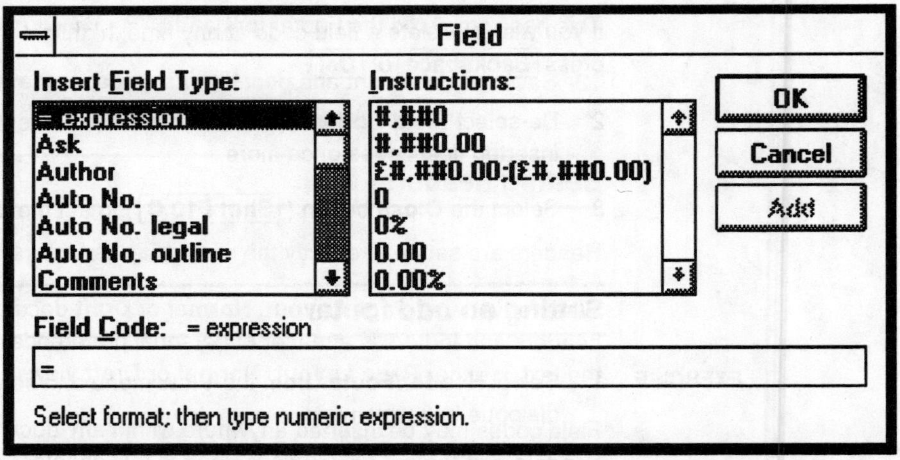

The *Insert Field Type:* area provides an extensive list of useful fields (*field codes*) which may be inserted into a document.

Any available options for the currently selected field type (in the *Insert Field Type:* area), will be displayed inside the *Instructions:* area.

As field types and options are selected, these will appear inside the *Field Code:* text box.

5 Select **No. of words** from the *Insert Field Type:* area. The *Field Code:* text box indicates that the *Field Code* {NUMWORDS} will be entered into the footer. This prints the total number of words in the document. Accept when ready.

You may wish to select **Field Codes** from the **View** menu which will display the field code. De-select **Field Codes** before continuing.

6 Press **Tab** to move to the centre of the footer line.

7 Type **Page :**
Add a space as before.

8 Select **Field** from the **Insert** menu and select the *Insert Field Type:* **Page**. From the *Instructions:* box, select the page number format: **1 2 3....** Accept when ready (you may also need to accept an information box).

9 Add another space and type **of.**
Add another space.

10 In the same way as above, insert the *Field:* **No. of pages**. The text in the centre of the footer should read: 'Page 1 of 5'. If the number of pages comprising the document changes, the items in the footer will automatically be updated each time you open this document (number of words and number of pages).

11 Press Tab to move to the right of the footer line and insert the *Field:* **Author**. This will place your name (as set up as a default value on page 18) on the right of the footer.

This has completed the Footer for page 1.

12 Save the document and print the first page, or the whole document if required.

Setting headers

Headers are set up in exactly the same way as footers.

Whether you use **Page Layout, Normal** or **Draft** document views for setting up headers and footers is a matter of personal preference. Fields may be placed into the text in either **Page Layout, Normal** or **Draft** views.

Field codes may be inserted anywhere within any document and not just in headers and footers as you have done in this chapter. You may wish to experiment with different field codes using a new document.

10.3 Date and time

You have previously seen how the page number, date and time may be inserted into a header or footer. These may be placed anywhere in the text by inserting the appropriate field code or selecting the appropriate buttons found on the Icon bars in the header or footer Panes. Word for Windows provides an additional method of inserting the date, time or both anywhere within a document.

When you select the **Date and Time** command found in the **Insert** menu (Alt I T), the following dialogue box is displayed:

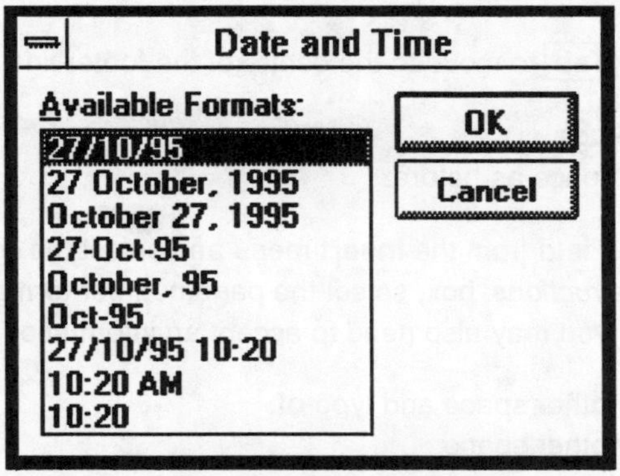

To insert a date or time at the current insertion point position, simply select the appropriate option in the *Available Formats:* area.

10.4 Practice exercise

EXERCISE

1. Load the **MEMBERS2.DOC** document from the Samples Disk. This was prepared as a consolidation exercise to Part I of this guide (page 101).
2. Set up a header containing the page number aligned to the right-hand side of the page, starting at page number 5.
3. Set the character formatting of the page number in the header to **Helv 8pt, bold.**
4. Using either a field code or the **Date and Time** command, insert a date at an appropriate position in the document.
5. Print a copy of the document.
6. Save the document using the same name as before.

11 Styles, stylesheets and templates

Paragraph styles provide a powerful, time-saving method of setting all the values (including paragraph and character formatting) associated with particular paragraphs of text within a document. In addition, paragraph styles may provide a consistent approach to the formatting of text across a range of similar documents.

A paragraph style consists of a label (name), to which is attached all the details concerning the alignment, character formatting, tabs and positioning of a paragraph on the page.

Once set, a paragraph style may be applied to any number of individual paragraphs within a document, which will all have exactly the same format.

All text within a document is assumed to take on the characteristics of the **Normal** paragraph style (which is displayed in the Ruler) until it is set to another paragraph style.

One or more paragraph styles is referred to as the *stylesheet.*

The stylesheet (made up of one or more paragraph styles), the page layout, breaks, paragraph and character formatting are all stored with a document when you save it to a disk. This is referred to as the document *template.*

Templates may be stored separately from the document, for use with other documents which will use the same page layout and stylesheet. This leads to consistent presentation across a range of similar documents.

11.1 Changing an existing paragraph style

EXERCISE 1 Open the **FORTUNE** document if necessary and move the insertion point into the footer at the bottom of page 1, using the **Page Layout** document view.

When you created the *First Page Footer* on pages 119-121, a paragraph style called **'footer'** was automatically created by the Word for Windows program. The name **'footer'** will be displayed in the text box found on the left-hand side of the Ribbon. This paragraph style was attached to all the footers in the document and determines their formatting.

2 Move the insertion point anywhere in the document above the footer. Notice that the *Style* text box now reads **'Normal'**. All text in the document is assumed to take on the characteristics of the **Normal** paragraph style unless changed to another style, as in the case of the footer.

3 Move the insertion point into the footer at the bottom of page 2. The style should once again read '**footer**'. This is the same for the footer at the bottom of each page of the document.

All the paragraphs with the **footer** paragraph styles attached will now have their character formatting changed in one operation.

Displaying the paragraph style dialogue box

The dialogue box used for changing the details of an existing paragraph style may be displayed in one of two ways:

- *Either* press **Ctrl S** followed by another **Ctrl S**.
- *Or* select **Style** from the **Format** menu (**Alt T Y**).

EXERCISE 1 Move the insertion point into the footer at the bottom of any page.

2 Display the *Style* dialogue box by using one of the methods described above.

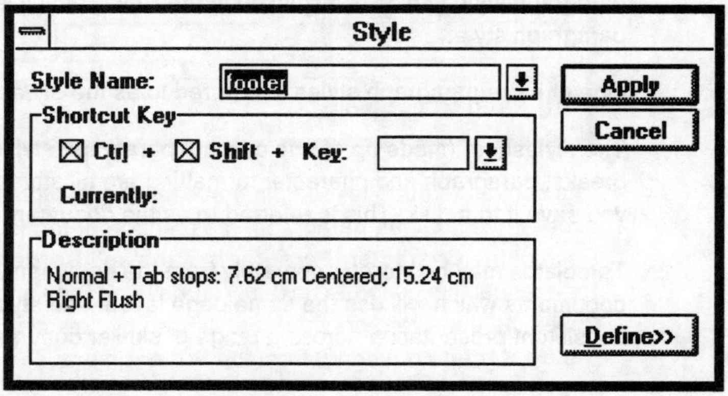

The paragraph style name '**footer**' should be highlighted in the *Style Name:* text box and a description of the paragraph style appears towards the bottom of the dialogue box in the *Description* area.

In this case, the description indicates that any paragraph marked with the **footer** paragraph style will have the same characteristics as the **Normal** paragraph style, with the addition of specific *Tab stops,* set with particular alignments.

You may assign your own keyboard sequence for any paragraph style by setting up the keys to be used in the *Shortcut Key* area. The shortcut key sequences include any combination of: **Ctrl**; **Shift**; alphabetic and numeric characters; and function keys. You may, for example, set up the shortcut key code of **Ctrl Shift F** to apply the formatting associated with the footer style, to any paragraph of text.

3 Select the **Normal** paragraph style in the *Style Name:* text box. This will display its characteristics (*Font:* Tms Rmn 10 pt, Language: English (UK), Flush left).

4 Select **footer** once more and select the **Define** command button. The *Style* dialogue box will be extended to display the following:

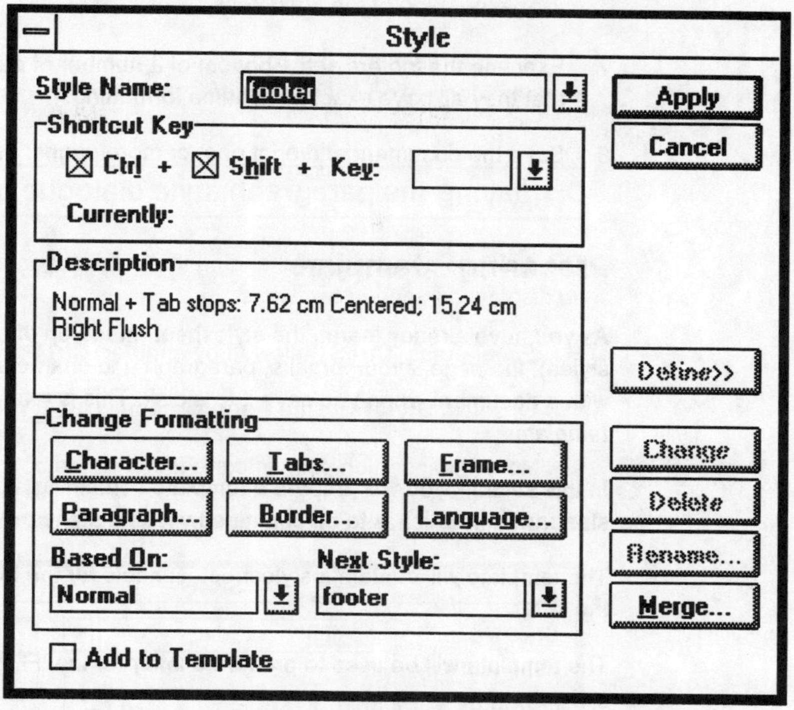

The command buttons found in the extended section of this dialogue box allow access to character, paragraph, tab and border formatting for the paragraph style. Each of the **Character**, **Paragraph, Tabs** and **Border** command buttons display their respective dialogue boxes. You have already encountered these dialogue boxes, as they were previously displayed by selecting the appropriate option (e.g. the **Character** command) from the **Format** menu.

The **Language** command button allows you to mark paragraphs as consisting of text written in a foreign language. If available, the appropriate dictionaries for the language will then be used when using the spelling and grammar checks or thesaurus.

The **Frame** command button displays a *Frame* dialogue box which will be explored at a later point, in the context of graphics.

The **Delete** and **Rename** command buttons allow you to delete or rename a paragraph style.

Two or more paragraph styles may be joined together when required, by use of the **Merge** command button.

5 Select the **Character** command button to change the character formatting of the **footer** style.

6 Set the *Font:* to **Helv 8pt**, and **italic**. Accept when ready, to return you to the *Style* dialogue box. Accept once more to return you to your document.

7 Examine the footers at the bottom of a number of pages and note that they all have exactly the same formatting.

8 Save the document and print one, or more pages, as required.

11.2 Preparing a template

As you have already learnt, the stylesheet (made up of one or more paragraph styles), the page layout, breaks, paragraph and character formatting are all stored with a document when you save it to a disk. This is referred to as the document *template*.

In this section, you will prepare a template containing a letterhead and other standard text which is to be contained within a standard letter document.

The template will contain a stylesheet, suitable for the formatting of the text within the letter.

The template will be used to prepare a letter for the 'Flying Wheels Motoring Club'.

EXERCISE

1 Select **New** from the **File** menu and select **Template** from the *New* area. This will open a new document as a template, which will be based upon the **NORMAL** (default) template. This should be highlighted. Accept when ready.

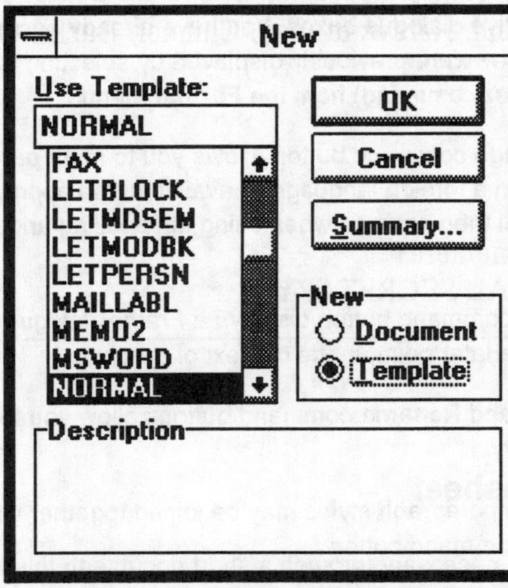

2 Select either a **Normal** or **Page Layout** view of the document.

3 Set the *Top:* page margin to **1**cm (by selecting **Page Setup** from the **Format** menu *or* **Alt T U**), leaving all the other values as set.

4 In order for you to understand more clearly the formatting of this template, display the **Paragraph Marks** if necessary by selecting the **Options** command found in the **Tools** menu (**Alt O O**), *Category:* **View**. Alternatively, select the **Hidden Characters** button in the Ribbon.

5 Type in the following three lines of text, pressing **Enter** at the end of each line:

The Flying Wheels
Motoring Club
Maple End, Hareward Way, Chinnor, Bucks. OK2 3MB

6 On the fourth line, insert the **Date** *Field* (**Field** from the **Insert** menu *or* **Alt I D**), with the *Instructions:* **d MMMM,yyyy** (date format). Accept when ready to insert the current date into the text.

7 Press **Enter** twice and type: **Dear**
Add a space with the **Spacebar** and press **Enter** twice again.

8 Type: **Yours**
Add an additional space as before, and press **Enter** to move onto the next line where you should type your name.

9 Press **Enter** once more and type: **GENERAL SECRETARY**.

The document should appear similar to that shown below:.

The Flying Wheels¶
Motoring Club¶
Maple End, Hareward Way, Chinnor, Bucks. OK2 3MB¶
4 October 1995¶
¶
Dear ¶
¶
Yours ¶
Your name here¶
GENERAL SECRETARY¶

11.3 The stylesheet

Although not necessary for such a short document, this letterhead template will be set up to include the character and paragraph formatting (*paragraph styles*) for a number of different types of paragraph within the document.

Setting a new paragraph style

EXERCISE

1 Place the insertion point in the top line of text.

2 Select **Style** from the **Format** menu (**Ctrl S** **Ctrl S** *or* **Alt T Y**) to display the *Style* dialogue box that you have seen previously.

3 In the *Style Name:* text box, type the new *paragraph style* name: **Letterhead 1**. Select the **Define** command button to extend the dialogue box as before.

4 Select the **Character** button to display the *Character* dialogue box seen before.

5 Set the character formatting to: **Tms Rmn 36pt, Bold** and **Italic**. Accept when ready, to return to the *Style* dialogue box.

6 Select the **Paragraph** command button to display the *Paragraph* dialogue box.

7 Set the following values:
Alignment: **Right**
Indentation *From Left:* **–2.0 cm** (minus 2.0cm)
Indentation *From Right:* **–2.0 cm** (minus 2.0cm)
Spacing *Before:* and *After:* to **0 li** (zero lines)
Accept when ready to return to the *Style* dialogue box.

8 Select the **Border** command button and set:
Border: **above**
Line: **medium, single**
From Text: **4 pt**

The details attached to this paragraph style name (Letterhead 1) will be displayed in the *Description* area of the dialogue box.

9 Select the **Add** command button to add this paragraph style to the document template. Select the **Apply** command button when ready, to return to the document. Note that the first line of the text in the document will be re-formatted according to the details set up for the **Letterhead 1** style. Note also that the new style name, **Letterhead 1**, appears in the *Style* text box found in the Ribbon.

10 Display the list of available styles in the *Style* box in the Ribbon (click on the arrow found to the right of the box *or* press **Ctrl S** and use the cursor control keys). The new **Letterhead 1** paragraph style should now be included in a list of available paragraph styles which were included in the **NORMAL** (default) template on which the current template is based.

Changing an existing paragraph style

EXERCISE

1 Move the insertion point into any paragraph underneath the letterhead.

2 Select **Style** again from the **Format** menu. The **Normal** paragraph style name should appear in the *Style Name:* text box. Keeping the name the same, select the **Define** command button followed by the **Character** command button. Set the style to **Tms Rmn 12 pt**. Accept to return to the *Styles* dialogue box.

3 Select the **Paragraph** command button and set the *Spacing Before:* to **1ll** (one line). Accept when ready.

Select the **Apply** command button (you do not need to add this style with an **Add** command button, since you are modifying an existing style). An information box will be displayed which reminds you that you are changing one of the styles that was originally in the **NORMAL** template on which this template is based. Accept to return to the document.

Note that the text will automatically change to correspond to the new values set for the **Normal** paragraph style. Since the insertion point was positioned inside the first paragraph, the first line of text will be reformatted according to the attributes of the **Normal** style.

Adding further paragraph styles

EXERCISE 1 Set up the following new paragraph styles in the same way as on page 128 (using **Style** from the **Format** menu), changing only the values mentioned below. Make sure that you select the **Add** command button after setting the attributes of each paragraph style.

Note: the attributes of all the new paragraph styles may be set together, without the need to return to your document after you have set a single style.

Paragraph *Style Name:* **Letterhead 2**
Character formatting: **Helv 12 pt, bold**
Paragraph formatting:
Alignment: **Right**
Indentation *From Left :* **–2.0 cm**
Indentation *From Right :* **–2.0 cm**
Spacing *Before:* **0 ll** (zero lines)
Border: **medium thickness, single line** border below the paragraph
From Text: **4 pt**

Paragraph *Style Name:* **Date & Name**
Paragraph formatting:
Spacing *Before:* **5 ll** (five lines)

Paragraph *Style Name:* **Address**
Paragraph formatting:
Spacing *Before:* **0 ll** (zero lines)

Paragraph *Style Name:* **Title**
Character formatting: **Bold**

Paragraph formatting:
Spacing *Before:* **0 li** (zero lines)

The new paragraph styles (**Letterhead 1, Letterhead 2, Date & Name, Address** and **Title**) should now be set up and the **Normal** paragraph style has been modified.

Deleting and renaming paragraph styles

Should you ever wish to delete a paragraph style, the *Style* dialogue box provides a **Delete** command button which allows the removal of the currently selected paragraph style. The paragraph styles from the original template (NORMAL) cannot be deleted in this way.

The same dialogue box contains a **Rename** command button which may be used to rename any paragraph style other than those which were in the original template.

Applying paragraph styles to text

Having now set the paragraph styles, they may be applied to paragraphs of text whenever required. This may be accomplished as follows:

Using the **Keyboard**:

- *Either* move the insertion point into the paragraph, *or* highlight the group of paragraphs that you wish to format according to a particular paragraph style.
- Press **Ctrl S** to activate the *Style:* box in the Ribbon and use the up and down cursor control keys to display the available paragraph styles.
- Press **Enter** when the appropriate paragraph style is displayed.

Using the **mouse**:

- *Either* move the insertion point into the paragraph, *or* highlight the group of paragraphs that you wish to format according to a particular paragraph style.
- Click on the arrow to the right of the *Style:* box in the Ruler, and select from the list of available paragraph styles which appears.

EXERCISE

1 Highlight the top two lines of text and select the **Letterhead 1** paragraph style from the *Ribbon* using one of the methods described above.

2 If the second paragraph (line) has a border drawn above it, as with the first, then remove the border for this paragraph by using the **Border** command from the **Format** menu.

3 Move the insertion point into the third line and apply the **Letterhead 2** paragraph style.

4 Move the insertion point into the paragraph containing the date and apply the **Date & Name** paragraph style. Repeat for the line containing your name.

5 Move the insertion point into the fifth line, immediately below the date and apply the **Address** paragraph style.

6 Move the insertion point into the last line of text immediately below your name and apply the **Title** paragraph style. The top section of this template should now appear as below:

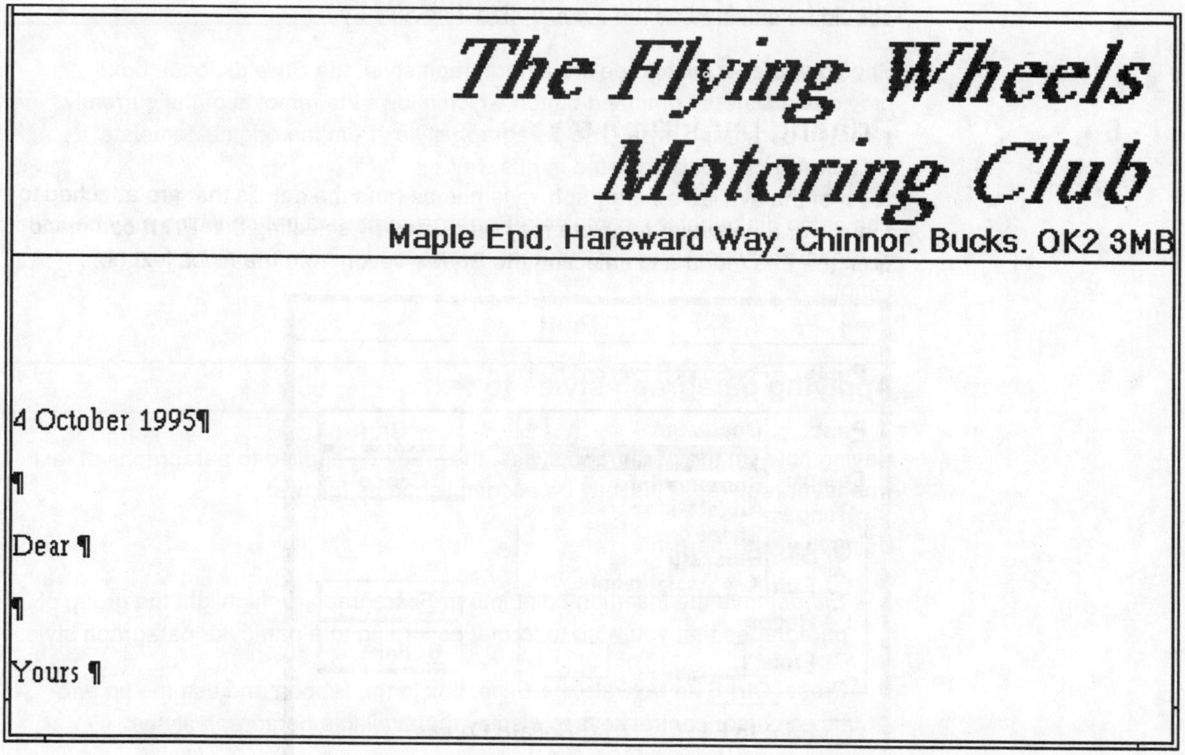

The Flying Wheels Motoring Club

Maple End, Hareward Way, Chinnor, Bucks. OK2 3MB

4 October 1995¶

¶

Dear ¶

¶

Yours ¶

11.4 Saving a template

EXERCISE

1 Select **Save As** from the **File** menu and type **FWLETR** for the template file name and accept.

2 Enter any appropriate details into the dialogue box which appears and accept to save the file.

Word for Windows saves all templates in the \WINWORD directory (where the Word for Windows program resides) of your hard disk and does not give an option to save the template elsewhere (although the template may be copied elsewhere using the **File Find** command – see page 95).

The program automatically adds .DOT to the end of the filename, thus FWLETR.DOT is the full name of the template stored in this case.

11.5 Printing a template

Should you wish to print a copy of the template for reference, it may be sent to the printer in the normal way by selecting **Print** from the **File** menu. **Document** should be selected as the *Print:* option if necessary.

11.6 Printing paragraph styles

A list of the available paragraph style names (and the details that are attached to them), for a particular template may be printed by selecting the **Print** command from the **File** menu and selecting the **Styles** option from the *Print:* text box.

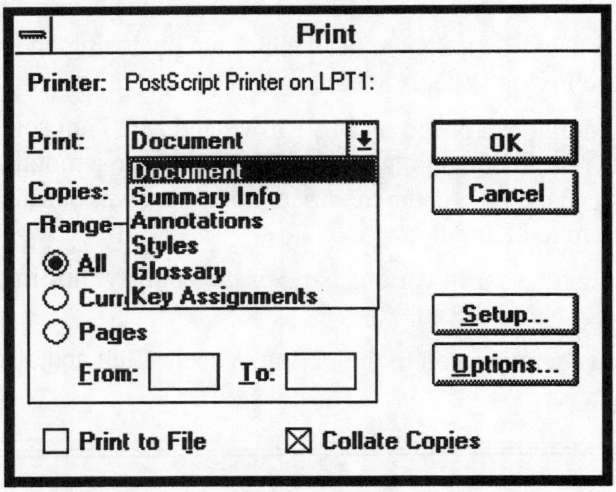

11.7 Opening a document with a template

The **FWLETR** template prepared previously will be used to produce a letter for the 'Flying Wheels Motoring Club'.

EXERCISE

1 Open a new document by selecting **New** from the **File** menu (**Alt F N**).

2 Select the **FWLETR** template from the *Use Template:* text box and accept. All the text and its formatting included in the original template will now be placed into the document.

11.8 Using a template

EXERCISE

1 Move the insertion point to the beginning of the line immediately under the date. This is to contain the address. Note that the **Address** paragraph style appears in the *Ruler*.

2 Type the following address, pressing **Enter** as usual, at the end of each line:

Mr. J. Clifford
Thatchers Way
Stubbs
Lincs. PE19 7JE

3 Move the insertion point to the right of 'Dear ' and type: **Mr. Clifford,**

4 Move the insertion point into the next line down and type the following four paragraphs, pressing **Enter** once to start each new paragraph:

> In reply to your letter dated 12th September 1995, I am enclosing an application form for membership of the Flying Wheels Motoring Club.
>
> This Club was formed nine years ago by Mr. Brown and Mr. Timpson. The main meeting place is at 'Wells' Garage in Chinnor. We meet once a month, but obviously not all our members can attend. As the membership has grown, our members come from all parts of the United Kingdom.
>
> We hold events during the year in various parts of the country. Information about these appears in our monthly News Sheet.
>
> We look forward to welcoming you to the Flying Wheels Club and also to viewing your famous Lagonda car.

5 Add **sincerely** to the end of the line beginning 'Yours '.

Notice that no formatting of the text within the document is necessary since all the details have been prepared within the template.

6 Edit the text within the document, including a spell check. You may wish to replace some words with the assistance of the thesaurus facility.

7 Save the document (using **Save As** from the **File** menu) on the Samples Disk in drive A:, under the name of **LETTER1**. Print the document if required.

8 You may wish to open another new document using the same FWLETR.DOT stylesheet and experiment with the preparation of another letter using appropriate text of your own. This would have exactly the same layout and formatting as in the previous letter.

12 Graphics and frames

Graphics (pictures) may be included within a document. They may be placed accurately and sized within the Word for Windows program. If the graphic contains unwanted areas, these may be *cropped* (removed).

There are two basic ways of placing and positioning a graphic within a document.

Method 1 simply places a graphic at the current cursor position as though it were a paragraph. Once placed, the graphic can be displayed on the page, re-sized, cropped and any of the normal paragraph formatting facilities applied to it. This therefore, allows you to set the positioning of the graphic on the page (using tabs and indents), borders etc.

Method 2 involves the use of a frame (box) into which the graphic is placed. As with the first method, the graphic can be re-sized and cropped within the frame, but the big advantage is that the frame may then be dragged to a new position anywhere on the page and may also be made to interact with surrounding text in a variety of different ways.

The following exercises explore both methods of placing and positioning graphics.

Graphics may be imported into a document from many different sources. These may include scanned or digitised images, drawings from line-art packages (Windows Paintbrush is an example), graphics from spreadsheet or database packages, clip-art libraries (commercially available, pre-prepared collections of graphics and symbols) and so on.

If you have installed a full version of the Word for Windows program on your system, four additional programs will be available to you which will allow you to create (and modify) graphics of different types. In addition, a full installation will include a clip-art library containing various symbols (such as arrows) and pictures. The additional graphics oriented programs include:

- Microsoft Draw which is a line-art drawing program, providing a range of drawing tools;
- Microsoft WordArt which allows you to create special effects with text;
- Microsoft Graph which allows you to create graphs with data in a document or from other sources;
- Microsoft Equation Editor which allows you to create and edit equations to be placed inside a document.

Since these programs are designed to run from within the Word for Windows program, they are called *embedded applications* and provide the wordprocessor with facilities that it otherwise would not have. Other embedded application programs are available commercially, which provide further specialist facilities.

Graphics, pictures and images may be stored to a disk in a variety of different data formats depending on the program/s that you use to generate them. Word for Windows recognises data stored in a number of different formats and these include: .PCX, (Paintbrush); .WMF (Windows Metafile); .EPS (Encapsulated PostScript); .TIF (Tagged Image File Format); .BMP (Windows Bitmaps); .PIC (Lotus 1-2-3 Graphics); WPG (DrawPerfect); .HGL (HP Graphics Language) and others. When installing Word for Windows, the data format *filters* may be chosen for both graphics and text file formats. A filter provides a method of converting information stored in one data format to another. These allow the program to import information from a variety of sources without the need for you to modify it.

An additional method of importing a graphic (other than using filters) is to cut the graphic to the clipboard in one program (such as Windows Paintbrush) and paste it into the Word for Windows program.

The range of acceptable data formats for text and graphics that you have access to will depend upon the data format filters chosen when Word for Windows was installed on your system. If a full, automatic installation of the program was chosen, then all the import (and export) filters will be available. This chapter will assume that any sample graphics stored on your Samples Disk are saved in the .BMP data format (which may originate from a range of Paintbrush line-art programs such as Windows Paintbrush). If alternative graphics are used, or if the images are stored in a different data format, make the necessary adjustments to the text. The sample graphics should be found in a subdirectory of the Samples Disk, called GRAPHICS.

The graphics shown above, come supplied on a Samples Disk available from the Publisher. If you are using your own Samples Disk, the graphics may be scanned if a scanner is available. Alternatively, you may have suitable clip-art images (including those that may have been installed with the Word for Windows program) that you may choose to use in their place. If none of these options are appropriate, suitable graphics may be created using any line-art package that you may have available (including Windows Paintbrush or Microsoft Draw mentioned above).

12.1 Importing a picture

The **Picture** command found in the **Insert** menu (**Alt I P**) allows you to place a graphic into your document at the current cursor position. Once placed using this command, the graphic may be considered as being a normal paragraph and all the usual paragraph formatting facilities may be applied to it.

In the following exercise, three sample clip-art graphics supplied with the Word for Windows installation will be placed into the CFORMAT.DOC document. These graphics will be used to illustrate the basics of manipulating images placed with the **Picture** command.

EXERCISE 1 Open the **CFORMAT.DOC** document and save it on the Samples Disk under the name of **PICTURE.** Continue to work with PICTURE.DOC.

2 Select either a **Page Layout** or **Normal** document view. Both of these views allow you to see any picture placed within a document (**Draft** view only indicates the position of placed pictures). You may also find it useful to display **Paragraph Marks.**

3 Move the text beginning 'The women are interested' from the first paragraph under the heading for January, onto a new line with an extra paragraph break between this and the preceding text (i.e. move the insertion point immediately to the left of the required text and press **Enter** twice).

4 In the same way, move the text beginning 'If born on or after the 21st' so that it begins a new line with an empty paragraph above it. Pictures are to be placed on these empty lines created between the paragraphs of text.

5 Move the insertion point into the empty line above the paragraph beginning 'The women are interested' and select **Picture** from the **Insert** menu (**Alt I P**). The following *Picture* dialogue box will be displayed:

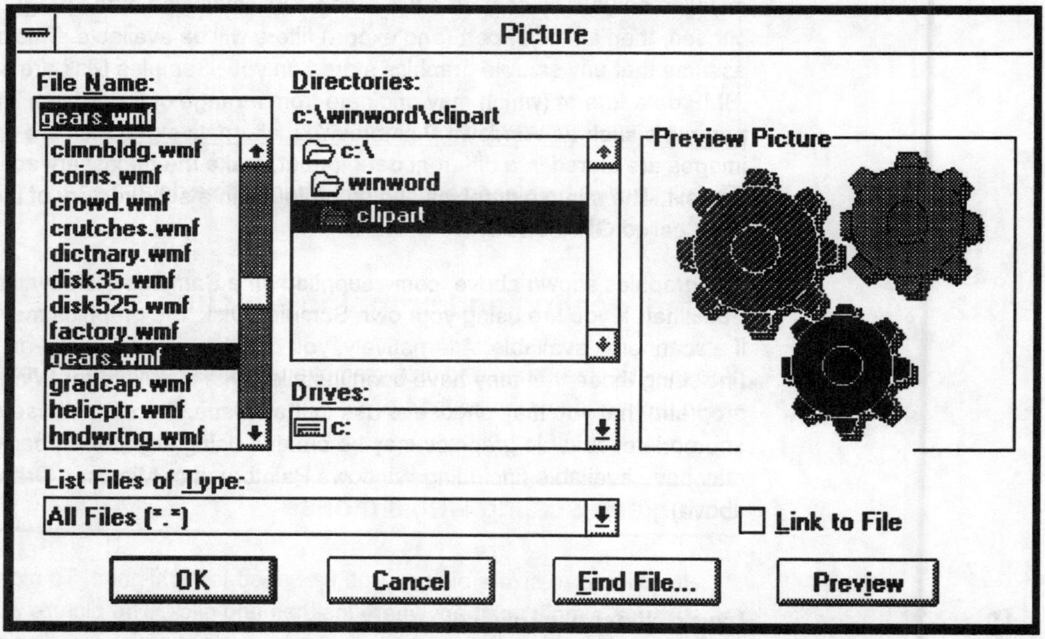

This dialogue box allows you to select a graphics file that you wish to place within the document. Word for Windows provides a clip-art collection which is stored in a **CLIPART** subdirectory of the **WINWORD** directory in which the program is normally installed.

6 Locate and select the **CLIPART** subdirectory if necessary in the *Directories:* area of the *Pictures* dialogue box. A list of pictures (using a .WMF data file format) will be displayed in the *File Name:* area of the *Picture* dialogue box.

Any picture file may be viewed in the *Preview Picture* area by first selecting it in the *File Name:* area and then selecting the **Preview** command button. You may like to try this.

7 Select the **WOMAN.WMF** picture file, preview it if you wish and accept to place the picture into the document at the current cursor position.

MONTHS AND THEIR FORTUNE

JANUARY

Those who have a birthday in January are ambitious, proud, loyal, careless as to appearances; reserved, averse from showing their feelings. They have good business ability, if born in the second half of the month.

The women are interested in engineering.

The picture will be placed into the document with a default size.

12.2 Sizing, scaling and cropping a picture

You may re-size, scale and crop (remove unwanted areas of the image) pictures using the mouse or the keyboard.

Sizing and scaling with a mouse

- In order to re-size a picture, you first need to highlight it. To highlight a picture, simply point anywhere inside it and click. The picture will be displayed with a picture border containing eight *sizing handles* as shown on the next page.

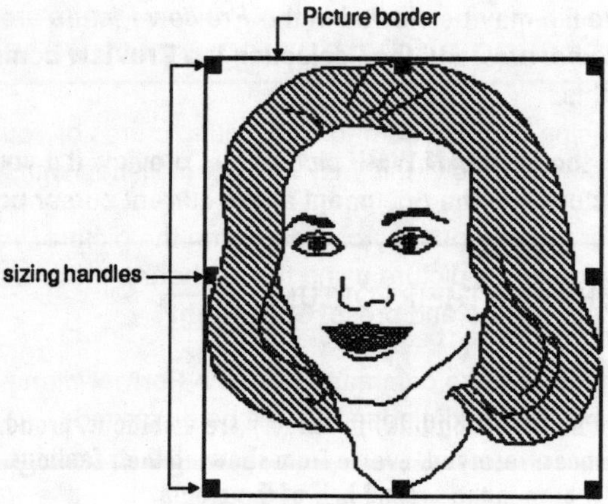

Picture resized proportionally by dragging a corner handle

- If you drag one of the corner handles, the picture will be scaled up or down, keeping the aspect ratio constant (the horizontal and vertical scaling is kept proportionally the same).
- If you drag one of the side handles, the picture will be scaled up or down, changing only the horizontal scaling. The picture will thus become proportionally taller (squashed) or wider (stretched).

- If you drag one of the top or bottom handles, the picture will be scaled up or down, changing only the vertical scaling. The picture will thus become proportionally taller (squashed) or wider (stretched).

Cropping with a mouse

Unwanted areas of a picture may be removed by the process of cropping. This may be carried out as follows:

- Highlight the picture as above.
- Hold down the **Shift** key.
- Drag any one of the eight handles to reduce the area of the picture to be included in the document.

Sizing, scaling and cropping a picture with a command

If you are using the keyboard to work with pictures or you wish to size, scale and crop pictures accurately, this may be accomplished with a command as follows:

- In order to carry out any operations on the picture, you first need to highlight it. To highlight a picture using the keyboard, place the insertion point to the left of the picture and press **Shift Right**.

- Select the **Picture** command from the **Format** menu (**Alt T R**). The following *Picture* dialogue box will be displayed:

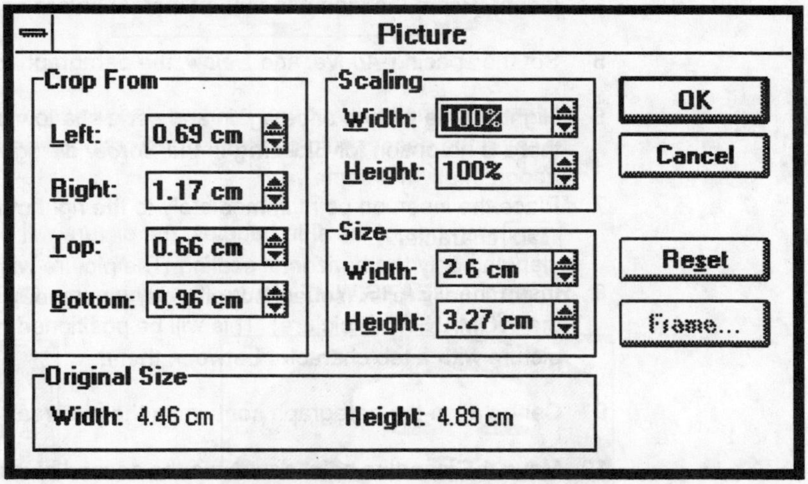

The *Size* area allows you to specify the *Width:* and *Height:* of the picture.

The *Scaling* area allows you to change the aspect ratio of the picture (scaling horizontally and vertically).

The *Crop From* area allows you to specify any cropping of the picture.

The **Reset** command button allows you to reset the picture back to its initial dimensions as indicated in the *Original Size* area.

EXERCISE 1 Using the **PICTURE.DOC** document and the methods outlined above for mouse and keyboard, experiment with the sizing, cropping and scaling of the WOMAN.WMF picture.

12.3 Positioning and formatting a picture

As has been previously mentioned, once you have inserted (sized, scaled and cropped) a picture inside a document using the method outlined above, you may treat the picture as though it was a normal paragraph. Therefore, you may alter the spacing above and below the picture, the indentation, alignment, borders around the picture and so on.

EXERCISE

1. Highlight the picture in the PICTURE.DOC document and use the **Paragraph** command in the **Format** menu or the appropriate button in the Ribbon, to set a centred paragraph alignment. The picture will be re-positioned to a central position across the page.
2. Reset the picture to left alignment.
3. Move the insertion point to the left of the picture and insert some **Tab** characters. The picture will be tabbed across the page.
4. Delete the **Tab** characters to return the picture to the left margin and adjust the left indent. The picture will be re-aligned to reflect the change in the indent. Reset the indent to the left margin before continuing.
5. Set the spacing *Above:* and *Below:* the paragraph to **0 li**,
6. Highlight the picture once again and set a shadow border around it. Notice that there is no option for **Shading** in the *Border* dialogue box.
7. Place the insertion point immediately to the right of the picture and insert a **Tab** character.
8. Insert the **GEARS.WMF** picture (from the same **CLIPART** subdirectory as the WOMAN.WMF picture). This will be positioned next to the previous picture with a tab character between them.
9. Centre align the paragraph containing the pictures.
10. Move the insertion point down into the second blank line in the text (created earlier).
11. Insert the **MAPMEN.WMF** picture.
12. Size, scale and crop the three pictures as you wish and experiment with their formatting. You may find it useful to view the document using different zoom levels.
13. When satisfied, save and print the first page of the document. A sample is shown on the next page.

You should have noticed that the picture has been behaving very much as though it were a paragraph. As with normal paragraphs, the following is also possible:

- **Deleting a picture**: any picture may be deleted from a document by first highlighting it and then either using the **Cut** command (sending it to the clipboard) or pressing **Del**.
- **Copying a picture:** any picture may be copied in the normal way using the **Copy** command.
- **Moving a picture:** any picture may be cut and pasted (using the **Paste** command) to a new position in the normal way or re-positioned using the **drag and drop** facility.

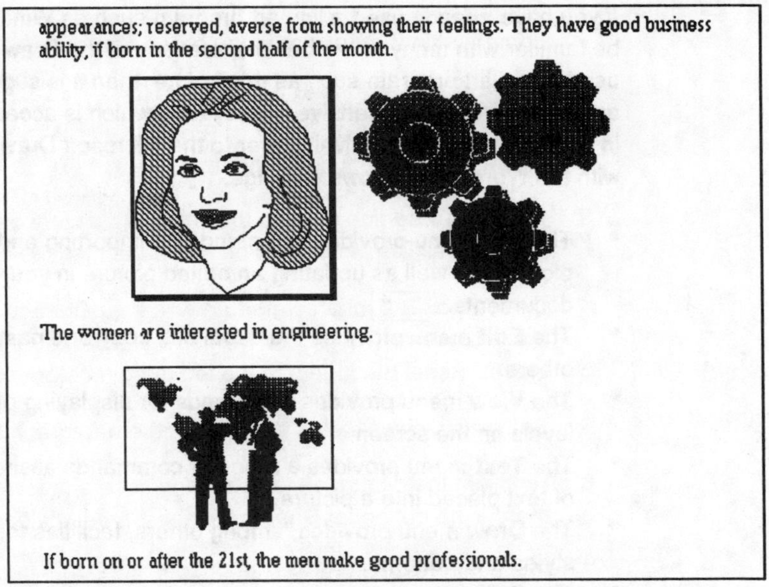
appearances; reserved, averse from showing their feelings. They have good business ability, if born in the second half of the month.

The women are interested in engineering.

If born on or after the 21st, the men make good professionals.

12.4 Editing a picture

Pictures may be created or edited using the Microsoft Draw embedded application program. This program requires a mouse, therefore only brief mention is made of the tools and commands offered by the program.

If you wish to edit an existing picture, the Draw program may be activated by: *either* highlighting the picture that you wish to edit and selecting **Picture** from the **Edit** menu (**Alt E I**) *or* double-clicking on the picture. When maximized, the Draw screen will be displayed as shown below:

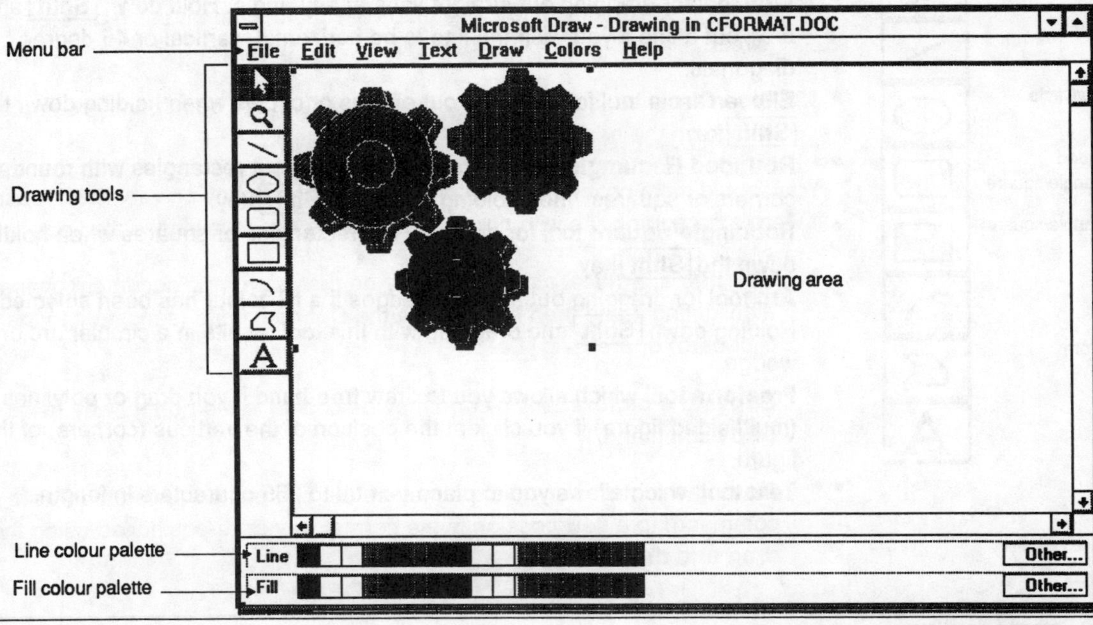

If you have already used a line art program such as Windows Paintbrush, you will be familiar with many of the basic operations of the Draw program. If you have not used a line-art program such as this before, then it is suggested that you obtain assistance from the extensive help system which is accessed via the **Help** menu in the menu bar. Alternatively, refer to the Microsoft Draw User's Guide supplied with the Word for Windows package.

- The **File** menu provides commands for importing and updating (saving) your pictures as well as updating an edited picture in your Word for Windows documents.
- The **Edit** menu provides the usual cut, copy and paste commands, among others.
- The **View** menu provides commands for displaying pictures at different zoom levels on the screen.
- The **Text** menu provides a range of commands associated with the formatting of text placed into a picture.
- The **Draw** menu provides, among others, facilities for changing drawing styles and patterns.
- The **Colors** menu contains commands for loading and saving different colour palettes which affect the **Line** and **Fill** colour palettes displayed towards the bottom of the Draw screen. These two colour palettes allow you to specify the drawing colour and any fill colour. A diamond inside a coloured box in either the Line or Fill palettes indicates the current selection. For example if a circle is to be outlined in one colour and filled in another, you may specify the colours in the appropriate colour palette.

The following drawing tools are also provided:

Pointer
Zoom
Line
Elipse/Circle
Rounded Rectangle/square
Rectangle/square
Arc
Freeform
Text

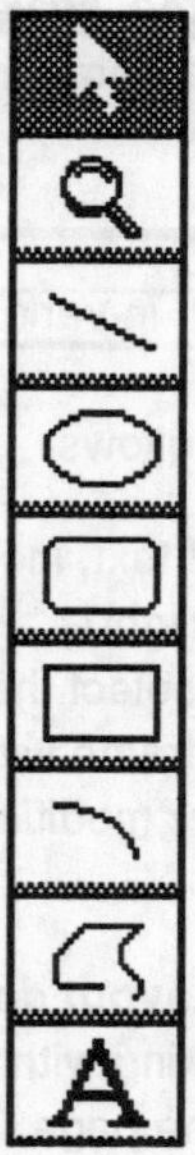

- **Pointer** tool for selecting and dragging objects in a picture.
- **Zoom** tool for zooming in and out of a picture. Select the tool and click to zoom out, or hold down Shift and click to zoom in.
- **Line** tool for dragging out straight lines at any angle. Hold down Shift and drag out a line if you wish the line to be horizontal, vertical or 45 degree diagonals.
- **Ellipse/Circle** tool for dragging out elipses or circles when holding down the Shift key.
- **Rounded Rectangle/Square** tool for dragging out rectangles with rounded corners or squares when holding down the Shift key.
- **Rectangle/Square** tool for dragging out rectangles or squares when holding down the Shift key.
- **Arc** tool for dragging out arcs (or wedges if a fill colour has been selected). Holding down Shift and dragging with this tool results in a circular arc or wedge.
- **Freeform** tool which allows you to draw free-hand if you drag or polylines (multi-sided figure) if you click at the position of the vertices (corners) of the figure.
- **Text** tool which allows you to place text up to 255 characters in length.

EXERCISE 1 Choose one of the pictures placed in the **PICTURE.DOC** document and activate the Draw program using one of the methods outlined above.

2 Obtain further assistance if necessary from the **Help** menu in the Draw program.

3 Experiment with editing the picture using the various tools and commands.

4 When ready, select the **Exit and Return to** command in the **File** menu. This will return you to your document. The picture will reflect any changes that you have made.

Note: the **Update** command found in the **File** menu of the Draw program is the equivalent of a **Save** command in the Word for Windows program. This would save an updated/edited version of the picture for future reference, over-writing the previous copy.

5 There is no need to save the document.

12.5 Placing an object into a frame

In Sections 12.1-12.4, you placed various sample pictures within a document. These pictures (apart from sizing, scaling and cropping) behave much like any other paragraph of text in the ways in which they may be formatted. Word for Windows provides another method of inserting *objects* such as pictures. This method makes use of *frames* (which look and behave much like a picture border) and the *objects* may be pictures, tables, graphs, mathematical equations, or text. Once an object has been placed within a frame, it may be sized, scaled and cropped in the same way as with picture borders. However, a frame may also be additionally:

- easily moved to any position on the page;
- made to interact with the rest of the text in the document, in various ways.

An existing document object may be placed into a frame as follows:

- Highlight the object (if the object is a whole paragraph of text, include the paragraph break at the end of the paragraph, in the highlight).
- *Either* select **Frame** from the **Insert** menu (**Alt I F**) *or* select the **Frame** button in the Toolbar. The object will be placed inside a frame with a default, single line border surrounding it (this may be removed, or modified as required).

EXERCISE 1 Load the **PICTURE.DOC** document and select a **Page Layout** document view if necessary. It is always best to use this view when working with frames since the actual location of each frame is displayed on the page.

2 Highlight the paragraph (including the paragraph break at the end) beginning 'The women are interested'.

3 Using the instructions above, place the highlighted object into a frame. Do not worry if other surrounding objects appear to be 'repelled' by this new frame.

Notice that the paragraph is placed into a frame which has a single line, box border surrounding it. This will be removed later.

4 In the same way, place the paragraph beginning 'If born on or after the 21st' into a frame.

5 Highlight the **MAPMEN.WMF** picture and place it into a frame. Again, do not worry if the main text in the documents seems to interact with the three new frames in a strange way. This will be explained on page 146.

As you have seen, it is a simple process to place any existing object into a frame.

12.6 Sizing, scaling and cropping a frame

As with picture borders, a frame may be sized, scaled and cropped using either a mouse or the keyboard.

Using a **mouse,** the processes of sizing, scaling and cropping a frame are the same as those for modifying pictures using the handles on the picture border (see page 138). A frame may be highlighted by pointing and clicking in the usual way.

A highlighted frame, just like a picture border, displays eight sizing handles. Any of these may be dragged (as with picture borders) to change the size and shape of the frame.

If the frame contains a picture or other graphic, then this may be cropped by dragging appropriate frame handles while pressing the **Shift** key (as with picture borders).

Frames containing text cannot be cropped, and when a frame is re-sized, only the frame dimensions are altered and not the contents.

If you wish to size, scale or crop a frame containing a picture using the **keyboard**, highlight the picture frame in the same way as you did for highlighting pictures (see page 137) and use the **Picture** command from the **Format** menu to make the required changes.

EXERCISE 1 Experiment with the picture frame (containing MAPMEN.WMF) inserted into the **PICTURE.DOC** document and see the effect of re-sizing, scaling and cropping it.

12.7 Positioning and formatting a frame

You have seen that frames may be manipulated in much the same ways as pictures, except that they may contain a number of different types of objects.

Frames may also be positioned anywhere on the page, much more easily than pictures placed as paragraphs. This is particularly true if you are using a mouse.

Moving a frame with a mouse

When using **Page Layout** document view, you may use a mouse to drag a frame (containing any type of object) to any new position on the page. This is accomplished as follows:

- Highlight the required frame (by pointing and clicking).
- Point to a position between any two frame handles on the frame border. The mouse pointer will turn into a four-headed arrow.
- Drag the frame to a new position A dotted frame border will indicate the position of the frame while you drag it.

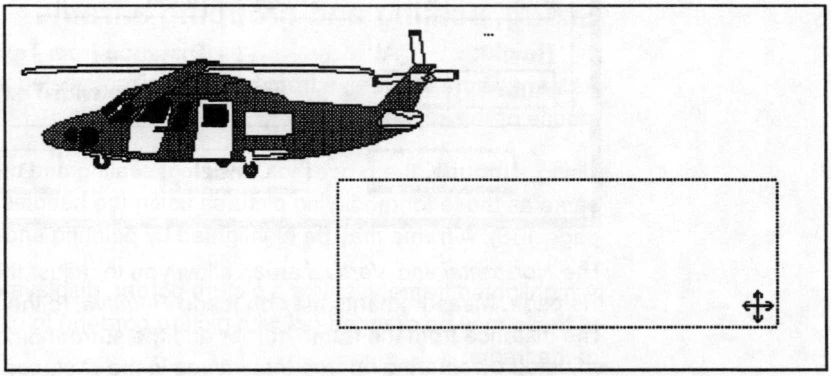

- Release the mouse button to fix the new position of the frame.

Sizing and positioning a frame with a command

If you are using the keyboard to work with frames or you wish to apply accurate changes to the characteristics of a frame, the **Frame** command found in the **Format** menu may be used as follows:

- Before you can operate on a frame using the **keyboard**, you must first *either* move the insertion point into the frame (if it contains text) *or* highlight it (if the frame contains a picture). This is best done using the **Normal** document view. When you have completed an operation on the frame you can switch back to **Page Layout** document view to see the effect of any changes.

  In **Normal** document view, framed objects have a small, non-printing, square bullet to their left to indicate that they are contained within frames.

  Moving the insertion point into frames which contain objects other than pictures (using the cursor control keys) is a simple process using this document view. Frames containing pictures may be highlighted in the normal way, or the insertion point may be positioned to the left of the frame.

If you are using a mouse, frames may be highlighted in the normal way.

- Select the **Frame** command from the **Format** menu (**Alt T F**). The following *Frame* dialogue box will be displayed.

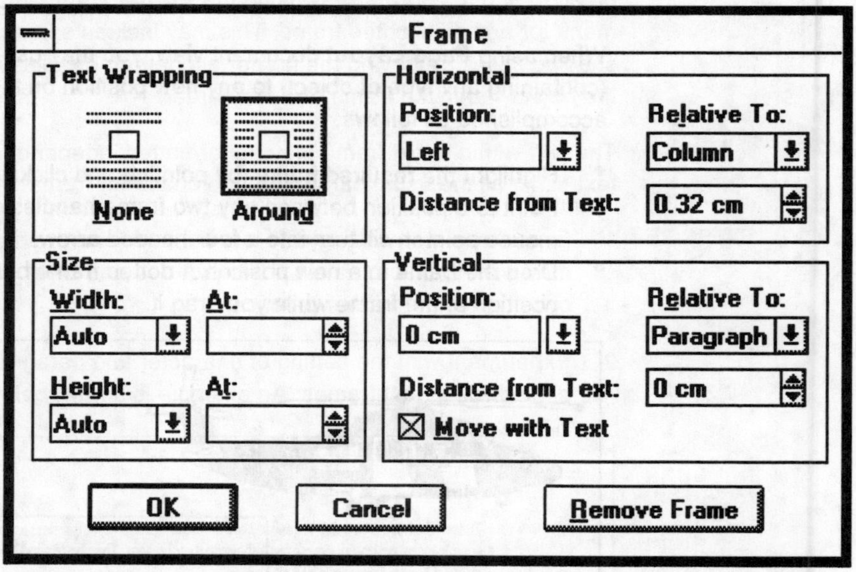

The *Horizontal* and *Vertical* areas allow you to adjust the position of the frame on the page. Measurements may be made *Relative:* to the **Column, Page** or **Margin.** The distance from the frame border and the surrounding text may also be adjusted by entering appropriate values in the *Distance from Text:* text boxes. The **Move with Text** option allows you to indicate whether or not the frame should automatically be repositioned if the surrounding text is moved.

The *Size* area allows you to adjust the dimensions of the frame.

The *Text Wrapping* area allows you to specify how the frame will interact with the surrounding text. The **None** option instructs the program to stop the flow of text above the frame and continue with the text below it. The **Around** option instructs the program to flow text around the sides of the frame (this is the default setting).

A frame may be deleted by selecting the **Remove Frame** command button. If the frame contains text, then the text will have the default border set around it.

- Make the required changes and accept.

EXERCISE

1. If you have a mouse, practice dragging the three frames in the **PICTURE.DOC** document around the page.
2. Practice using the **Frame** command in the **Format** menu (**Alt T F**) to re-size, and position the three frames.
3. Experiment with the *Text Wrapping* and *Distance from Text:* options. You may, for example, wish to move a frame into a normal paragraph of text with the *Text Wrapping* option set to **Around** and observe the effect.

Formatting a frame and frame contents

Each new frame is surrounded by a single line, box border by default. The border (and shading of frames containing objects other than pictures and graphics) may be altered in the normal way using the **Border** command found in the **Format** menu for any highlighted frame. This may include setting different line and shading styles, removing the border altogether, or adjusting the distance between the object within the frame and the border.

The text within a text frame may be formatted independently of any surrounding text using all the usual paragraph and character formatting facilities.

EXERCISE

1. Experiment with setting different borders (and/or shading) around frames. You may wish to place the other two pictures and other sections of text within their own frames, for further practice.
2. Experiment with the setting of character and paragraph formatting of the text placed within text frames. An example is shown below:

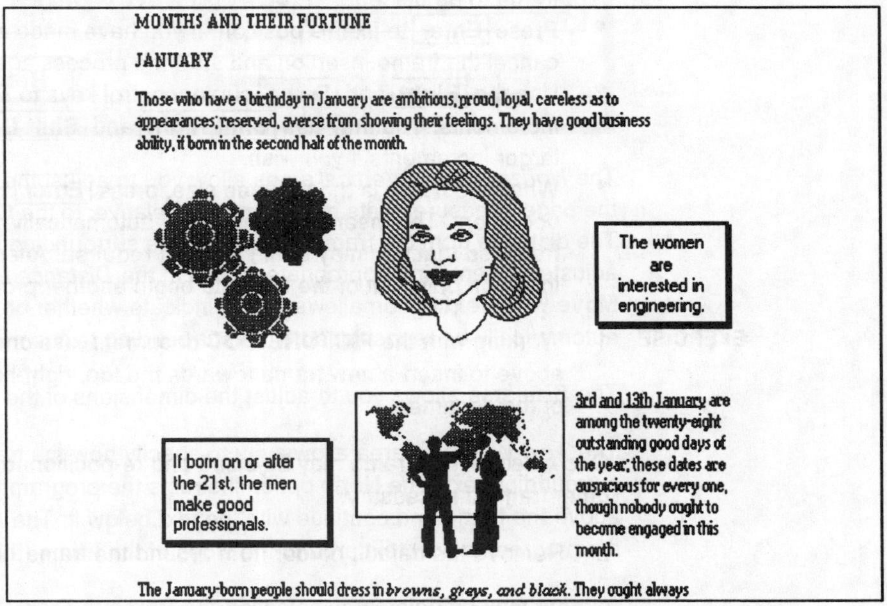

MONTHS AND THEIR FORTUNE

JANUARY

Those who have a birthday in January are ambitious, proud, loyal, careless as to appearances; reserved, averse from showing their feelings. They have good business ability, if born in the second half of the month.

The women are interested in engineering.

If born on or after the 21st, the men make good professionals.

3rd and 13th January are among the twenty-eight outstanding good days of the year; these dates are auspicious for every one, though nobody ought to become engaged in this month.

The January-born people should dress in *browns, greys, and black*. They ought always

12.8 Importing objects into frames

You have previously placed existing document objects into frames. Word for Windows however, allows you to define empty frames into which you may import and place other objects as required.

Inserting an empty frame

An empty frame may be inserted into a document using a **mouse** as follows:

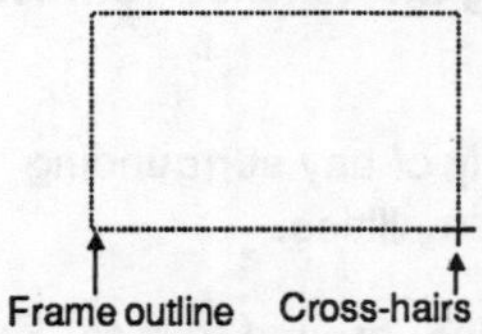

- Select the **Page Layout** document view, if necessary.
- Either select **Frame** from the **Insert** menu or select the **Frame** button on the Toolbar. The mouse pointer will be displayed as cross-hairs.
- Position the cross-hairs where you want the top, left-hand corner of the new frame to be placed.
- Drag out the new frame until it is the desired size and shape.
- Release the mouse button to complete the operation.

An empty frame may be inserted into a document using the **keyboard** as follows:

- Select the **Page Layout** document view, if necessary.
- Select **Frame** from the **Insert** menu (Alt I F). A cursor will be displayed as cross-hairs on the screen.
- Position the cross-hairs where you want the top, left-hand corner of the new frame to be placed.
- Press Enter to fix this position. If you have made a mistake, press Esc to cancel the frame insertion and start the process again.
- Use the Right and Down cursor control keys to size the frame in small increments. You may use Shift Right and Shift Down to size the frame in larger increments if you wish.
- When the frame is the required size, press Enter to insert the frame in the document. The insertion point will be automatically placed within the new frame so that you may begin typing if required. Alternatively, move the insertion point out of the frame to begin another process.

EXERCISE

1 Working with the **PICTURE.DOC** document, use one of the methods outlined above to insert a new frame towards the top, right-hand side of the first page of the document.

Once placed, this frame may be sized and re-positioned in the same way as any other frame if necessary.

2 Remove the default border from around the frame.

3 Save the document when ready.

Importing a picture into a frame

An object may be easily placed into any frame in much the same way as sample pictures were placed into documents earlier. The major advantage of placing an object into a frame (other than being able to re-position it easily) is that the object will be pre-sized according to the size of the frame. To import a **picture** into an empty frame, simply:

- place the insertion point inside the frame;
- select **Picture** from the **Insert** menu;
- select the appropriate picture file as before.

EXERCISE 1 Use the method outlined above to insert the **STAR.WMF** picture into the new frame placed at the top of the first page of the **PICTURE.DOC** document. This picture should be found in the **CLIPART** subdirectory as before.

2 Re-size and adjust the position of the frame as you feel necessary.

MONTHS AND THEIR FORTUNE

JANUARY

3 Save the document when ready.

Importing other objects

Apart from the Microsoft Draw program encountered on page 141, the full installation of Word for Windows has a number of additional embedded programs:

Microsoft WordArt allows you to create special effects with text. This program will be explored in the exercise that follows.

Microsoft Graph is used to generate graphs from data arranged in tables. This will be explored on page 225.

Microsoft Equation Editor allows you to generate mathematical equations. Due to the specialist nature of this program, it will not be examined in this text.

Any of the objects generated by these and other programs (including additional documents) may be imported into frames, using the **Object** command found in the **Insert** menu.

Using WordArt

EXERCISE 1 Open the PICTURE.DOC document if necessary and delete the first paragraph forming the document heading ('Months and their fortune').

2 If necessary, switch to a **Page Layout** document view and use a **Page Width** zoom level.

3 Move the **STAR.WMF** picture frame temporarily out of the way, to a location further down the page. Remove the frame highlight before continuing. Do not worry about the effect that this frame may have on other elements on the page, as it will be re-positioned later.

4 Insert a new, empty frame which should be dragged across the top of the first page (from the left to the right-hand margins) of the document as shown on the next page.

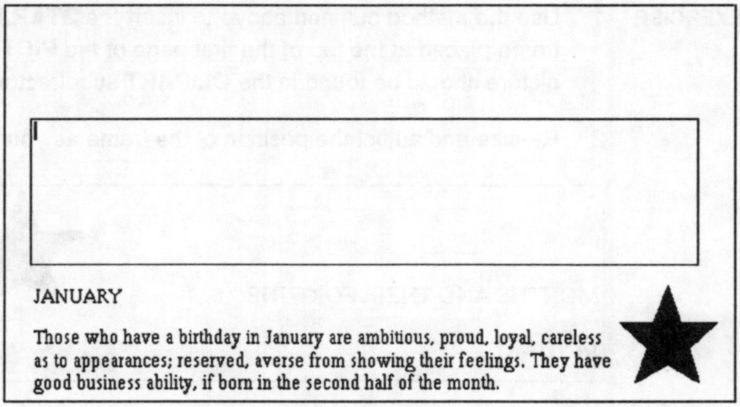

5 Remove the border surrounding this frame.

6 With the insertion point inside the frame, select the **Object** command from the **Insert** menu (**Alt I O**). The following *Objects* dialogue box will be displayed:

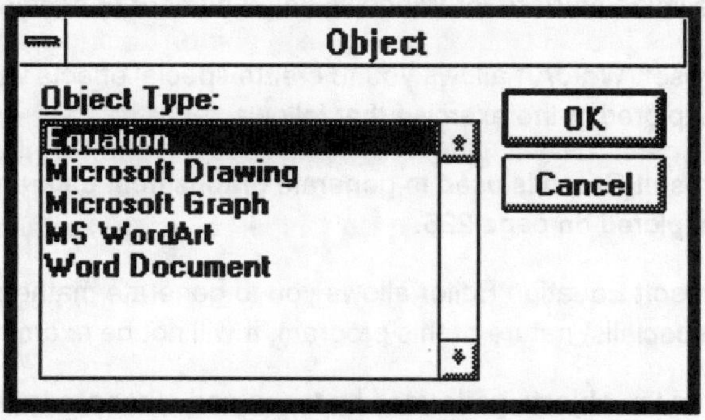

This dialogue box lists the embedded programs which have been installed with the Word for Windows program.

7 Select the **MS WordArt** option in the *Object Type:* list (double-click *or* select and accept). A WordArt screen will be displayed. This is shown on the next page.

8 Type **Months and their fortune** into the area at the top of the dialogue box. This text will appear inside the *Preview* area after a short pause.

9 Select a suitable font for the text using the pull-down list in the *Font* text box. Observe the change of font in the *Preview* area.

10 Select the **Arch Up** option in the *Style* pull-down list. Note the wide variety of different text styles available.

The drop-down list attached to the *Fill* text box allows you to change the colour of the text.

The *Align* drop-down list provides a variety of different text alignment options.

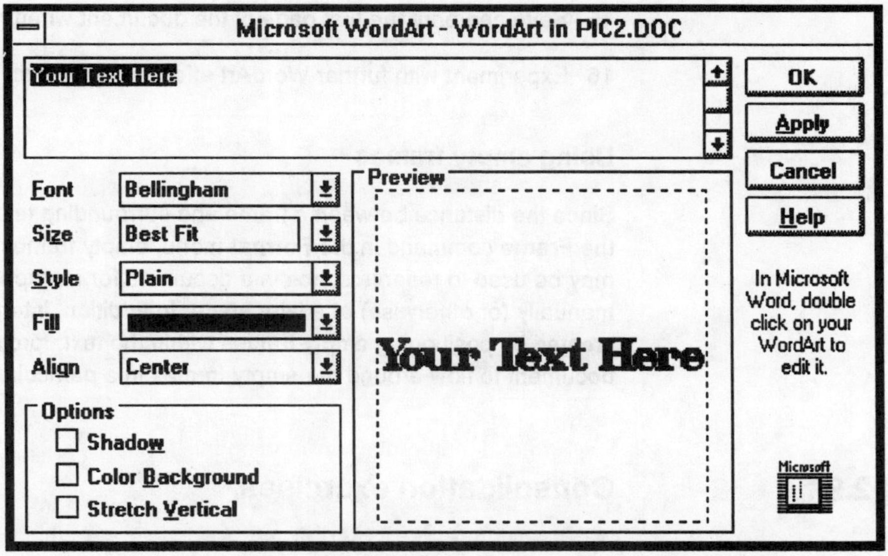

The *Options* area contains an option for creating a **Shadow** effect on the text, giving the text a coloured background (**Color Background**) and for increasing the height of the text characters (**Stretch Vertical**).

11 Experiment with different options, observing their effect in the *Preview* area. Before continuing, ensure that the following are set: *Size*: **Best Fit**; *Style*: **Arch Up**; *Align*: **Center**; **No** *Options* check boxes selected.

12 When ready, accept to return to the document. The WordArt effect will be placed into a default, large frame.

13 Re-size the WordArt frame so that it occupies the same area as the original empty frame inserted earlier. Note that the WordArt text is re-sized with the frame.

14 Move the **STAR.WMF** picture frame into position under the WordArt text and re-size as necessary.

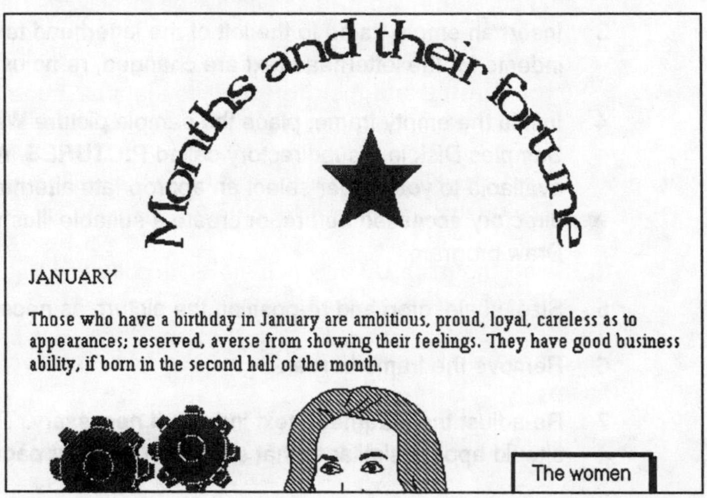

15 Save and print the first page of the document when ready.

16 Experiment with further WordArt effects as you wish

Using empty frames

Since the distance between a frame and surrounding text can be adjusted using the **Frame** command in the **Format** menu, empty frames (with or without borders) may be used to reserve space in a document for a graphic that is to be pasted in manually (or otherwise) at a later stage. In addition, interesting effects may be created by positioning empty frames within the text, forcing the text in the document to flow around the empty frames in a particular way.

12.9 Consolidation exercises

Including a graphic in a template

In the following exercise, the FWLETR.DOT template prepared on page 131 will be modified to include the graphic called WINGS.BMP stored in the GRAPHICS subdirectory, found on the Samples Disk in drive A:.

Loading and editing a template

EXERCISE

1 Open a new document, select **Template** in the *New* area of the *New* dialogue box and select the **FWLETR** template in the *Use Template:* list. The text making up the FWLETR.DOT template will appear.

2 Use a **Page Layout** document view and set the left indent for the three paragraphs making up the letterhead to the **5 cm** mark on the Ruler. The rules above and below the letterhead text will be shorter as a result. A logo (a picture) is to be placed to the left of the letterhead.

3 Insert an empty frame to the left of the letterhead text. If you find that the indents for the letterhead text are changed, re-adjust them.

4 Inside the empty frame, place the sample picture **WINGS.BMP** stored on the Samples Disk in a subdirectory called **PICTURES**. *Note:* if this picture is not available to you, either select an appropriate alternative from the **CLIPART** directory accessed before, or create a suitable illustration in the Microsoft Draw program.

5 Size, scale, crop and re-position the picture as necessary.

6 Remove the frame border.

7 Re-adjust the letterhead text indents if necessary. The top part of the template should appear similar to that shown on the next page.

The Flying Wheels
Motoring Club
Maple End, Hareward Way, Chinnor, Bucks. OK2 3MB

8 Use the **Save As** command to save the new template under the name of **FWLETGRF** (Flying Wheels letterhead with graphics). This will be used in Part III of this guide.

9 Print a copy of the template.

A newsletter document

The following exercise is used for the consolidation of basic wordprocessing skills developed in Part I and the more extensive skills developed in Part II of this guide.

The exercise is deliberately less prescriptive than has been the case previously. If necessary, refer to the appropriate pages in the text for assistance.

The completed sample document is shown on the next page and contains the following formatting ingredients:

- Character formatting;
- Column text;
- Paragraph, line, column and page breaks;
- Formatting with paragraph styles;
- Paragraph borders and shading;
- Indents and hanging indents;
- Numbered or bulleted lists;
- Frames containing pictures and text;
- Footer.

You may wish to follow the instructions found in the exercise that follows. Alternatively, you may wish to attempt to create a similar document (with or without the same layout) on your own.

EXERCISE 1 Open a new document with the **NORMAL** template.

2 Set the page margins to:

Top: **1 cm**
Bottom: **2.54 cm**
Left and Right: **1.5 cm**

3 Type the text shown on pages 155-156.

Flying Wheels The *Club News*

Chairman's Chatter

The Rallies organised during this past year have proved to be very enjoyable. The weather has been kind to us and the turn-out has been impressive. We have had fewer break-downs than in previous years. This is all credit to Mr. Timpson, who has proved to be a fountain of knowledge, particularly with the older engineering practices.

Once again, we have approached numerous Councils about the condition of some road surfaces, and hope that they will do something about them before next year.

We have had some complaints from the general public about the incorrect usage of hand signals by some of our members owning vehicles which do not possess modern indicators. I have taken the opportunity of including a description of accepted signals in this issue of the News Sheet, for those who seek clarification.

Thank you for all your continued support. Happy motoring!

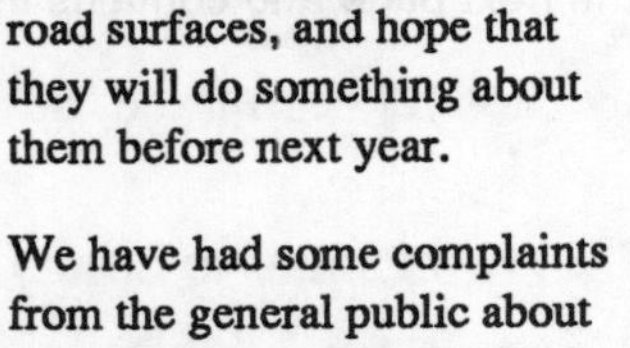

Events

Club events this year will all take place on Sundays. Dates have not yet been fixed, but you will be informed of them in the next issue of the News Sheet.

We aim to have at least four Rallies to National Trust properties, two Picnics to beauty spots and one Day Trip to France.

Event Results

Treasure Hunts

Overall winners:
the Chertsey family.

Runners up:
Mr. & Mrs. Parkin.

Best Car Award

Winner:
Mr. Swanson for his Morris 8.

Runner up:
Mrs. James for her Austin Ruby.

Congratulations to you all.

Facilities

- Wells' Garage in Bledlow is still available to our members every weekend from 8.30a.m. to 8.30p.m. Mr. Timpson will be on hand during these times to assist and offer advice.
- Please remember to provide your own consumables.
- Any spares not in the garage may be obtained for you at cost price.
- The Map Library has been transferred to Wells' Garage and members are welcome to borrow the maps at any time, but please return them - eventually!

Please note:

We will not be meeting during January next year.

Vol. 5 Issue 3 *Page 1*

Flying

Wheels

The

Club

News

Chairman's Chatter

The Rallies organised during this past year have proved to be very enjoyable. The weather has been kind to us and the turn-out has been impressive. We have had fewer break-downs than in previous years. This is all credit to Mr. Timpson, who has proved to be a fountain of knowledge, particularly with the older engineering practices.

Once again, we have approached numerous Councils about the condition of some road surfaces, and hope that they will do something about them before next year.

We have had some complaints from the general public about the incorrect usage of hand signals by some of our members owning vehicles which do not possess modern indicators. I have taken the opportunity of including a description of accepted signals in this issue of the News Sheet, for those who seek clarification.

Thank you for all your continued support. Happy motoring!

Events

Club events this year will all take place on Sundays. Dates have not yet been fixed, but you will be informed of them in the next issue of the News Sheet.

We aim to have at least four Rallies to National Trust properties, two Picnics to beauty spots and one Day Trip to France.

Event Results

Treasure Hunts

Overall winners:

the Chertsey family.

Runners up:

Mr. & Mrs. Parkin.

Best Car Award

Winner:

Mr. Swanson for his

Morris 8.

Runner up:

Mrs. James for her

Austin Ruby.

Congratulations to you all.

Facilities

Wells' Garage in Bledlow is still available to our members every weekend from 8.30 a.m. to 8.30 p.m. Mr. Timpson will be on hand during these times to assist and offer advice.

Please remember to provide your own consumables.

Any spares not in the garage may be obtained for you at cost price.

The Map Library has been transferred to Wells' Garage and members are welcome to borrow the maps at any time, but please return them – eventually!

Please note:

We will not be meeting during January next year.

4 Edit the text as necessary.

5 Save the document under the name of **NEWS** on the Samples Disk.

At the top of the page is a masthead. The term *masthead* is often used to describe the banner or wide title found on the front of a magazine, newsletter or newspaper.

There are two ways in which you could organise the newsletter document to contain the masthead and the rest of the text arranged into three columns.

Method 1:

- Format the document into three columns.
- Insert a new frame to cover the complete area of the masthead across the top of the document, from left to right margins. There should only be a bottom border set for this frame.
- Highlight the text to be placed on the left of the masthead and place it in a frame. Size and position this frame in the masthead. Repeat for the sections of text designated for the centre and right-hand positions in the masthead. These three frames should have no border.

Method 2:

- Divide the page into three sections using continuous breaks:
- Section 1 should contain the masthead containing the text 'Flying..' to '..News'.
  Section 2 should consist of a blank line with a border set above it, providing the rule underneath the masthead.
- Sections 1 and 3 should be formatted into three columns with **1cm** spacing between columns.
- Insert column breaks in section 1 (the masthead) as appropriate.

6 Set up the page layout using one of the methods outlined above.

7 Set **centred alignment** for the paragraphs in the masthead.

8 Set the text in the left and right-hand columns in the masthead to **Tms Rmn 36 pt, bold** and **italic.**

9 Set the character formatting of the word 'The' in the centre column of the masthead to **Tms Rmn 18 pt.**

10 Set the remaining text in the document to **Tms Rmn 12 pt** with **1 li** of spacing set above each paragraph.

11 The main headings in the text should be set at **Helv 14 pt, bold** and **centred.** A **shadow border** should be set around each heading paragraph. This would be best set up as a paragraph style.

12 The sub-headings in the 'Event Results' section should be set to **Helv 12 pt, bold.** The remaining text within this section should be set with **0 li** spacing above the paragraphs.

13 Italicise the appropriate text elements.

14 The last paragraph in this section should have a **shadow border** set around it and should be shaded with a light tint.

15 The text in the 'Facilities' section should be set to either a bulleted or numbered list.

16 'Please note:' should be set to **Helv 14 pt, bold** and a **double line border** set around the two paragraphs making up this section.

17 An empty paragraph between the 'Events' and 'Event Results' sections should be set to have a **Double line border** above it.

18 A footer should be positioned as shown, at the bottom of the page. The character formatting should be set at **Tms Rmn 10pt, italic.**

19 The **CAR1.BMP** graphic should be placed, cropped and sized at the bottom of the first column. Use column breaks as necessary.

20 The **CAR2.BMP** graphic should be placed, cropped and sized at the top of the right-hand column. Use column breaks as necessary. Similarly, the **WINGS.BMP** graphic should be placed into position in the masthead.

21 Adjust the spacing between all the elements on the page until a satisfactory result is obtained. Remember that you may use line breaks (**Shift Enter**) to move sections of text down onto another line if necessary, without inserting any paragraph spacing.

Part III

Advanced level

Introduction

The purpose of Part III of this guide is to introduce further formatting facilities, consistent with examination syllabuses at Advanced Level, offered by the Word for Windows program. In addition, advanced production methods are introduced and practiced.

The Word for Windows program offers many sophisticated facilities for the extremely efficient processing of documents and their production. In addition, the program provides facilities for the automation and customisation of processes, including the generation of an index and table of contents. Provision is also made for the generation of your own pull-down menu system.

The new document formatting included in Part III are as follows:

- Footnotes.
- Hyphenation.

The new production techniques include:

- Bookmarks and calculations;
- Advanced use of fields;
- Print-merging;
- Sorting and searching text;
- Use of the Glossary;
- Tables and forms;
- Multi-document processing;
- Outlining;
- Generating a table of contents;
- Automation by use of Macros.

In order to complete the exercises within Part III, the following files should be available on your Samples Disk: **CFORMAT.DOC** or **PFORMAT.DOC** (prepared on pages 60 and 64 respectively); **TABS1.DOC** (prepared on page 82); **MEMBERS.DOC** and **MEMBERS2.DOC** (prepared on pages 100 and 101 respectively).

In addition, one of the following templates should be available: **FWLETR.DOT** or **FWLETGRF.DOT**(prepared on pages 126 and 152 respectively).

13 Bookmarks and calculations

13.1 Bookmarks

A bookmark is a label attached to any amount of text, so that the text itself may be uniquely identified. Bookmarks are very much more than just simple place markers. They may be used to:

- Find text quickly using the **Go To** command (from the **Edit** menu *or* the F5 key).
- Mark text on which you wish to work, and automate editing and formatting functions applied to the text. This makes use of the macro facilities explored in Chapter 23.
- Mark the text and graphics that you wish to copy, move or delete.
- Mark text on which you wish to perform calculations.
- Mark text for cross-referencing, allowing for the automatic generation of a table of contents, or index.
- Mark places in a document for the insertion of text (which may change) taken from other documents. This is used in the print-merging process.

Bookmark names must begin with a letter, but may consist of up to 20 alphanumeric characters (letters and numbers). No punctuation is allowed (including spaces), however, the underline character may be used.

Bookmarks may be placed into a document by selecting **bookmark** from the **Insert** menu (ALT I M *or* Ctrl Shift F5).

Preparing a standard letter

EXERCISE

1 Open a **New** document and load the **FWLETR** or **FWLETGRF** template. The FWLETGRF letter template may take longer to print on some systems because of the inclusion of a graphic in the letterhead. If you are concerned about the length of printing time, choose the FWLETR template.

2 Type the following text into the appropriate positions in the letter template.

Mr. A. Davey

104, Mill House
Luton
Beds.
LU1 4RG

Dear Mr. Davey,

Please remember that your motor insurance, arranged for you by the Flying Wheels Motoring Club, is due for renewal on October 27 and your premium this year is £197.48, net of your no claims bonus.

The quotation excludes £8.00 for our special legal expenses cover. Should you decide to include this strongly recommended extra benefit, merely increase your payment accordingly to give a total of £205.48.

Thank you for your past custom. We hope that we can continue to be of service this year and if you would like any further help or information, please let us know.

Yours sincerely

3 In preparation for the use of bookmarks, delete the figure of **£205.48** (including the £ sign).

4 Save the letter on the Samples Disk under the name of **PREMIUM1**.

5 Ensure that **Field Codes** (in the **View** menu) is de-selected before continuing.

13.2 Inserting bookmarks

EXERCISE

1 Highlight the figure of **197.48** (not including the £ sign)

2 Select **Bookmark** from the **Insert** menu (**ALT I M** *or* **Ctrl Shift F5**). A *Bookmark* dialogue box will be displayed as shown on the next page.

3 Type the name **Premium** inside the *Bookmark Name:* text box and accept.

4 Highlight the figure of **8.00** (not including the £ sign) and insert the bookmark with the name of **LegalExpenses**.

5 Move the insertion point to the left of the full stop at the end of the paragraph which finishes with '**...give a total of ...**'.

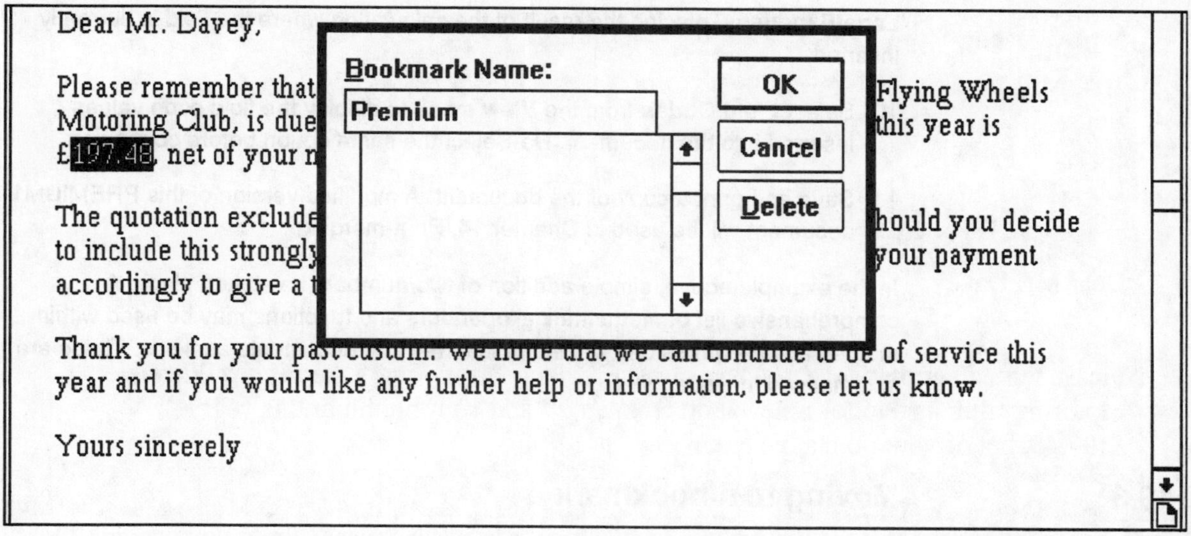

6 Insert a field by selecting **Field** from the **Insert** menu (**Ctrl F9**) as you have done before. The *Insert Field Type:* area of the *Field* dialogue box should have **= expression** highlighted.

7 Select the **£#,##0.00** number format from the *Instructions:* area of the dialogue box. This will display a number to two decimal places with a pound sign prefix.

8 Type the following inside the *Field Code:* text box:
Premium+ LegalExpenses

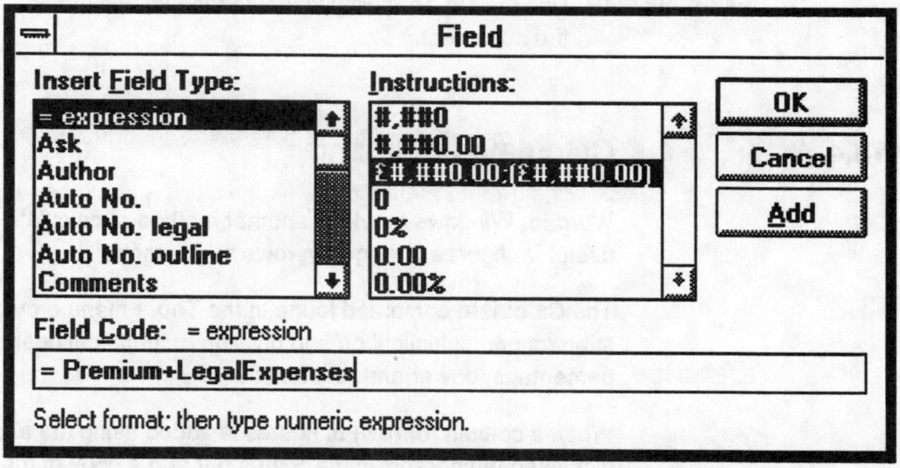

9 Accept when ready.

When you return to the document, the correct total figure should appear where you inserted the field.

In this case you instructed Word for Windows to add the number represented by the bookmark label **Premium**, to the number represented by the bookmark label

LegalExpenses, placing the result of the calculation where the field is currently inserted.

10 Select **Field Codes** from the **View** menu to display the field code values inserted into the document. De-Select the same option before continuing.

11 Save and print a copy of the document. A modified version of this PREMIUM1 document will be used in Chapter 14, Print-merging.

In the example above, simple addition of two numbers has taken place. A comprehensive list of mathematical operators and functions may be used within mathematical expressions which are inserted into documents as fields. These are summarised in *Appendix B.*

13.3 Moving to a bookmark

Once a bookmark has been defined, you may use the **Go To** facilities to locate and move to it quickly. As a reminder:

- Pressing [F5] once will allow you to type a bookmark name into the Status bar. On pressing [Enter], the bookmark will be located if it exists.
- Pressing [F5] [F5] will display the **Go To** dialogue box from which existing bookmarks may be selected. Double-clicking on the Status bar or selecting **Go To** from the **Edit** menu have the same effect.

EXERCISE 1 Use the **Go To** facility to locate the two bookmarks that you have inserted into the document.

13.4 Calculate command

Word for Windows provides another method of calculation which is particularly useful for figures arranged in rows or columns.

The **Calculate** command found in the **Tools** menu provides for the addition, subtraction, multiplication and division arithmetical operations and includes percentage, power and root functions.

When a column (or row) of figures is added using the above command, the total is displayed temporarily in the Status bar and a copy of the result is sent to the clipboard. A copy of the answer may therefore be pasted into the document (from the clipboard) at any point in the document.

Calculations across rows

EXERCISE 1 Open the **MEMBERS** document stored on the Samples Disk, which was produced on page 100.

2 Delete all the '**Total**' figures in column 5 of the table, except for 'Social Members:' and 'New Members:'. Delete also, the total figures across the bottom row of the table for '**Total End 1995**'.

3 Highlight the 3 figures in the row labelled **Austin 'Ruby'** and select **Calculate** from the **Tools** menu (**ALT O C**). The result of the calculation will be displayed temporarily in the Status bar and a copy will be sent to the clipboard.

4 Move the insertion point into the **Total** column, keeping to the same row of the table.

5 Select **Paste** from the **Edit** menu (**ALT E P** *or* **Ctrl V** *or* select the **Paste** button in the Toolbar) to paste a copy of the answer from the Clipboard to the current insertion point position.

6 In the same way, total the remaining rows in the top part of the table.

Any text included with numbers in a highlighted section (apart from exclamation marks, which may need to be deleted for satisfactory calculation) is ignored by the **Calculation** command.

Without the presence of mathematical operators, addition of numbers is assumed.

Calculations in columns

Word for Windows provides the facility to work with columns rather than blocks of text as is the norm. When in column mode operation, **COL** appears in the Status bar.

Column mode may be activated (or deactivated) by pressing **Ctrl Shift F8**. In order to perform calculations on the figures in the **MEMBERS** document, you will need to turn **column mode** on.

EXERCISE 1 Place the insertion point immediately to the right of the first number found at the top of the column for **Full** membership.

Since **Decimal** tabs have been set for the alignment of the figures in this table, care must be taken to highlight the figures within a particular column from right to left, otherwise certain digits may not be included in the subsequent calculation.

2 Press **Ctrl Shift F8** to turn column mode **on**. Notice that **COL** appears in the Status bar.

If you ever wish to cancel column mode, simply press **Esc** .

3 Highlight the numbers in the column for **Full** members (remember to highlight from right to left). The screen should appear as shown on the next page.

Make of car	Full	Family	Junior	TOTAL
Austin 'Ruby'	17	6	2	25
Austin 7 'Chummy'	9	3	0	12
Morris Minor Traveller	35	5	0	40
Morris Minor Saloon	99	20	5	124
Morris 8	4	4	2	10
Riley 1.5	16	7	0	23
Jowett Javelin	6	2	0	8
Ford 8	9	4	2	15
Rover 14	10	6	1	17
Social Members				15
New Members	41	6	3	50
Total End 1995				

4 In the same way as before, use the **Calculate** command to total the figures and **Paste** the answer into the appropriate position in the last row of the table. Note that column mode is automatically turned **off** when the calculation is complete.

5 Repeat for the remaining three columns. Be careful to position the insertion point at the top-right (or bottom) of the appropriate column first. You will then need to turn column mode **on** for each column to be totalled.

6 Embolden the figures in the last row of the table if necessary.

7 Save the document.

Column mode may also be useful in highlighting columns of text within tables for copying, moving and deleting purposes.

Calculations using a range of arithmetical operators

Numbers in rows or columns involved with calculations, may be preceded with the + (plus), – (minus), * (multiplication), / (division), % (percentage) and ^ (exponentiation – to the power of) arithmetical operators. These will be acted upon by the **Calculate** command. Negative numbers may be represented by enclosing them in brackets.

EXERCISE 1 Open a **New** document and type the following lines of text:

37 – 3 + 4 =
4 * 5 =

2 For each line, use the **Calculate** command to perform the calculation and **Paste** the answer into position. Do not include the = sign in the calculation.

3 Type the following lines of text:
Cost of goods = £5.60
V.A.T. rate = * 1.175
Cost inc. V.A.T. =

4 Highlight the first two lines of text in this section and place the calculated answer into position in the third line.

5 Type the following line of text:
Twenty percent of three hundred pounds is £300 * 20% =

6 Highlight this line, calculate the answer and paste it into position at the end of the line .

7 Type the following two lines of text:
6 to the power of ^2 =
48 to the power of ^0.5 will give the square root of the number. This is:

8 Paste the calculated answers into position on the appropriate line.

37 - 3 * 4 = 25
4 * 5 = 20

Cost of goods £5.60
V.A.T. rate = * 1.175
Cost inc. V.A.T. = £6.58

Twenty percent of three hundred pounds is £300 * 20% = £60.00

6 to the power of ^2 = 36

48 to the power of ^0.5 will give the square root of the number. This is: 6.9

9 Save the document (using **Save As**) under the name of **CALC.**

Hidden text

If the figures and text involved in a calculation are no longer required (you are only interested in the result), then they may be deleted without affecting the result of the calculation. However, it may be prudent in certain situations to keep the details of figures involved in calculations, for checking purposes. Word for Windows has a character format called **Hidden**. Any highlighted text may be hidden from view on the screen and any printouts, by selecting **Hidden** from the *Character* dialogue box accessed via the **Format** menu.

Hidden text may also be useful in adding comments or explanatory notes to a document for example, in explaining a particular Field code.

Selecting the **Options** command button from the **Print** command (**File** menu) provides an option to print any hidden text if required.

EXERCISE

1 Using the **CALC.DOC** document, highlight lines three to five, not including the result of the calculation for 'Cost inc. V.A.T.'.

2 Select **Character** from the **Format** menu and select the **Hidden** option in the *Style* area of the *Character* dialogue box. When you accept to return to your document, the highlighted text is not displayed and the result of the calculation only is shown. If printed normally, what you see on the screen is what would be printed out.

If you wish to re-display the hidden text, highlight the line containing the result of the calculation and de-select the **Hidden** character formatting from the *Character* dialogue box.

3 With the text hidden, select **Print** from the **File** menu and select the **Options** command button in the *Print* dialogue box which appears. The *Options* dialogue box for *Category:* **Print** will be displayed. This contains a **Hidden Text** check box which, when selected, will print any hidden text in a document. Accept to return to the *Print* dialogue box and either select the **Close** command button to cancel the operation or accept to print.

4 Save or close the document as you wish.

14 Basic print-merging

Print-merging (often called *mail-merging*) involves the combining of information stored in one or more documents with the information contained in another.

You probably receive large amounts of 'junk mail' on a regular basis because your name and address is to be found on one or more mailing lists. These have been gathered together and sold commercially. The lists continue to grow and are bought and sold by marketing departments and others, causing a movement of information from one company to another.

Whenever a particular company needs to 'mail-shot' potential customers, a standard document is prepared with certain specific details missing (such as name, address etc.). This standard document is then merged with the appropriate mailing list to produce as many individualised documents as are listed in it. This process is obviously very efficient.

Christmas card lists for the addressing of envelopes (printing either directly on the envelope or on sticky labels) would be another example of the use of print-merging.

The main document in the print-merging process consists of the basic text and graphics that are to be printed on each copy of the document. Any information that is to change from copy to copy, is entered as a special field code known as a *merge field*.

The information to be placed individually into the main document is prepared separately and is referred to as the *data file*. You can envisage a data file as a two-dimensional table consisting of rows and columns. The table is organised as follows:

Each column within the data file is called a *field* and the column headings are, as a result, referred to as *field names*.

Each complete row across the data file table is known as a *record* and contains all the separate items of information that are to be included within a single copy of the main document when printed.

The very first row (record) across the data file table contains all the field names (column headings) and is known as the *header record*.

The illustration on the next page shows the structure of a typical data file consisting of 8 fields, 1 header record and 3 records.

Word for Windows provides a facility which allows you to set up easily a suitable data file (in the form of a table, for up to 31 fields) and link this information to the main document for the print-merging process.

Field name

Header record →

Records (3)

Title	Initials	Surname	Addressline1	Addressline2	Town	County	PostCode
Mr.	A.	Davey		104 Mill House	Luton	Beds.	LU14RG
Mr.	K.	Wright		102 Bedford Road	Harpenden	Herts.	HY43RG
Ms.	D.	Burke	The Maltings	17 Whitehorn Way	Biggleswade	Beds.	SG173AB

Fields (8)

In the following exercises, the **Print Merge** command found in the **File** menu will first be used to create a simple data file. This data file will then be used to assist in creating a main document. Finally the data file will be print-merged with the main document to print individualised copies of the main document.

Approaching print-merging in this way simplifies the process. However, you may prepare the main document first if you wish. This approach might be useful if you are not entirely sure as to the exact nature of the information that you want to save in the data file for merging with the main document.

14.1 Preparing a data file

There are four stages involved in the preparation of a data file:

- Attach a data file to a main document.
- Define the field names in the header record for the data file.
- Enter the data records.
- Save the data file as a document.

The data file to be produced in the next exercise consists of 11 fields, a header record and 5 data records. This data file will be print-merged with a main document at a later stage.

EXERCISE

1. Open the **PREMIUM1.DOC** document and save a copy under the name of **MAILLETR** on the Samples Disk. The MAILLETR.DOC document will be modified later and is to form the main print-merge document.

2. Continue to work with the **MAILLETR.DOC** document. Select **Print Merge** from the **File** menu (**ALT F M**). The following *Print Merge Setup* dialogue box will be displayed as shown on the next page.

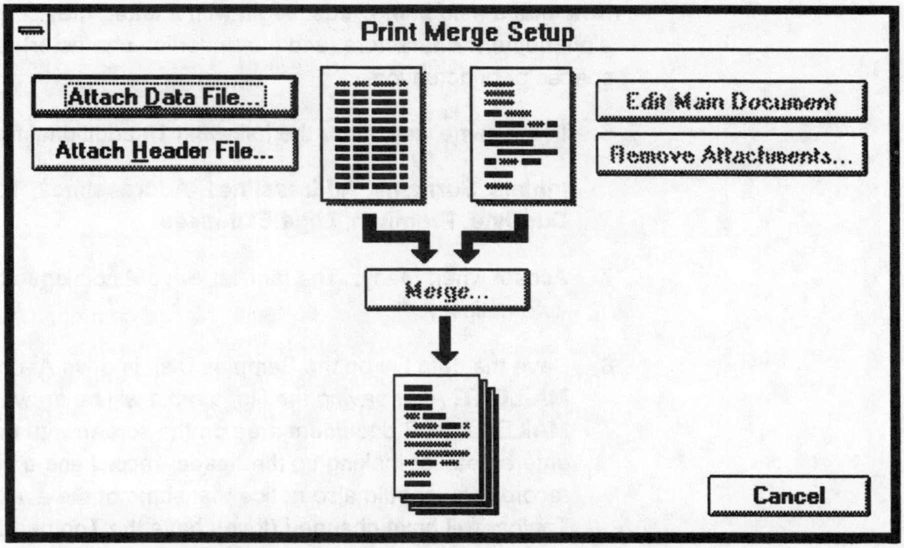

3 Select the **Attach Data File** command button to begin setting up the data file. The *Attach Data File* dialogue box should be displayed at this point.

4 Select the **Create Data File** command button. This will display the *Create Data File* dialogue box shown below:

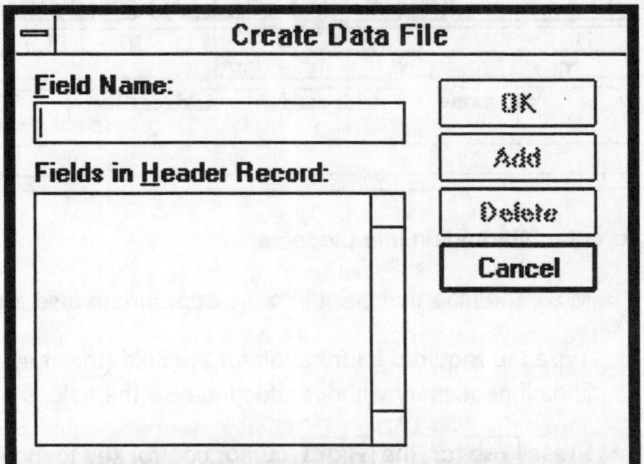

This dialogue box allows you to enter the field names (column headings forming the header record) for the data file. These are typed into the *Field Name:* text box.

You may select the **Add** command button *or* press **Enter** to add the current field name (inside the *Field Name:* text box) to the *Fields in Header Record:* area.

If you wish to delete a field name inside the *Fields in Header Record:* area, highlight the appropriate field name and select the **Delete** command button.

5 Type **Title** into the *Field Name:* text box and select the **Add** button (*or* press **Enter**). The field name 'Title' will appear inside the *Fields in Header Record:* area.

Note that a *field name:* must begin with a letter; may consist of up to 32 alphanumeric characters (and the underline character); and cannot include any spaces or punctuation.

6 In the same way, enter the following 10 additional field names:

Initials, Surname, Addressline1, Addressline2, Town, County, PostCode, DueDate, Premium, LegalExpenses.

7 Accept when ready. The familiar *Save As* dialogue box will be displayed automatically.

8 Save the data file on the Samples Disk in drive A: under the name of **MAILDAT**. After saving the file, a table will be drawn inside the MAILDAT.DOC document area on the screen with the field names that you entered earlier making up the header record and a blank row for a data record. You should also notice that some of the available buttons in the Toolbar will have changed (If you have the Toolbar displayed). These buttons are used to edit a data file and their function will be explained on page 182.

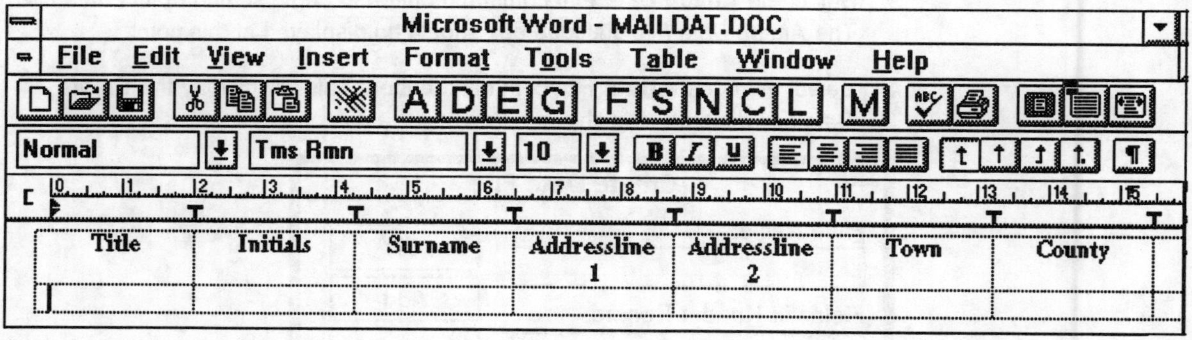

To enter information into the table:

- Move the insertion point into the appropriate field for a record.
- Type the required information for the field (this may wrap-around onto more lines if necessary without affecting how the field is printed).
- Press Tab or the Right cursor control key to move to the next field. Alternatively, move the insertion point with the mouse. If there is no information for a particular field, move to the next field to contain information.
- Enter all the information for the data record into the appropriate fields.
- Press Tab to start entering information for another record.

If you press Enter by mistake, you will need to move the insertion point to the last field in the last record of the file and press Tab.

9 Enter the following five data records, using the instructions above. The screen will scroll left and right as you proceed. Do not worry if your data items wrap-round onto the next line.

Title	Initials	Surname	Addressline1	Addressline2	Town	County	PostCode	DueDate	Premium	LegalExpenses
Mr.	A.	Davey		104 Mill House	Luton	Beds.	LU1 4RG	October 16	197.48	8.00
Mr.	K.	Wright	The Dell	102 Bedford Road	Harpenden	Herts.	HY4 3RG	October 19	745.37	45.00
Mrs.	A. F.	Norton		99 Wilton Road	Letchworth	Herts.	SG22 3JM	October 23	127.50	7.00
Ms.	D.	Burke	The Maltings	17 Whitehorn Way	Biggleswade	Beds.	SG17 3AB	October 22	375.99	12.00
Mrs.	A. N.	Other		66 Frederick Street	Stevenage	Herts.	SG1 3BE	October 17	599.99	63.27

10 Save the file (use **Save**) when ready. Fill in the *Summary Info* form as usual.

14.2 Preparing a main document

The main document, MAILLET.DOC, now needs to be modified in order to accept data from the data file. This document contains names, addresses and other values which need to be removed from the document. These pieces of information will be replaced by merge fields in the next exercise.

EXERCISE 1 If **MAILDAT.DOC** is the current document:

Either select **MAILLETR.DOC** from the **Window** menu

or select **Print Merge** from the **File** menu and select the **Edit Main Document** command button in the *Print Merge Setup* dialogue box which appears.

The document will be displayed as normal but an additional *Print merge bar* will be displayed above the Ruler.

2 Edit the letter in the following ways:

- If your letter contains the WINGS graphic in the letterhead, you may wish to delete this as this will save time in printing multiple copies of the document later.
- Delete the text in the address block (including the name). Insert an extra line to give 6 empty lines under the date.
- Delete the name after 'Dear'.
- Delete the date for policy renewal, leaving the spaces either side between which you will insert a new date from the data file later.

- Insert a *soft return* (Shift Enter) before the **£** symbol of the **Premium** figure. A soft return forces the text onto a new line, ignoring any paragraph spacing. This may be necessary as the figure is close to the end of the line and it is possible that it may be split over two lines. This is therefore, just a precaution.
- Delete the two sums for premium and legal expenses (retaining the £ symbol).

3 Save the document.

14.3 Inserting merge fields

The final stage in the print-merging preparation stages is to place merge fields, containing appropriate field names (corresponding to those in the header record of the data file), into position within the main document.

When placing merge fields, you should have an awareness of what spacing, if any, is required either side of the information that will be ultimately inserted into the main document from the data file, before printing.

Merge fields create the link between the main document and specific items of information in the data file. There are two methods of inserting a merge field into a document at the current insertion point position:

Method 1
Select the **Insert Merge Field** command button (ALT Shift F) found in the *Print Merge bar*. This displays the *Insert Merge Field* dialogue box shown below.

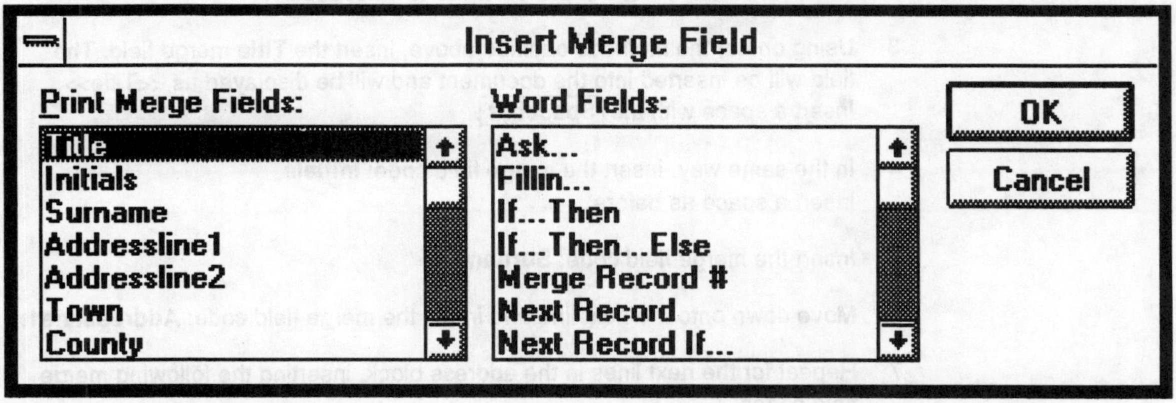

The *Print Merge Fields:* area contains a list of the field names that you prepared for the header record in the data file earlier. The *Word Fields:* area gives more advanced options which will be explored on page 188.

To select a field for insertion into the document, *either* double-click on the required field name *or* select and accept it.

Method 2

Select **Field** from the **Insert** menu (ALT I D) to display the familiar *Field* dialogue box.

Inside the *Insert Field Type:* area of the dialogue box, select **Merge Field.** The list of field names entered into the header record of the data file earlier are shown in the *Instructions:* area. This is shown below:

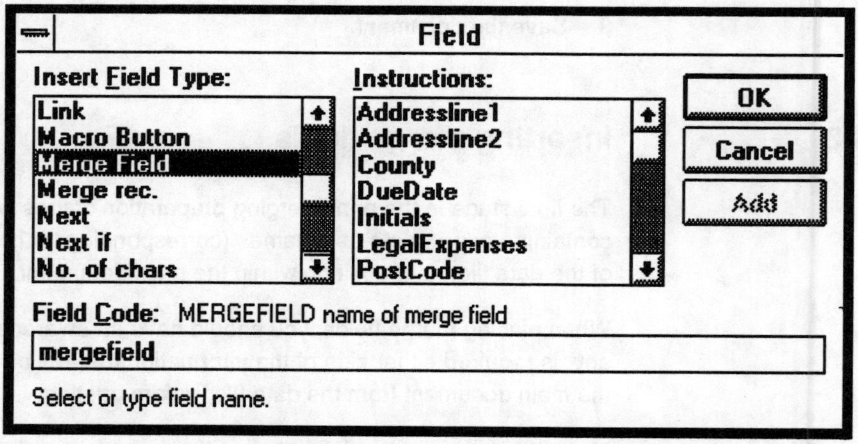

To select a field for insertion into the document, *either* double-click on the required field name *or* select and accept it.

EXERCISE

1 Load the **MAILLETR.DOC** document if necessary and move the insertion point into the first line of the address block.

2 De-select **Field Codes** in the **View** menu if necessary.

3 Using one of the methods outlined above, insert the **Title** merge field. The field will be inserted into the document and will be displayed as <<Title>>. Insert a space with the Spacebar

4 In the same way, insert the merge field code: **Initials.** Insert a space as before.

5 Insert the merge field code: **Surname.**

6 Move down onto the next line and insert the merge field code: **Addressline1.**

7 Repeat for the next lines in the address block, inserting the following merge field codes:
Addressline2
Town
County
PostCode

8 Insert the following merge field codes at the end of the line beginning '**Dear** ' (insert a space between the two codes):
Title and **Surname**
Add a comma. The document should appear as shown on the next page.

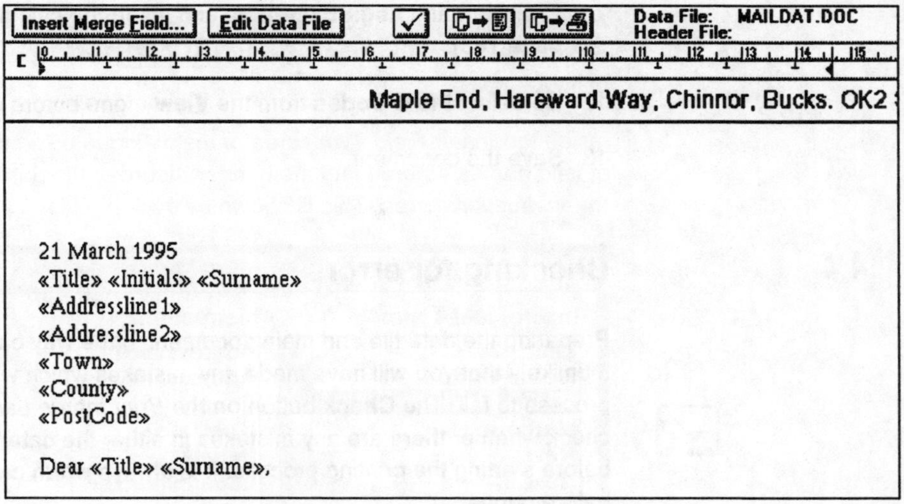

Maple End, Hareward Way, Chinnor, Bucks. OK2

21 March 1995
«Title» «Initials» «Surname»
«Addressline1»
«Addressline2»
«Town»
«County»
«PostCode»

Dear «Title» «Surname»,

9 In the same way, insert the merge field codes into position for:
DueDate
Premium
LegalExpenses

10 Select **Field Codes** from the **View** menu and examine the merge field codes. The bottom section of the document should appear as shown below.

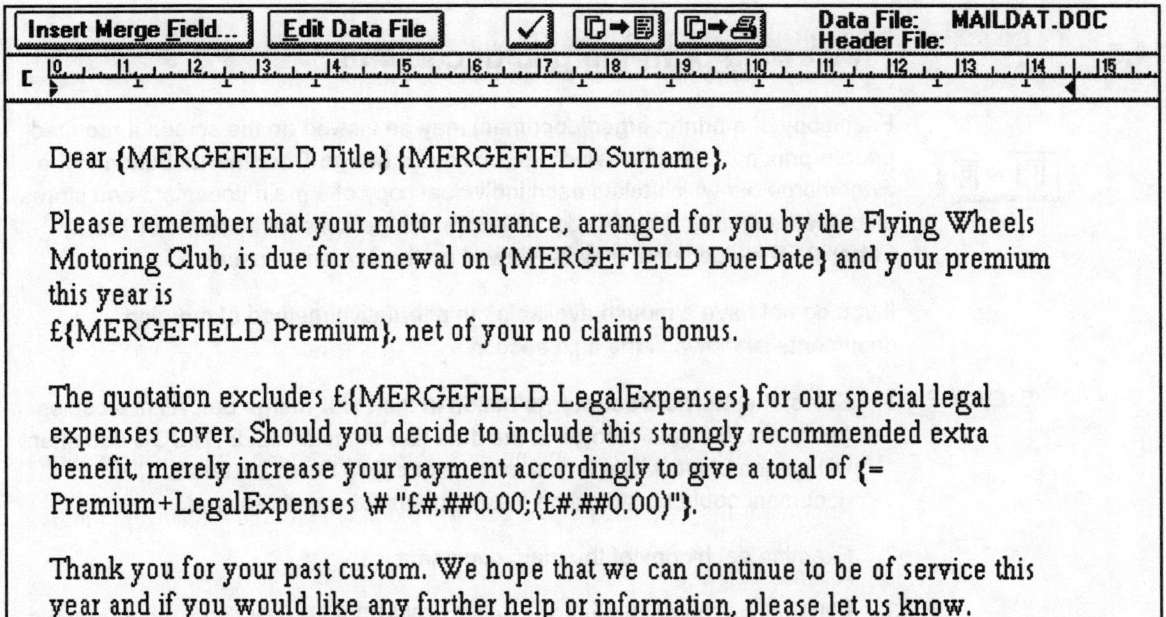

Dear {MERGEFIELD Title} {MERGEFIELD Surname},

Please remember that your motor insurance, arranged for you by the Flying Wheels Motoring Club, is due for renewal on {MERGEFIELD DueDate} and your premium this year is
£{MERGEFIELD Premium}, net of your no claims bonus.

The quotation excludes £{MERGEFIELD LegalExpenses} for our special legal expenses cover. Should you decide to include this strongly recommended extra benefit, merely increase your payment accordingly to give a total of {= Premium+LegalExpenses \# "£#,##0.00;(£#,##0.00)"}.

Thank you for your past custom. We hope that we can continue to be of service this year and if you would like any further help or information, please let us know.

11 Check the document carefully. Any field codes may be edited in the same ways as normal text, if necessary. If the calculation field at the end of the middle paragraph of the main text is not present (you have inadvertently deleted it), then you may need to redefine the bookmarks for

Premium and **LegalExpenses** and insert the calculation field again (see page 163).

12 De-select **Field Codes** from the **View** menu before continuing.

13 Save the document.

14.4 Checking for errors

Preparing the data file and main document in the way carried out above will make it unlikely that you will have made any mistakes which will cause the print-merging process to fail. The **Check** button on the *Print merge bar* however, allows you to check whether there are any mistakes in either the data file or main document before starting the printing process. It is always worth carrying out this process before printing.

If you do not have a mouse available, an alternative method of checking for errors is shown on page 179.

EXERCISE 1 Use the **Check** button on the *Print merge bar* to check your **MAILLETR.DOC** document for errors. When the checking process is complete, an information box will be displayed giving a report of the check.

14.5 Previewing print-merged documents

Each copy of a print-merged document may be viewed on the screen if required, prior to printing. Word for Windows provides a **Merge Documents** button in the *Print merge bar* which takes each individual copy of a main document and stores all of them together in a new document (which defaults to the name of **Form Letters**). This document may be viewed on the screen as usual.

If you do not have a mouse available, an alternative method of merging documents is shown in the next section.

EXERCISE 1 Select the **Merge Documents** button in the **Print** merge bar. All five copies (there are five data records in the data file) of the MAILLETR.DOC document will be combined within a new document called **Form Letters2**. This document could be stored on disk in the usual way if required.

2 Examine each copy of the main document.

3 Either close the document or select the **MAILLETR.DOC** document from the **Window** menu to return to your main document.

14.6 Print-merging the main document

There are two methods of printing print-merged documents. The first time you print, it is better to use the **Print Merge** command in the **File** menu as this provides a range of useful printing options. Once the printing options have been set, the **Merge and Print** button found in the *Print merge bar,* provides a convenient method of print-merging on subsequent occasions.

EXERCISE

1 Using the **MAILLETR.DOC** document, select **Print Merge** from the **File** menu. The *Print Merge Setup* dialogue box will be displayed as before.

2 Select the **Merge** command button. The *Print Merge* dialogue box will be displayed as below:

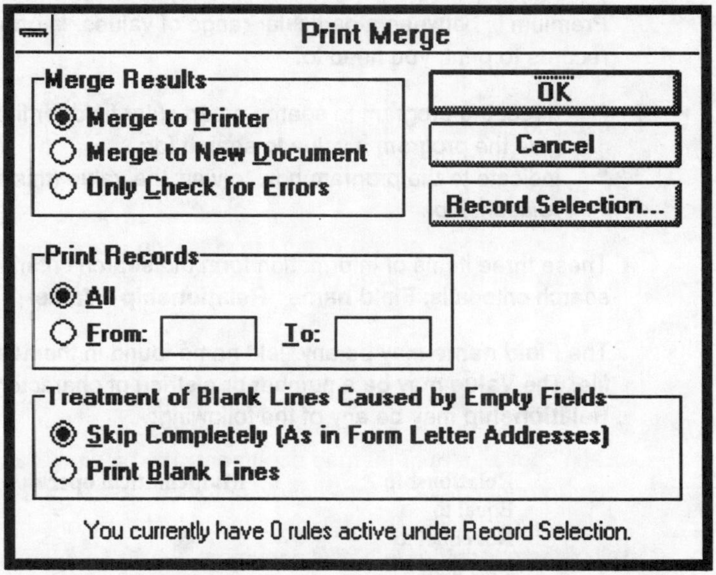

The *Merge Results* area provides an alternative method, other than using buttons in the Print merge bar, of checking for errors or merging to documents (page 178).

Each data record in the data file has its own record number. The first data record has record number 1, the next data record has record number 2 and so on. The *Print Records* area allows you to specify a range of record numbers to print. *From:* **2** *To:* **4** for example, would print records 2 to 4 inclusive.

The *Treatment of Blank Lines Caused by Empty Fields* area allows you instruct the program not to print a blank line in the main document if a field in a data record is empty. This may be useful when printing addresses as some address records are likely to contain empty fields (see the MAILDAT data file for an example).

The **Record Selection** command button allows you to select specific records to be printed. This is explored in the next section.

3 Ensure that the values in the *Print Merge* dialogue box are set as shown above and accept to start the print-merge process. Five individualised letters will be printed. Note that a blank line in the address block will not be printed where there is an empty field in the data record.

14.7 Selecting records

It is unlikely that you will always require an individualised copy of the main document for every data record that you have in the data file. More usually, you will wish to select records based upon information stored in the data file. This is referred to as the *search criteria*. Taking the MAILDAT data file as an example, you may want to print out letters for people that live in Herts. or where the Premium is between a particular range of values. In order to specify which records to print, you need to:

- direct the program to search a particular field (or fields) within the data file;
- give the program a value to search for;
- indicate to the program how to view the value (this is often called the *relationship*).

These three items of information form the search criteria. The general form of search criteria is: **Field name Relationship Value**

The **Field name** may be any field name found in the header record of the data file. The **Value** may be a number or a string of characters (*text string*). The **Relationship** may be any of the following:

Relationship	Mathematical operator equivalent
Equal to	=
Not equal to	<>
Less than	<
Greater than	>
Less than or equal to	<=
Greater than or equal to	>=
Blank	no equivalent
Not blank	no equivalent

The search criteria: **County Equal to Herts.** for an example, would instruct the program to search in the **County** field of the data file for a value which is exactly **Equal to Herts.**

The words **And** and **Or** (called *logical operators*) may be used to join together different search criteria. An example of this would be:

Premium Greater than 200 And Premium Less than 300.

This would instruct the program to search the **Premium** field for values which are **Greater than 200** and values (in the same field) which are **Less than 300.**

The following exercise demonstrates the use of the *Record Selection* dialogue box to set up easily the search criteria.

EXERCISE

1 Using the **MAILLETR.DOC** document, select **Print Merge** from the **File** menu.

2 Select the **Merge** command button to display the *Print Merge* dialogue box.

3 Select the **Record Selection** command button. The following *Record Selection* dialogue box will be displayed:

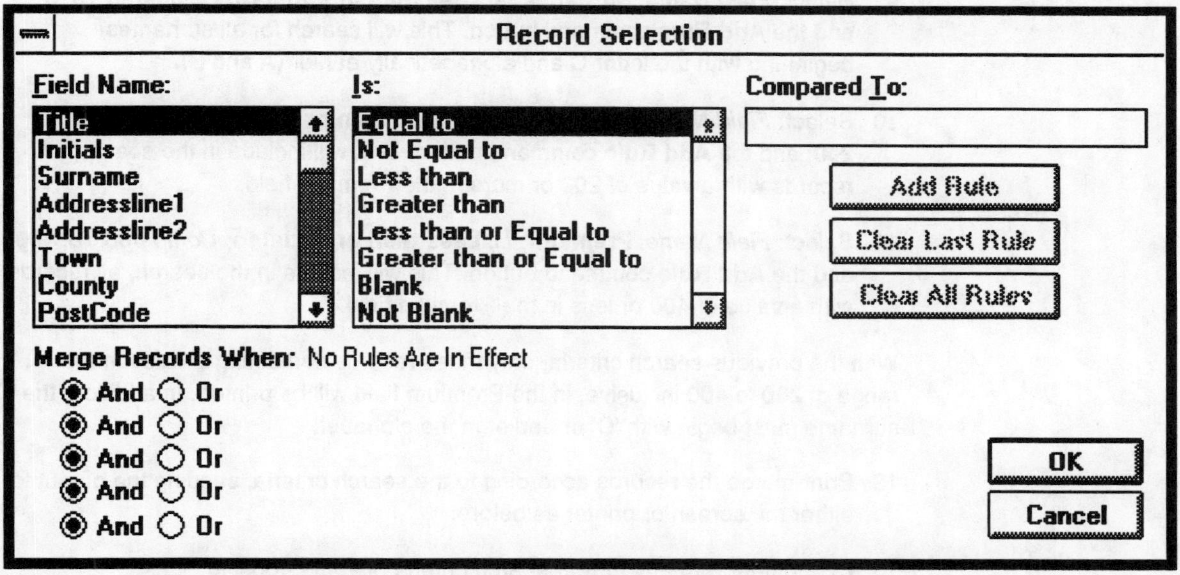

The *Field Name:* area allows you to select conveniently the field name to be involved in the search.

The *Is:* area allows you to select the relationship used in the search criteria.

The *Compared To:* text box allows you to enter the value used in the search criteria.

The *Merge Records When:* area displays the current search criteria (referred to in the dialogue box as a *rule*).

4 Select the **County** *Field Name:* and select the **Equal to** relationship in the *Is:* area.

5 Type the value **Herts.** into the *Compared To:* text box and select the **Add Rule** command button. The search criteria (rule) will appear in the *Merge Records When:* area.

You have set up search criteria which will print merge only those records where Herts. appears in the County field in the data file.

6 Accept when ready to return to the *Print Merge* dialogue box.

7 If you wish to view the print-merged documents on the screen rather than printing them out, select the **Merge to New Document** check box and accept,

otherwise just accept. Print-merging will only occur for those records where Herts. appears inside the County field (3 records).

8 Display the *Record Selection* dialogue box again and select the **Clear All Rules** command button. This will remove all search criteria.

9 Select: *Field Name:* **Surname**; *Is:* **Less than or equal to**; *Compared To:* **C**; and the **Add Rule** command button. This will search for all surnames beginning with the letter C and alphabetically earlier (A and B).

10 Select: *Field Name:* **Premium**; *Is:* **Greater than or Equal to**; *Compared To:* **200**; and the **Add Rule** command button. This will include in the search, all records with a value of 200 or more in the Premium field.

11 Select: *Field Name:* **Premium**; *Is:* **Less than or Equal to**; *Compared To:* **400**; and the **Add Rule** command button. This will include in the search, all records with a value of 400 or less in the Premium field.

With the previous search criteria, only those records containing a value in the range of 200 to 400 inclusive, in the Premium field will be printed. In addition, the surname must begin with 'C' or earlier in the alphabet.

12 Print-merge the records according to the search criteria, sending the output to either the screen or printer as before.

13 Experiment with any further search criteria of your choosing.

14.8 Editing a data file

As you use data files over a period of time, you will need to modify the information that they contain. This may involve adding extra records and fields, editing or deleting individual records or fields, changing the header record, sorting the data file into some order and so on.

When you create a data file using the **Print Merge** command, the DATAFILE.DOT template is automatically attached to the data file document. This provides a number of additional facilities (*macros* are discussed in Chapter 23) which are designed to ease the process of editing data files.

You may display a data file for editing in one of two ways:

- Load the document containing the data file in the normal way *or* select it from the **Window** menu if it has been previously loaded.

Edit Data File

- Select the **Edit Data File** button found in the *Print merge bar* above the main print-merge document.

When you view a data file, the buttons in the Toolbar change to provide the functions shown on the next page.

In addition, the **Tools** menu changes to contain two extra commands: **Record Management Tools** (ALT O N) and **Database Management Tools** (ALT O D).

If the **Record Management Tools** command is selected, the following dialogue box is displayed:

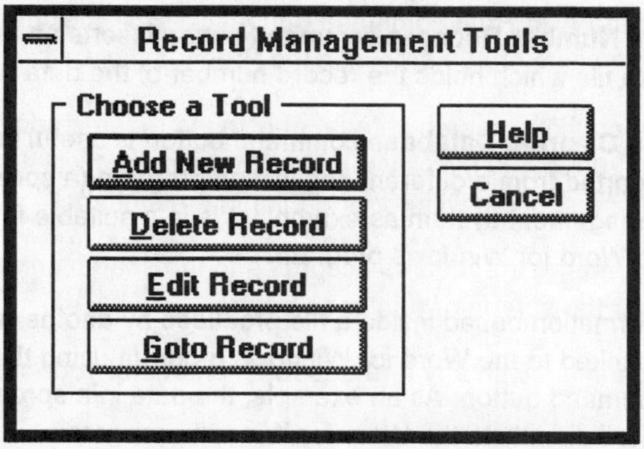

This dialogue box provides a number of command buttons to:

- Add a new record to the end of the data file (**Add New Record**).
- Delete specified records either at the current position of the insertion point or by record number (**Delete Record**).
- Edit specified records either at the current position of the insertion point or by record number (**Edit Record**).
- Move to a record specified by its number (**Goto Record**).

If the **Database Management Tools** command is selected, the dialogue box shown on the next page is displayed.

This dialogue box provides a number of command buttons which affect the structure of the data file:

- The **Add New Field** command button allows an additional field to be inserted into the data file.
- The data file may be sorted into some order determined by up to three fields (known as *key fields*) using the **Sort Records** command button. This is explored in Chapter 16.

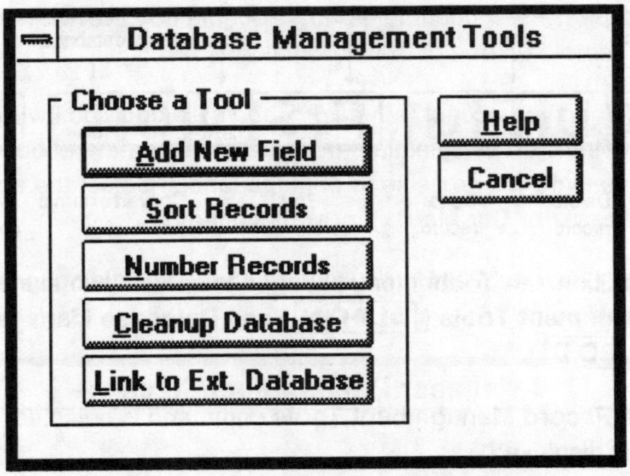

- The **Number Records** command button inserts an additional field into the data file which holds the record number of the data records.
- The **Cleanup Database** command button is useful in ensuring that a data file imported from a different application program (a spreadsheet or database management system as examples) is in a suitable format to be recognised by the Word for Windows program.
- Information based inside a file produced by another application program may be linked to the Word for Windows program using the **Link to Ext. Database** command button. As an example, the data in a spreadsheet file might be linked directly to the Word for Windows program.

EXERCISE

1 View the **MAILDAT.DOC** as described above and save a copy to the Samples Disk under the name of **TESTDAT**.

2 Using the **TESTDAT.DOC** document, experiment with the various editing options as described above, using either the Toolbar or appropriate commands in the **Tools** menu.

3 Close all open files at this point. You do not wish to save any changes that you may have made.

14.9 Printing mailing labels

Word for Windows provides a MAILLABL.DOT template which provides a simple method of printing either a single label or sheets of address labels. For most purposes, the template is flexible enough to cope with most standard label and address label sheet sizes. In some instances however, other methods need to be used to gain a satisfactory result. Different ways of print-merging documents, labels and envelopes are explored on page 187.

In the following exercise, a new document will be opened with a suitable template (MAILLABL.DOT) to print mailing labels using appropriate information from the MAILDAT.DOC data file.

EXERCISE 1 Open a new document and select the **MAILLABL** template in the *Use Template:* area of the *New* dialogue box.

2 When you accept, a *Mailing Labels* dialogue box will be displayed, asking you to indicate by selecting an appropriate command button, the type of printer that you will be using to print the labels. Select the appropriate type of printer (**Laser** or **Dot Matrix**) for your system.

3 A *Laser* (or *Dot Matrix*)*Printer Label Sizes* dialogue box will be displayed at this point.

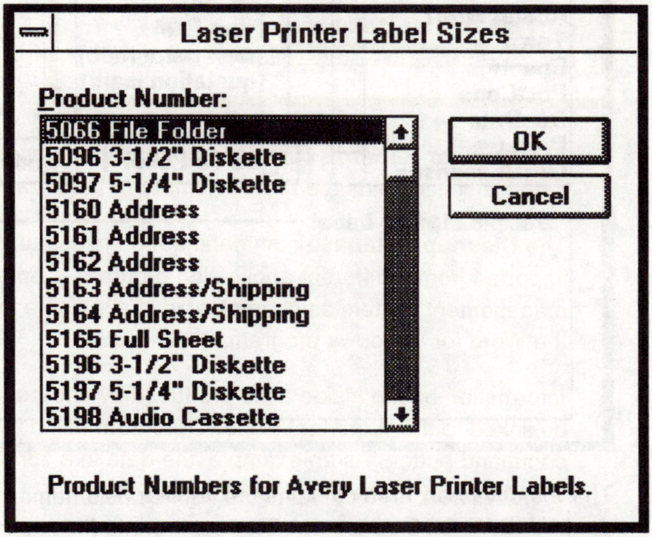

4 Select the *Product Number:* **7160** if you are using a laser printer or *Product Number:* **4603** if you are using a dot-matrix printer. These are a suitable A4 size, with labels arranged into three columns. It is intended that the resulting labels from this Exercise will be printed on normal A4 sheets rather than mailing label sheets. *Note:* if you were producing 'real' mailing labels, then you would need to experiment to find appropriate sheet and label sizes. Accept when ready.

The document will be divided up into a table, each empty square (or *cell*) in the table representing the area of one label.

5 After a short pause, you will be prompted to choose whether to print a **Single Label** (in which case you provide the information to be printed on the label) or **Multiple Labels** using information from a data file.

Since the information is to be extracted from the MAILDAT.DOC data file, select the **Multiple Labels** command button.

6 You will be further prompted to indicate whether the header record and the data records are held in two separate files or not. Select the **No** command button to indicate that all the necessary information is in one file. The *Attach Data File* dialogue box, seen previously, will be displayed.

7 Select the **MAILDAT.DOC** data file stored on the Samples Disk in drive A: and accept. The following *Layout Mailing Labels* dialogue box will be displayed:

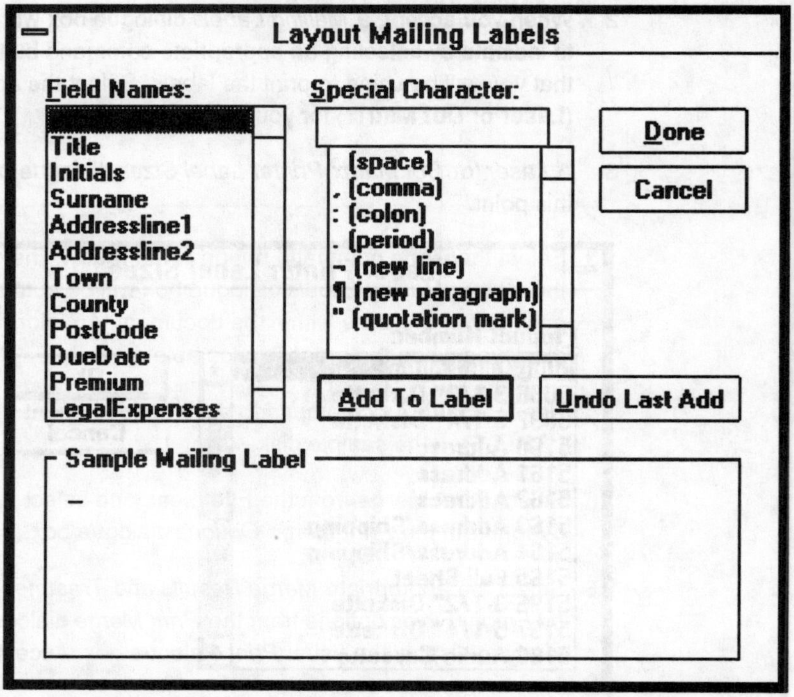

The *Field Names:* area contains the familiar field names in the header record of the MAILDAT.DOC document. The appropriate field names to be included in the mailing label may be selected from this area in turn.

The *Special Character:* area contains various items which may be used to separate and position the fieldnames on the mailing label.

8 Select the **Title** field from the *Field Names:* area and select the **[space]** *Special Character:*.

9 Select the **Add To Label** command button. The effect of this will be shown in the *Sample Mailing Label* area of the dialogue box.

10 Select the field name **Initials**, another **[space]** character and select the **Add to Label** command button.

11 Select the **Surname** field name, the **[new line]** character and **Add To Label** command button. This has built up the first line of the mailing label and contains the name of a person.

12 In the same way, build up the mailing label so that the *Sample Mailing Label* area is displayed similar to that shown on the next page.

You may use the **Undo Last Add** command button if you make a mistake.

Sample Mailing Label

«Title» «Initials» «Surname»-
«Addressline1»-
«Addressline2»-
«Town»-
«County» «PostCode»_

13 Select the **Done** command button when ready. The merge codes entered into the *Layout Mailing Labels* dialogue box will be automatically duplicated in each cell of the table within the document. An information box will be displayed when the process is complete.

14 Use the **Save As** command to save the document under the name of **LABELS** on the sample disk.

15 Select **Print Merge** from the **File** menu and select the **Merge** command button from the *Print Merge Options* dialogue box.

16 Select the appropriate *Merge Results* and *Treatment of Blank Lines Caused by Empty Fields* options from the *Print Merge* dialogue box. Accept when ready to display the usual *Print* dialogue box. Accept to begin the print-merging process.

The address labels for the five data records in the MAILDAT.DOC data file will be printed. Search criteria may be applied to this print-merge process if required in the normal way.

15 Advanced print-merging

For most print-merging applications, the **Print Merge** command provides sufficient flexibility. Further facilities are offered however, by the use of special bookmark field codes which may be inserted into a document for specialised print-merging tasks. These special bookmark fields may be embedded in the text when you set up a main document using the **Print Merge** command, or when you select the **Insert Merge Field** button found in the Print-merge bar of the main document (see the *Word Fields:* area of the *Insert Merge Fields* dialogue box on page 175). The **Field** command from the **Insert** menu provides an alternative method of inserting appropriate field codes.

Each of the special field codes will be explored during the exercises in this chapter. A brief explanation of their purpose follows.

Note: The *condition* referred to below is similar in structure to that of search criteria introduced on page 180 (Field name, Relationship, Value). In this case, condition refers to: bookmark name, mathematical operator, value. An example would be LegalExpenses = 8.00 where LegalExpenses is the bookmark name, = is the mathematical operator and 8.00 is the value.

{Ask *bookmark name "prompt"***}** This field code instructs the program to prompt you for certain information prior to printing. This information is assigned to a bookmark name.
Example: {Ask DueDate "Print this message as a prompt"} asks the user to enter the DueDate with the message inside double quotes being printed as a prompt on the screen.

{Data *file name***}** This is used to specify the name of the data file to be used in the print merging process.
Example: {Data MAILDAT} use the MAILDAT.DOC data file.

{Fill-in "*prompt text"***}** This field code prompts you for some information prior to printing. This information is placed into the document at the {Fill-in} field position.
Example: {Fill-in "Place this text into the document"}

{If *condition "text"***}** if the condition is met, this field code will print the text inside the double quotes, at the position where the field is placed in the document.
Example: {If DueDate < October 4 "Urgent action required"} the text will be printed if the DueDate is before October 4.

{If *condition "text 1" "text 2"***}** If the condition is met, this field code will print the *text 1* text found inside the first set of double quotes, otherwise the text inside the second set of double quotes ("*text 2*") will be printed. The appropriate text will be inserted at the position where the field is placed in the document.
Example: {If DueDate > October 10 "Take your time" "Urgent action required"}

{Next} This field code instructs the program to take the remaining items for the current copy of the main document from the next record in the data file. This field code allows you to print two or more records in the same document. This is useful for printing mailing labels as an example.

{Nextif *condition***}** This field code instructs the program to take the remaining items for the current copy of the main document from the next record if the condition is met.
Example: (Nextif DueDate = October 4} take the details from the next record if the DueDate is equal to October 4).

{Quote "*text***"}** The text inside double quotes is printed in the document at the {Quote} field position.
Example: {Quote "inclusive of VAT"}

{Set *bookmark name***}** assigns a value to a bookmark. The bookmark needs to be inserted in the document at the position where it is to be printed.
Example: {Set VAT "17.5} assigns the value of 17.5 to the bookmark name VAT.

{SkipIf *Expression***}** Instructs the program to move to the next record if the condition within the expression is met.
Example: {Skipif Premium < 350} move to the next record if the value of Premium is less than 350).

These field codes effectively allow for the searching of data files, the selective printing and further individualisation of main documents.

The field codes shown above are those which appear in the *Insert Field Type:* area of the *Field* dialogue box accessed via the **Insert** menu. When you select the **Insert Merge Field** button in a Print merge bar attached to a main document, the fields appear slightly differently in the *Word Fields:* area of the *Insert Merge Field* dialogue box. The following is a list of the similarities and differences:

***Field* dialogue box:**	***Insert Merge Field* dialogue box:**
Ask	Ask
Fill-in	Fillin
If	If...Then
	If... Then... Else
Next	Next Record
Nextif	Next Record If
Quote	Quote
Set	Set Bookmark
Skipif	Skip Record If

15.1 Inserting special merge fields

As has been mentioned previously, merge fields may be placed into a document using a variety of methods as follows:

Using the Insert Merge Field button

This method is only suitable for inserting merge codes into a document that has already been attached to a data file since the Print merge bar is only displayed when this has occurred.

- **Move the insertion point to the position where the field code is to be placed.**
- **Select the Insert Print Merge button (ALT Shift F) in the Print merge bar to display the familiar *Insert Merge Field* dialogue box.**
- **Either double-click on the appropriate special field code in the *Word Fields:* area or select the appropriate field code and accept. A template field code (such as {SKIPIF Expression}) will appear in the document.**
- **Edit the field code to erase unwanted information (such as 'Expression') and enter any appropriate details.**

Entering a merge field code in this way results in the field code name being capitalised e.g. SKIPIF.

Using the Insert Field key

This method is suitable if you are already familiar with field codes and their structure.

- **Move the insertion point to the position where the field code is to be placed.**
- **Press Ctrl F9 to insert a blank field into the document (denoted by {}). *Note:* you cannot enter a field in this way by simply typing { and } using the respective keys on the keyboard.**
- **Edit the contents of the empty field to include the field name and any other additional information required, according to the nature of the field.**

Using the Field command from the Insert menu

This method is particularly useful if you have no data file attached to the main document.

- **Move the insertion point to where the field code is to be placed.**
- **Select Field from the Insert menu.**
- **Select the required field from the Insert *Field Type:* area of the *Field* dialogue box.**
- **Select the appropriate option in the *Instructions:* area if necessary.**
- **Type any additional information into the *Field Code:* text box as may be required by the field type.**
- **Accept to place the field code in the document.**

Entering a merge field code in this way results in the field name being set in lower case e.g. skipif.

Using {Skipif}

The SKIPIF merge field provides an alternative method to that practiced in Chapter 14, of printing selected records from a data file.

EXERCISE

1 Open the **MAILLETR.DOC** document and select **Field Codes** from the **View** menu if necessary.

2 Move the insertion point to the beginning of the document and set the character formatting (for the insertion point position only) to something more sensible, such as **12 pt** normal text. You will be inserting a field code at this position in the document. As the paragraph was set at 36 pt text size it is sensible to reduce the size of the new text (which will be a field code) to make it more readable.

3 Select the **Insert Merge Field** command button in the Print merge bar.

4 Select the field type **Skip Record If** in the *Word Fields:* area of the *Insert Merge Field* dialogue box and accept. {SKIPIF Expression} will be inserted into the document.

5 Delete **Expression** in the field code and type **Surname <> "Burke"** in its place. The complete field code should read:
{SKIPIF Surname <> "Burke"}.

The new field code will skip all records which do not have the Surname of Burke. The field code means 'skip this record if the Surname is not "Burke"'. Notice that the field type is displayed in capitals.

6 **Print Merge** the document, sending the output either to the printer or to a document for screen viewing (**Record Selection** is not necessary since the inserted field code will selectively print-merge the document). Only the document for Ms. D. Burke will result.

7 Delete the field by highlighting the complete code and press **Del**.

8 Select **Field** from the **Insert** menu and select the **Skipif** field in the *Insert Field Type:* area.

9 Move into the *Field Code:* text box and type **Premium >= "200"**.
Accept when ready. The field code will be inserted into the document and will read as: **{skipif Premium >= "200"}**. You may find it necessary to reduce the font size used to display the field code. Notice that the field name is displayed in lower case.

This field code means 'skip this record if the Premium is greater than, or equal to "200"'. Thus only documents with a record containing a Premium value of less than £200 will be printed.

10 **Print Merge** the document. Copies to Mrs. A.F. Norton and Mr. A. Davey should be printed.

11 Edit the field code so that it reads: **{skipIf County = "Herts."}**.

12 **Print Merge** the document as before.

13 Experiment as you wish, using any of the appropriate data file field names, mathematical operators and values.

14 Abandon the document or save it under a different name as you wish.

15.2 Print-merging without data files

Using the field code **{ASK}**, it is possible to modify the MAILLTR document in such a way that you are prompted for the information to be inserted for that copy of the letter, instead of merging data from a data file.

The {ASK} field may be used in conjunction with the print-merging of data files in order to add specific, individualised items to documents which are not included in the data file itself.

When the {ASK} field code is encountered by the Word for Windows program (while print-merging) an *Ask* dialogue box is displayed on the screen. You may enter the text which is to be inserted into the document at another point, into this dialogue box.

The {ASK} field code provides for the addition of a prompt which is displayed in the *Ask* dialogue box. This allows you to give a clear message, indicating the type of information to be entered.

The *syntax* (structure) of the {ASK} field is as follows:

{ASK Bookmarkname "prompt" \Switch "Default text"}

The prompt (optional) which is to appear in the *Ask* dialogue box should be placed after the name of the bookmark, inside double-quotes.

The **\O** switch (optional) would prompt for information once only, before printing the first document in the print-merging process.

The **\D** switch (optional) specifies the default information (which follows the \D switch, placed inside double-quotes) for that bookmark.

When inserting the {ASK} field code using the **Field** command, the \D switch may be chosen by selecting the **Default** option found in the Instructions: area of the *Field* dialogue box and selecting the **Add** command button. Similarly, the \O switch may be chosen by selecting the **Once** option.

Examples:

{ask DATAFILE "Which data file to print-merge?"}

This could be placed at the beginning of a main document, giving an opportunity to choose the name of the data file to be merged with this document. This would be useful if you had a number of similar mailing lists. The prompt 'Which data file to print-merge?' would appear in the *Ask* dialogue box. The bookmark name in this case would be DATAFILE.

{ask Title "Enter the persons Title" \D "Sir/Madam"}

The bookmark name is Title and the prompt to appear inside the *Ask* dialogue box is 'Enter the persons Title'. The \D switch sets the default value for Title as 'Sir/Madam'. This might be useful if the name was unknown.

The following exercise modifies a main letter document produced earlier so that you are prompted for the appropriate information to be inserted into the document prior to printing.

Preparing the main document

EXERCISE

1 Make a copy of **MAILLETR.DOC**, naming it **ASKLTR**. Continue to work with **ASKLTR.DOC** with the **Field Codes** displayed on the screen.

2 Delete the field code at the beginning of the document.

3 Edit all the field codes in the document so to remove any reference to MERGEFIELD. For example, {MERGEFIELD Initials} would be edited to read {Initials}. This will remove the connection between the main document and the data file for each field code.

4 Move into the **{Title}** field and edit it so that it reads as: **{REF Title}**.

If a chosen bookmark field name conflicts with an existing field name, as is the case with Title (Title already exists as a field name and appears in the *Insert Field Type:* area of the *Field* dialogue box), then the bookmark field name must be preceded with **REF** to indicate that this is the case.

5 Select **Print Merge** from the **File** menu and select the **Remove Attachments** command button. An information box will be displayed as a 'double-check' to this operation. Accept to remove all connection of the main document with the data file. The Print merge bar will be removed from the screen.

6 Set the paragraph style for the **Date** field code to normal (reducing the spacing above the paragraph. Add a blank paragraph above the **Date** field and move the insertion point into this new line.

7 Use the **Field** command method of adding a field to the document and insert an **{ASK}** field. Type the following additional information into the *Field Code:* text box so that it reads as: **ask Title "Enter the Title of the person"**. Accept. when ready. An *Ask* dialogue box will appear as shown on the next page.

Note that the prompt entered into the {ASK} field is displayed towards the top of the dialogue box.

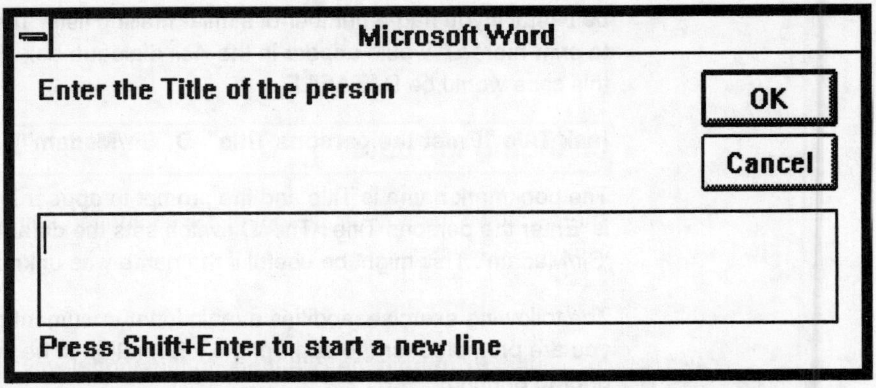

This dialogue box allows you to enter the bookmark value (for Title) immediately.

8 Enter a suitable value such as **Mr.** and accept.

The letter to be printed is to be sent to:

Mr. I. Morris
67, New Forest Rd.
Newcastle
Stoke-on Trent
Staffs.
SB2 4NJ
Duedate: **October 19**
Premium: **347.50**
LegalExpenses: **8.00**

9 In the same way, insert the following {**ASK**} fields, one after the other, as shown below:

The Flying Whee
Motoring Clu

Maple End. Hareward Way. Chinnor. Bucks. OK

{ask Title "Enter the Title of the person"}{ask Initials "Enter the Initials"}{ask Surname}{ask Addressline1 "1st line of the address?"}{ask Addressline2 "2nd line of the address}{ask Town}{ask County}{ask PostCode}{ask Duedate "Date when policy expires?"}{ask Premium "Enter the Premium"}{ask LegalExpenses "Enter the value for Legal Expenses}

{date \@ "d MMMM, yyyy"}

{REF Title} {Initials} {Surname}

10 Save and print a copy of the letter. All the values input, and any calculations resulting from them should be printed.

Changing the data

There are two methods of changing the data inserted into the main document using {ask} fields:

Method 1: **Using Print**

- Select **Print** from the **File** menu in the normal way. An *Ask* dialogue box will appear for each {ASK} field. Type the new data and accept, or accept to take the current value.
- Repeat the process if you wish to print another individual document.

Method 2: **Using the update field keycode**

- Place the insertion point inside the {Ask} field which contains the bookmark field of which you wish to change the value.
- Press the **update field** key : F9
- Change the bookmark value in the *Ask* dialogue box that appears.
- Change any other bookmark values contained within the appropriate {ASK} fields as required.
- Print the document in the normal way.

EXERCISE 1 Using the **Print** command, print a letter to:

Mrs. I. Morris
Pear Tree Farm
Thirkleby
York
N. Yorks.
YO4 2AB
Duedate: **October 19**
Premium: **321.45**
LegalExpenses: **8.00**

2 Using the **Update Field key,** change the Premium value to **199.99** and the PostCode to **YO7 3TL.**

3 Print the letter.

You have been working with a document without any data file attached. You may, however, use {Ask} fields within a main print-merge document, prompting for additional information not included within the data file.

15.3 Mailing labels

You used an address label template on pages 184-186 to print labels. In this section, you will set up a simple address label document for print-merging with the MAILDAT data file. This will give you an understanding of additional field codes and how to modify existing mailing label templates.

EXERCISE

1 Open the **MAILLETR** document and with the **Field Codes** displayed, highlight all the field codes in the address block ({MERGEFIELD Title} to {MERGEFIELD Post Code}).

2 Copy the text to the *clipboard.*

3 Open a **New** document using the **NORMAL** stylesheet. Select a **Page Layout** view and display the paragraph marks.

4 Format the section to consist of three columns (**Columns** from the **Format** menu or use the **Columns** button in the Toolbar).

5 Paste a copy of the contents of the *clipboard* at the beginning of the document.

6 Add three blank lines at the end of the pasted text and insert a **Column Break** (**Break** from the **Insert** menu).

7 Insert the field code: **{Next}**, to the left of the text in the first line. To remind you, this field type instructs the program to take data from the next record in the data file and print it in the current document, rather than starting a new document.

8 Highlight all the text in the left-hand column and copy it to the **Clipboard**.

9 Paste the contents of the *Clipboard* at the top of the second column. Insert the blank lines and **Column Break** as before. Repeat for the third column.

10 Insert a **Continuous Break** at the bottom of the third column.

11 Highlight the text in all three columns (which will include the Column Breaks) and copy to the clipboard.

12 Place the insertion point into section 2 (bottom of the left-hand column) and paste the contents of the clipboard.

13 In a similar fashion, paste three further copies of the clipboard, to fill the page with five rows and three columns of address block field codes.

14 Move to the top of the document and edit the first {Next} field so that it reads: **{data MAILDAT}**. This field type ({data}) simply names the data file to be used in the print-merging process. An alternative would be to select the **Attach Data File** command button in the *Print Merge* dialogue box and select the appropriate data file. This would have exactly the same result as above.

The top part of the document at this stage should appear similar to that shown on the next page.

{data MAILDAT}	{next }{MERGEFIELD	{next }{MERGEFIELD
{MERGEFIELD Title}	Title} {MERGEFIELD	Title} {MERGEFIELD
{MERGEFIELD	Initials}	Initials}
Initials}	{MERGEFIELD	{MERGEFIELD
{MERGEFIELD	Surname}¶	Surname}¶
Surname}¶	{MERGEFIELD	{MERGEFIELD
{MERGEFIELD	Addressline1}¶	Addressline1}¶
Addressline1}¶	{MERGEFIELD	{MERGEFIELD
{MERGEFIELD	Addressline2}¶	Addressline2}¶
Addressline2}¶	{MERGEFIELD Town}¶	{MERGEFIELD Town}¶
{MERGEFIELD Town}¶	{MERGEFIELD	{MERGEFIELD
{MERGEFIELD	County}¶	County}¶
County}¶	{MERGEFIELD	{MERGEFIELD
{MERGEFIELD	PostCode}¶	PostCode}¶
PostCode}¶	¶	¶
¶	¶	¶

15 Save the document on the Samples Disk under the name of **LABELS1**.

16 **Print Merge** the document. Address labels will be printed for the 5 records in the MAILDAT data file.

By adjusting the number of columns, margins, horizontal and vertical spacing, any layout for address labels is possible. Printing directly to envelopes is also feasible.

If only certain labels are required for printing, then searching and matching criteria may be set up as embedded field codes, as practiced on page 191, or alternatively using the searching facilities offered by the **Print Merge** command.

16 Sorting

It is often useful to be able to organise sections of text into a particular order. You may have produced a table for example which would be more comprehensive if it was re-organised into an alphabetical or numerical order.

Word for Windows provides two sorting facilities: one may be used to sort data files (such as those produced on pages 170-173); the other may be applied to columns or paragraphs of text within a document.

16.1 Sorting data files

It is useful to be able to sort a data file into a particular order. This is particularly true of a large data file where locating a record for editing purposes may be made more cumbersome if the file is not sorted. Printing mailing labels in alphabetical order provides a practical example of the additional use of a sorted data file.

As was discussed on page 181, when you create a data file using the **Print Merge** command, the DATAFILE.DOT template is automatically attached to the data file document. This provides additional **Record** and **Database Management Tools** which may be used with data files. These tools includes the facility to sort a data file using up to three fields (called *key fields*) on which the sorting process will be based.

The MAILDAT.DOC data file produced on pages 170-173 will be used to illustrate the data file **Sort Record** facility.

EXERCISE

1 Load the **MAILLETR.DOC** document .

2 Select the **Edit Data File** button in the Print merge bar if you have a mouse available. Alternatively, load the **MAILDAT.DOC** document.

3 Select the **Database Management Tools** command in the **Tools** menu.

4 Select the **Sort Records** command button in the *Database Management Tools* dialogue box which appears. A *Sort Records* dialogue box will be displayed. This is shown on the next page.

Up to three key fields may be used to sort the records in the data file. The *Sort Key 1, 2* and *3* areas display the field names found in the header record of the data file. You may type or select from the list, the field(s) on which the sorting will be based. The *Sorting Order* areas allow you to specify whether the sorting on a particular key field will be in ascending or descending order. The numbers 1, 2 and 3 reflect an ascending order. Similarly the letters A, B and C also reflect an ascending order.

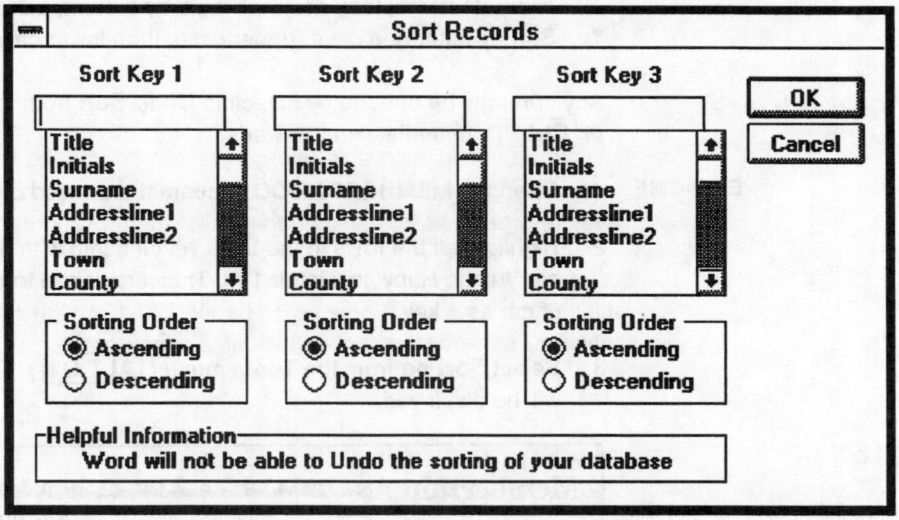

The sorting process will be based on the *Sort Key 1* field first, followed by the *Sort Key 2* field and so on.

5 In the *Sort Key 1* area, type or select **Surname** and select **Ascending** order if necessary. Sorting will be based on surname.

6 In the *Sort Key 2* area, type or select **Initials** and select **Ascending** order if necessary. If two surnames are the same, then the initials will be 'taken into account' to provide a final position in the data file.

7 Accept when ready, the table will be sorted according to the values above.

Note: It is not possible to reverse the order of the records in a data file (back to an unsorted form) by using the **Undo** button in the Toolbar or the **Undo** command in the **Edit** menu.

8 Experiment with sorting the data file using different key fields and sort orders. It is not necessary to save the data file document if not required.

16.2 Sorting paragraphs

The **Sorting** command found in the **Tools** menu (ALT O I) allows you to sort any text, whether arranged as standard paragraphs or in tables. Unlike the data file sorting seen in the previous Section, the **Sorting** command only allows for re-ordering of paragraphs based upon one key field. This facility provides the following options:

- Sort alphabetically, chronologically, numerically.
- Sort in ascending or descending order.

- Sort columns or paragraphs, based upon a particular key field. Paragraphs may be sorted by a key field, providing that if the paragraphs contain separate items, they are separated by a comma or tab character.
- Sort by letter and case (upper case, then lower case).

Any sort may be undone by selecting **Undo Sort** from the **Edit** menu.(ALT E U *or* Ctrl Z) immediately afterwards.

EXERCISE

1 Open the **MEMBERS2.DOC** document produced on page 101.

2 Highlight all the rows in the table which begin with different makes of car 'Austin Ruby' to 'Rover 14'). These rows are to be sorted using the make of car as a key.

3 Select **Sorting** from the **Tools** menu (ALT O I). The following dialogue box will be displayed:

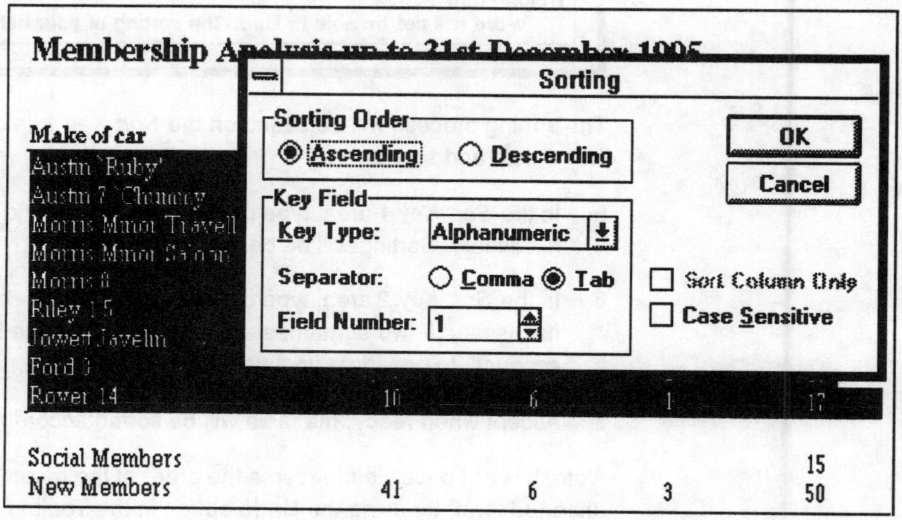

The *Key Field* area allows you to indicate the field on which you wish to sort. As the table in the document is arranged into fields (separated by tab characters in this case), any one of the five possible fields may be chosen as the sort field by entering its number in the *Field Number:* text box. The numbering of fields takes place from left to right across the table, thus *Field Number:* **1** corresponds to the 'Make of Car'.

The *Separator:* check boxes allow you to indicate whether items in the table are separated by comma or tab characters (in this case tab characters).

The *Key Type:* text box contains a drop-down list from which Alphanumeric, Numeric or Date options may be selected. These refer to the type of sorting (alphabetic, numeric or chronological respectively) to be carried out on the chosen key field.

The *Sorting Order* area contains the familiar Ascending and Descending check boxes.

You may instruct the program to take account of the case of the information in the key field by selecting the **Case Sensitive** check box.

When operating in column mode, you may choose to sort the columns by selecting the **Sort Column Only** check box.

4 Set all the values in the *Sorting* dialogue box to those shown in the illustration above. Accept when ready. The highlighted rows will be sorted into alphabetical order based upon the 'Make of Car' column.

5 Experiment with further sorts on the text within this and other documents. Switching to column mode (**Ctrl Shift F8**) provides for further possibilities.

17 Footnotes

Footnotes provide additional information concerning points raised in the main text. Footnotes are traditionally placed at the bottom of the page (within the bottom margin), separated from the main text. The aim is to avoid interrupting the main flow of the text with side issues.

Footnotes consist of a reference mark placed within the main text and the footnote text itself.

Word for Windows allows for the placement of footnotes: at the bottom of the page; directly beneath the main text if there is room; and at the end of the text or section.

If footnotes are placed at the bottom of the page, then a short rule (which may be edited) is automatically drawn across the page, separating footnote and main text.

If there is not enough room for footnotes at the bottom of a particular page, then they will continue onto the next and subsequent pages. In addition, continuation notices (e.g. 'Continued on page 10') may be added automatically.

The **Footnote** command from the **Insert** menu (**ALT I N**) is used to set up a footnote and allows you to establish its position on the page.

17.1 Entering a footnote in page layout view

EXERCISE

1 Open the **PFORMAT.DOC** or **CFORMAT.DOC** document, re-saving it as **FOOTNOTE** on the Samples Disk.

2 Using **Page Layout** document view, locate the word **'garnet'** in the section for January and place the insertion point either to the left or right of the word.

3 Select **Footnote** from the **Insert** menu. A *Footnote* dialogue box will be displayed as shown below:

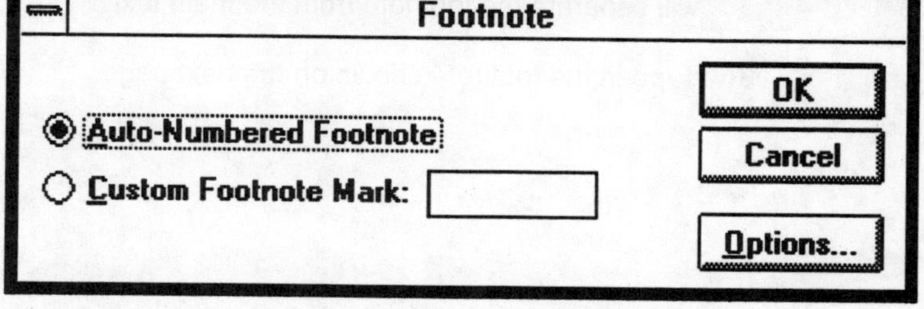

This dialogue box allows you to use a customised footnote mark in the text with a corresponding mark at the beginning of the footnote by entering characters into the *Custom Footnote Mark:* text box. Alternatively, footnotes will be automatically numbered by the program (this is the default). If you change the starting number of footnotes within the document, this value will be automatically updated.

4 Select the **Options** command button. The *Footnote Options* dialogue box will be displayed.

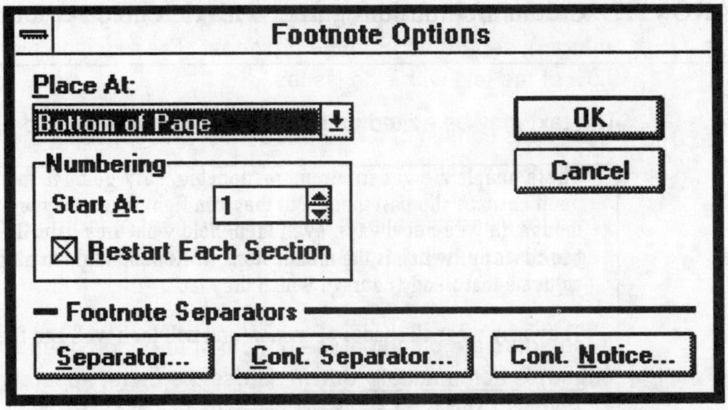

The *Place At:* area allows you to change the position on the page at which the footnote will be printed.

The *Numbering* area allows you to choose a different starting number for the footnote. If the *Restart Each Section* check box is selected, then the numbering of footnotes will be reset at the beginning of each section in the text (where there is a section break).

The *Footnote Separators* area contains three command buttons. The **Separator** command button allows you to adjust a short rule which is placed between the text in the main part of the document and footnote, separating them. If a footnote continues onto another page, a longer rule is drawn between the footnote and main text. The **Cont. Separator** command button allows you to adjust this line. A continuation notice (e.g. 'Continued on next page') may be entered by selecting the **Cont. Notice** command button.

5 Accept the default values and return to the *Footnote* dialogue box. Accept again to return to the document. The insertion point will be placed at the bottom of the page, at the beginning of the footnote area. A short, ruled line will separate the footnote from the main text.

6 Type in the footnote shown on the next page.

GROSSULARITE: Calcium/aluminium garnet, coloured white to yellow, mainly found in marble. PYROPE: Magnesium/aluminium 'precious' garnet, coloured red. Clear, perfect specimens are found alongside diamonds in South Africa. ALMANDITE: Iron/aluminium 'common garnet' with variable colours. Sometimes mistaken for Pyrope. SPESSARTITE: Manganese/aluminium, rare, violet tint. ANDRADITE: Calcium/iron 'common' garnet, coloured: yellow; green; red; black. Green form is a gem. UVAROVITE: Calcium/chromium garnet with rich green colour.

The text may be edited as normal. The footnote should appear as shown below:

> These people are generous, impressionable, easy-going in money matters, apt to let good chances slip past them. But they can fight when they are really up against it, though they do not always, even then, hold what they gain. To wear the noble **bloodstone**, which is the month-stone of March, ought to help the March-born to cultivate that steady courage which they lack.
>
> They may wear all shades of *green* and will look well and feel happy when dressed in
>
> ---
>
> [1]GROSSULARITE: Calcium/aluminium garnet, coloured white to yellow, mainly found in marble. PYROPE: Magnesium/aluminium 'precious' garnet, coloured red. Clear, perfect specimens are found alongside diamonds in South Africa. ALMANDITE: Iron/aluminium 'common garnet' with variable colours. Sometimes mistaken for Pyrope. SPESSARTITE: Manganese/aluminium, rare, violet tint. ANDRADITE: Calcium/iron 'common' garnet, coloured: yellow; green; red; black. Green form is a gem. UVAROVITE: Calcium/chromium garnet with rich green colour

7 With the insertion point inside the footnote text, select the **footnote text** paragraph style (this was automatically generated) from the *Ribbon.*

Change the **footnote text** style (**Style** from the **Format** menu) to another character format such as **Tms Rmn 8 pt**, if desired.

8 Move up to the word **'garnet'** again in the main text. Notice that the word has a reference number attached to it, which corresponds to the footnote reference number.

17.2 Entering a footnote in other page views

EXERCISE

1 Select **Normal** or **Draft** document view.

2 Locate, and place the insertion point next to **'amethyst'** in the text for February. Insert another footnote, accepting the default values.

The screen will split into two Panes, one for the document (the footnote reference should be visible), one for the footnote. Note that the footnote reference number has automatically increased.

3 Type the following into the footnote Pane:

The violet colour may be due to traces of manganese. Deeper coloured specimens are cut as gems. Once highly prized, amethysts lost much of their value when large deposits were found in Brazil.

The screen should appear as shown below:

They should wear *purples, bluish purples and black* if born in the first part of the month; those born in late February will find the *red purples* more lucky for them than the blues; and should always wear an [2]**amethyst**. Those born in the first part find 3 their lucky number; but those born in the latter half may take the number 9.

<u>Tuesdays</u> <u>and</u> <u>Saturdays</u> are good for the February-born, and March is a good month for them to enter on new enterprises. They happily marry partners born either in January or October.

Footnotes **Close**

[2]The violet colour may be due to traces of manganese. Deeper coloured specimens are cut as gems. Once highly prized, amethysts lost much of their value when large deposits were found in Brazil.

You may switch to and from the document and footnote Panes with the keyboard, by pressing **F6**. Alternatively point and click with the mouse.

4 Remove the footnote Pane by selecting the **Close** button.

5 Change back to a **Page Layout** document view and examine the two footnotes at the bottom of the page.

6 Save and print the document.

18 The glossary

The glossary provides a convenient method of constructing documents from standard text (often referred to a *boiler-plating*), graphics or a mixture of text and graphic elements. glossary entries consist of a label to which is attached the standard element. This could be a standard closure to a letter or standard paragraphs making up a contract, for example.

Whenever a standard element is required within a document, the appropriate glossary entry may be selected conveniently from a list of labels (called up by pressing the glossary key [F3]). The text or graphics associated with the label is then placed within the document.

In effect, standard elements need only be prepared once. If they are required again in the same or other documents, they may be selected from the glossary.

The glossary allows many entries to be stored, for as long as they are required. This forms a much more flexible arrangement than the process of cutting and pasting, where only the last element to be cut or copied is saved to the Clipboard.

In this Section, you will be using glossary entries to construct dinner menus at the 'Flying Wheels Motoring Club' Motel.

18.1 Defining glossary entries

EXERCISE

1 Open a **New** document with the **NORMAL** stylesheet.

2 Type in the following text in **italics** (character formatting may be saved with a glossary entry):

A Selection of Hors d'Oeuvres
*****

Saffron Soup with Fine Herbs

Red Onion Soup with Cheese Sippets

Deep Fried Mushrooms filled with Stilton

Leg of Lamb roasted with Rosemary & Thyme

Two Vegetable Dishes

Two Potato Dishes

*****

A Selection of Homemade Sweets

*****

A Selection of English & Continental Cheeses

*****

Coffee & Mints

A number of glossary entries will be made using different sections of this text.

3 Highlight the text in the first two lines and select **Glossary** from the **Edit** menu (ALT E O). A *Glossary* dialogue box will be displayed as shown below:

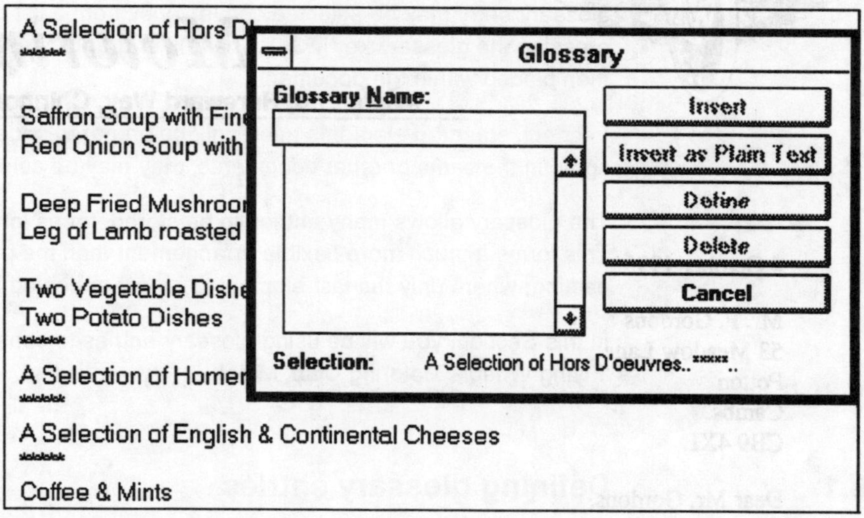

Glossary entries may consist of up to 31 characters in length and can contain spaces. The *Selection* area found towards the bottom of the dialogue box, displays the currently selected text.

4 Type: **hors** in the *Glossary Name*: text box and select the **Define** command button (*or* press Enter). This will take a copy of the highlighted text and store it as a glossary entry under the label of **hors**.

5 Highlight the third line and set up a glossary entry as above with the name of **saffron**. Repeat for the next line, giving a glossary entry name of **onion**.

6 Enter the next two lines of text under the glossary names of **mush** and **lamb** respectively.

7 Highlight the remainder of the text and enter the glossary name of **standard**.

You have now set up glossary entries for: hors; saffron; onion; mush; lamb and standard.

8 You do not need to save this document.

18.2 Preparing the main document

EXERCISE 1 Open a **New** document using either the **FWLETR** or **FWLETGRF** stylesheet.

2 Type the letter as shown below with an extra (empty) paragraph before 'Yours sincerely':

The Flying Wheels Motoring Club

Maple End, Hareward Way, Chinnor, Bucks. OK2 3MB

4 October 1995

Mr. F. Gordons
53 Meadow Lane
Potton
Cambs.
CB9 4XL

Dear Mr. Gordons,

I write to confirm that a reservation has been made in your name for an over-night stay in the Gourmet Cottage, at the Flying Wheels Motoring Club Motel, on the evening of October 27.

Your order for dinner will be delivered to the cottage kitchen by 6.00pm and will include cooking instructions. We confirm the following selections:

Yours sincerely

Your name here
MOTEL MANAGER

18.3 Inserting glossary entries into documents

EXERCISE

1 In the empty paragraph above 'Yours sincerely' type **hors** and press the glossary key F3. The word 'hors' will be replaced by the glossary entry.

2 Move down onto the next line and type either **saffron** or **onion** and press F3. Insert five '*' characters on the next line.

3 In the same way, type either **mush** or **lamb** on the next line and press F3.

4 On the next line type **standard** and press F3.

5 Set the menu block of text (apart from the first line) so that there is no line spacing above the paragraphs. **Centre** the entire menu block of text.

6 Place the menu block into a frame with a shadow border.

7 Size and position the frame enclosing the menu text block.

The letter should appear similar to that shown on the page 210.

8 Save and print the document if you wish.

9 You may wish to prepare a similar letter using a different menu, by preparing and inserting different glossary entries.

Note: When you later exit from the Word for Windows program, you will be prompted with the message 'Do you want to save the global glossary and command changes?'. The glossary entries that you have set will always be available for insertion into any document if you select the **Yes** command button. If you select the **No** command button they will be lost.

18.4 Deleting glossary entries

Should you wish to delete any glossary entries, display the *Glossary* dialogue box, then highlight the appropriate glossary name and then select the **Delete** command button.

The Flying Wheels Motoring Club

Maple End, Hareward Way, Chinnor, Bucks. OK2 3MB

4 October 1995

Mr. F. Gordons
53 Meadow Lane
Potton
Cambs.
CB9 4XL

Dear Mr. Gordons,

I write to confirm that a reservation has been made in your name for an over-night stay in the Gourmet Cottage, at the Flying Wheels Motoring Club Motel, on the evening of October 27.

Your order for dinner will be delivered to the cottage kitchen by 6.00pm and will include cooking instructions. We confirm the following selections:

A Selection of Hors d'Oeuvres
*****
Saffron Soup with Fine Herbs
*****
Deep Fried Mushrooms filled with Stilton
Two Vegetable Dishes
Two Potato Dishes
*****
A Selection of Homemade Sweets
*****
A Selection of English & Continental Cheeses
*****
Coffee & Mints

Yours sincerely

Your name here
MOTEL MANAGER

19 Hyphenation

Word for Windows will allow you to hyphenate text manually, semi-automatically and fully automatically.

Hyphenation reduces the 'ragged' appearance towards the right-hand margin of Left aligned text.

- *Manual Hyphenation* involves the insertion of one of three types of hyphen into the text:

  Regular Hyphens are used for words which are always hyphenated and which can be split at the end of a line. These are typed as the normal hyphen key [-].

  Optional Hyphens are those inserted manually to fill out a line, with part of the word being taken over to the next line. These are entered using [Ctrl -].

  Non-breaking Hyphens allow you to keep hyphenated words together on the same line. These are entered using [Ctrl Shift -].

- *Semi-Automatic Hyphenation* allows Word for Windows to indicate where hyphenation may take place, but requires confirmation from you before actually placing a hyphen within the text.

- *Fully Automatic Hyphenation* allows Word for Windows to hyphenate text automatically, without confirmation from you.

The *hot zone* is an area between the right-hand margin and the end of a line of text in which words will be hyphenated, if possible. If the space left at the end of a specific line of text is greater than the value associated with the hot zone, then the first word on the next line will be hyphenated. The larger the hot zone, the less ragged the text (at the right-hand margin) becomes.

You may choose whether to hyphenate text which is in capitals or not. This means that you may for example, instruct Word for Windows to ignore headings that are typed in capitals.

Hyphenation options are set using the **Hyphenation** command from the **Tools** menu ([ALT O H]).

EXERCISE

1 Open the **CFORMAT.DOC** document and notice the 'ragged' nature of the text towards the right-hand margin.

2 Select **Hyphenation** from the **Tools** menu ([ALT O H]). A *Hyphenation* dialogue box will be displayed as follows:

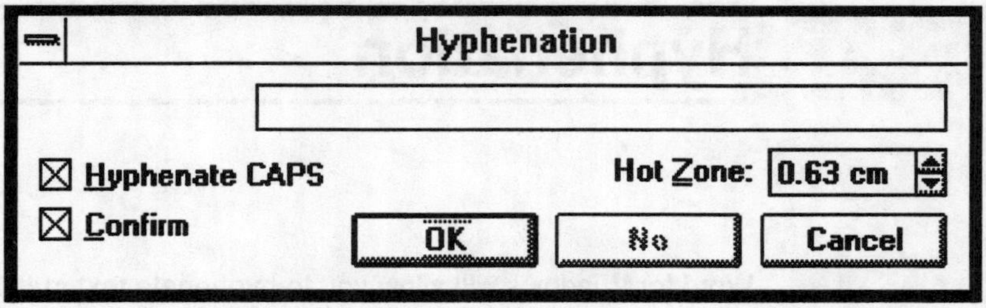

The **Hyphenate CAPS** checkbox allows you to include words in capitals or not in the hyphenation process.

When the **Confirm** check box is selected, hyphenation will be carried out semi-automatically, otherwise hyphenation will be fully automatic. Word for Windows will display alternative positions for hyphens (inside the *Hyphenate At:* text box) for any words that it judges should be hyphenated.

3 Select the **Confirm** check box and de-select the **Hyphenate CAPS** check box if necessary. Accept to begin the hyphenation process. Any word which may be hyphenated will be displayed in the *Hyphenate At:* text box.

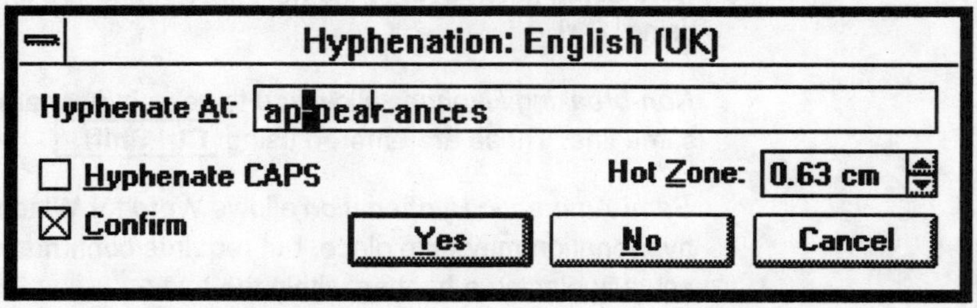

4 For each word, *either* select the required position for the hyphen (if there is more than one indicated) and accept *or* select the **No** command button to skip the word.

5 Divide the text into 3 columns (**Columns** from the **Format** menu) and hyphenate the text fully automatically (de-select the **Confirm** check box).

6 Experiment with hyphenation using different *Hot Zone:* values.

7 Experiment with the three different manual hyphenation keyboard codes.

It is suggested that the document is not, on this occasion, saved.

20 Tables and forms

On pages 80-86, you were introduced to the use of tabs and paragraph borders in the production of simple tables. However, Word for Windows provides much more versatile table facilities giving far greater flexibility in the presentation of forms and tables of many different kinds.

You will already have used a simple table when you created a data file on pages 170-173. The table facilities in this case, were automatically employed by the program to assist you in the preparation of a data file used in the print-merging process,

A table consists of a grid of rows and columns. At the intersection of a row and column, referred to as a *'cell'*, is a position where any item may be entered and displayed. A cell may be envisaged as a 'box' inside which may be placed text, and/or graphics.

If using a mouse, a table may be conveniently placed within a document at the current insertion point position, by using the **Table** button in the Toolbar. This is explored on page 223.

Commands affecting the organisation of tables are found in the **Table** menu. These various commands allow you to do the following:

- Set the numbers of rows and columns in a table.
- Adjust column widths.
- Set character and paragraph formatting of text within a table.
- Merge together one, or more cells.
- Split merged cells.
- Perform calculations as if a table were a simple spreadsheet.
- Convert existing text-based tables (as set up with tabs) into a table.
- Convert a table into a text-based table.

In addition, the **Border** command in the **Format** menu allows you to:

- Draw borders of various types around a table, individual and groups of cells.
- Add shading to individual and groups of cells.

Also, the usual commands in the **Edit** menu allow you to: cut, copy, and paste parts of a table.

Once a table has been formed, each cell has its own unique reference (*cell reference*) described by row and column. For example, the cell found at the top, left-hand side of a table would be in position Row 1, Column 1. This cell reference is useful in describing the position of figures, found within a table, particularly if the values are involved in calculations. Cell references are written in the following form: **[R1C1]** for Row 1, Column 1.

20.1 Tables and Ruler views

When you are working with a table, three different views of the Ruler are possible. The **Ruler Scale** icon found on the left-hand side of the Ruler switches between indent, margin and table Ruler scales. You are already familiar with indent view (used for setting indents and tabs) and margin view (used for setting margins).

The table Ruler view is used for setting the width of columns within a table, by dragging the column icons using a mouse (it is not possible to use the keyboard to affect column widths in this Ruler view).

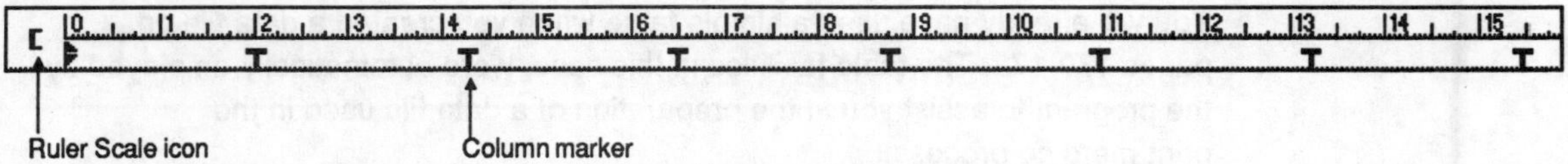

20.2 Converting text to a table

The following exercise takes the tabular text found in the TABS1.DOC document produced on page 82 and converts it into a simple table. This will be used to practice the basic skills required for the manipulation of tables.

EXERCISE

1. Open **TABS1.DOC** and highlight all the text.
2. Select **Convert Text to Table** from the **Table** menu (ALT A T). A dialogue box will be displayed as shown below:

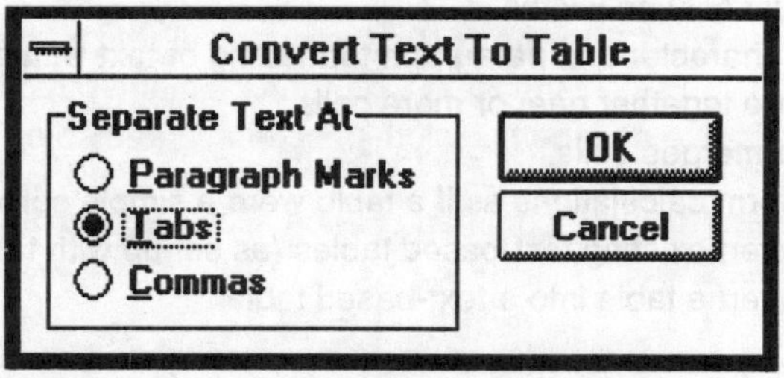

This *Convert Text To Table* dialogue box allows you to indicate the character which was used to separate items of information in the original text.

3. Since tabs were used originally to place the text within columns, the **Tabs** check box should be selected if necessary in the *Separate Text At area.* This means that the program will place items separated by tabs into separate columns.
4. Accept when ready. The text will be placed into a table consisting of three columns and thirteen rows, corresponding to the original tab text.

Do not be surprised at this point that the third column appears to spread downwards – the width of the column is likely to be narrower than required. This will be adjusted in the next section. For now, leave the table highlighted on the screen.

20.3 Adjusting column widths

There are three methods of adjusting the width of highlighted columns within a table:

Changing column widths with the keyboard

Select **Column Width** (ALT A W) from the **Table** menu. The following *Column Width* dialogue box will be displayed:

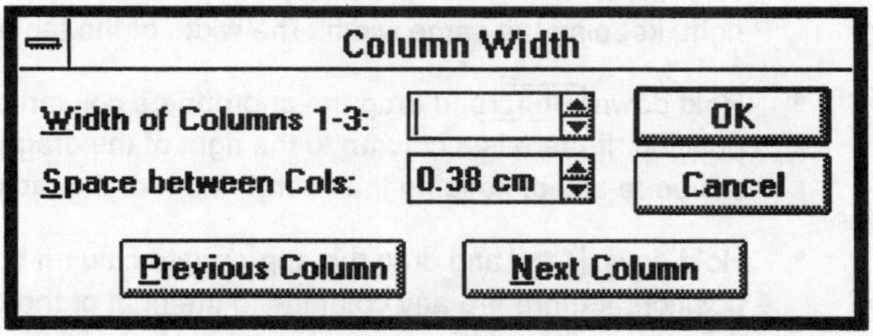

With more than one column highlighted, the *Width of Columns* text box allows you to set the width of all columns to a similar value in one operation.

Selecting the **Next Column** command button allows you to change the width of column 1. If you select the **Next Column** command button for a second time you will be allowed to change the width of column 2 and so on.

The **Previous Column** command button allows you to move to a previous column and change its width.

The space automatically inserted between columns may also be adjusted by setting an appropriate value inside the *Space between Cols:* text box.

Changing column widths with the mouse and Ruler

If the table scale of the Ruler is not displayed, click on the **Scale** icon on the left of the Ruler. The following options are available:

- Drag the appropriate column marker to the required position on the Ruler. If there are any columns to the right of the dragged column marker, they will be moved to the right along the Ruler, keeping the same width. The width of the table will thus be increased.

- Hold down **Shift** and drag the appropriate column marker to the required position on the Ruler. If there is a column to the right of the dragged column marker, then it will be re-sized, keeping the overall width of the table the same.

- Hold down **Ctrl** and drag the appropriate column marker to the required position on the Ruler. If there are any columns to the right of the dragged column marker, then they will each be re-sized proportionally, keeping the overall width of the table the same.

Changing column widths with the mouse and column borders

If the borders around the table are not displayed, select **Gridlines** from the **Table** menu. The following options are available:

- Drag the appropriate column border to the required position. If there are any columns to the right of the dragged column border, they will be moved to the right, keeping the same width. The width of the table will thus be increased.

- Hold down **Shift** and drag the appropriate column border to the required position. If there is a column to the right of the dragged column border, then it will be re-sized, keeping the overall width of the table the same.

- Hold down **Ctrl** and drag the appropriate column border to the required position. If there are any columns to the right of the dragged column border, then they will each be re-sized proportionally, keeping the overall width of the table the same.

EXERCISE

1 If the entire table is not highlighted, move the insertion point into any cell in the table and press **Ctrl 5** (5 on the numeric keypad) to highlight the whole table. This is similar to using the keyboard to highlight a whole document.

2 Use one of the methods outlined above, to set the width of column **3** to **3 cm** (this should correspond to 13.75 cm on the Ruler). The table will be re-formatted.

Month	Colours	Birth Stone
January	brown, grey, black	Garnet
February	purple, blue-purple, black	Amethyst
March	green, green and red	Bloodstone
April	blue, grey, green, red, white	Diamond
May	emerald green	Emerald
June	red, yellow, white	Agate
July	all colours of the roses	Ruby
August	grey, tomato red, deep yellow	Sardonyx
September	primrose, violet, pale green	Sapphire
October	grey, dark blue, red, red-mauve, pink-red	Opal
November	yellow, gold-brown	Topaz
December	light blue, pink	Turquoise

3 Save the document on the Samples Disk under the name of **TABLE1**.

20.4 Highlighting cells

Should you wish to reformat cells and their contents by changing their borders, column widths, height etc., then as for character and paragraph formatting, you need to indicate the specific cells that you wish to effect. This, as before, is seen as highlighted text and/or graphics within cells on the screen.

Highlighting cells within a table may be accomplished in a variety of ways using a mouse. Highlighting using the keyboard is carried out in a similar fashion to selecting parts of paragraphs and columns of normal text.

Highlighting table selections

- A **single cell** may be selected by pointing and clicking to the left of any text or graphics placed in the cell ([Shift End]).
- A **range of cells** may be selected by dragging across the required cells (hold down [Shift] and press a cursor control key).
- A **single row** may be selected by:

(a) Dragging across the required row ([ALT A R]).

(b) Double-clicking immediately to the left of the left table border.

(c) Double-clicking on the *selection bar* (the space between the left border and the text) of any cell in the row.

- **Multiple rows** may be selected by dragging down and across the table.
- A **section of a column** may be selected by dragging down the column.
- An **entire column** may be selected by:

(a) Dragging down the column ([ALT A C]).

(b) Clicking the **right** mouse button whilst pointing to any cell in the required column.

(c) Clicking directly above the top table border for the required column.

- The **whole table** may be selected by dragging from the top-left to the bottom-right of the table ([ALT A A] *or* [Ctrl 5] on the numeric keypad).

EXERCISE

1 Practice highlighting sections of the table.

2 Use the **Border** command from the **Format** menu to experiment with different borders surrounding cells and cell shading.

3 Experiment with the setting of different column widths for different parts of the table.

20.5 Inserting and deleting columns, rows and cells

Inserting columns

Columns may be inserted to the left of a selected column within a table, or to the right of the table.

- If inserting a *column into a table*, highlight a column immediately to the right of where you wish to insert a new column (or on the right of where you wish to insert a number of columns, highlight as many columns as you wish to insert).
- If inserting a *column to the right of a table*, point to an end-of-row mark on the right-hand side of the table and press the **right** mouse button to select all the end-of-row marks.
- Select the **Insert Columns** command from the **Table** menu (ALT A I).

Deleting columns

Highlighted columns may be deleted as follows:

- Highlight the column/s that you wish to delete.
- Select the **Delete Columns** command from the **Table** menu (ALT A D).

Inserting rows

New rows may be inserted above a highlighted row in a table, or at the bottom of a table.

To insert a *row at the bottom of a table:*

- Move into the right-most cell in the bottom row of the table and press Tab.

To insert a *row within a table:*

- Highlight a row immediately below where you wish to insert a new row (or below where you wish to insert a number of rows, highlight as many rows as you wish to insert).
- Select the **Insert Rows** command from the **Table** menu (ALT A I).

Deleting rows

- Highlight the rows that you wish to delete.
- *Either* select **Delete Rows** from the **Table** menu (ALT A D) *or* select **Cut** from the **Edit** menu.

Inserting cells

The following may be used to add as many cells as you require and may also be used to add rows and columns:

- Highlight the cells that you wish to add (across rows and columns if required).
- Select **Insert Cells** from the **Table** menu (**ALT A I**). The following *Insert Cells* dialogue box will be displayed:

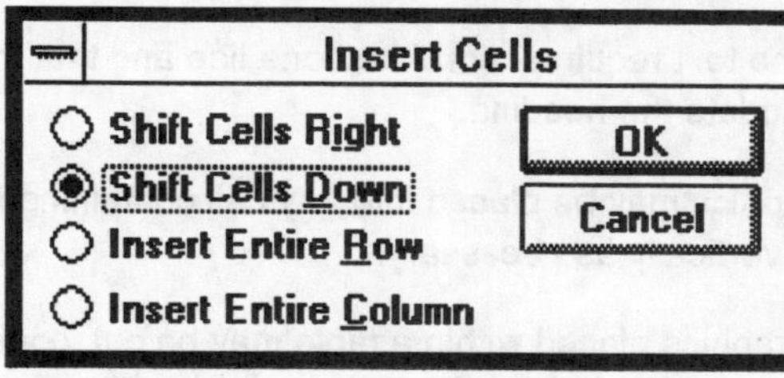

- Select one of the options.

Shift Cells Right inserts a corresponding number of cells to the left of the highlighted cells (the highlighted cells being moved to the right).

Shift cells Down inserts a corresponding number of cells above the highlighted cells (the highlighted cells are moved down).

Insert Entire Row inserts a row above the highlighted cells.

Insert Entire Column inserts a column to the left of the highlighted cells.

Deleting cells

- Highlight the cells that you wish to delete.
- Select **Delete Cells** from the **Table** menu (**ALT A D**). A *Delete Cells* dialogue box will be displayed which is similar to the *Insert Cells* dialogue box.

Select the appropriate option in the *Delete Cells* dialogue box, indicating how the program is to move the remaining cells or whether a row or column is to be deleted.

EXERCISE 1 Practice methods of inserting and deleting columns, rows and blocks of cells in the **TABLE1.DOC** document.

20.6 Inserting text or graphics into a cell

Text or graphics may be placed into any cell by simply pointing at the required cell and clicking to position the insertion point. If the cell is highlighted rather than the insertion point being visible, then try clicking towards the centre of the cell.

With the **keyboard**, **Tab** will move the insertion point from cell to cell across rows (left to right), working down the table. **Shift Tab** will move the insertion point from right to left across rows, working backwards towards the top of the table.

EXERCISE

1 Create a new row at the top of the table in the **TABLE1.DOC** document.

2 Place the insertion point into the top, left-hand cell (**[R1C1]**).

3 Type **Summary of Months and their Fortune**

Note that the text requires more than one line and that the row expands vertically to accommodate the heading.

Text or graphics may be placed into any cell containing the insertion point, the cell expanding vertically as necessary.

Text and graphics placed within a table may be cut, copied and pasted (using appropriate commands from the **Edit** menu) just like any other element within a document.

20.7 Merging and splitting cells

The heading created in the previous exercise would look better spread across the top of the three columns. This requires the merging of the three cells forming the top row of the table.

EXERCISE

1 Highlight the three cells forming the first row across the top of the table and select **Merge Cells** from the **Table** menu (**ALT A M**). The three cells will be merged to form one cell.

2 The merged cell contains the empty paragraphs that were placed by default into the original cells, [R1C2] and [R1C3]. Delete these empty paragraphs in the normal way using the **Backspace** or **Del** keys.

3 Centre the heading paragraph in the normal way and set any character formatting and/or paragraph spacing that you wish.

If previously merged cells need to be split into their separate cells, this may be carried out as follows:

- Highlight the merged cell/s.
- Select **Split Cells** from the **Table** menu (**ALT A P**).

20.8 Setting row height, table alignment and indents

Spacing between selected rows in a table may be set in the normal way by changing the space *Before:* and *After:* in the *Paragraph* dialogue box accessed via the **Paragraph** command in the **Format** menu. Alternatively, the appropriate paragraph style(s) may be changed.

The default height of a row in a table is dependent on the contents of the cells. However, the automatic row height adjustment may be altered using the **Row Height** command in the **Table** menu. To alter the height of rows:

- Highlight the rows that you want to adjust.
- Select **Row Height** from the **Table** menu (**ALT A H**). The following *Row Height* dialogue box will be displayed:

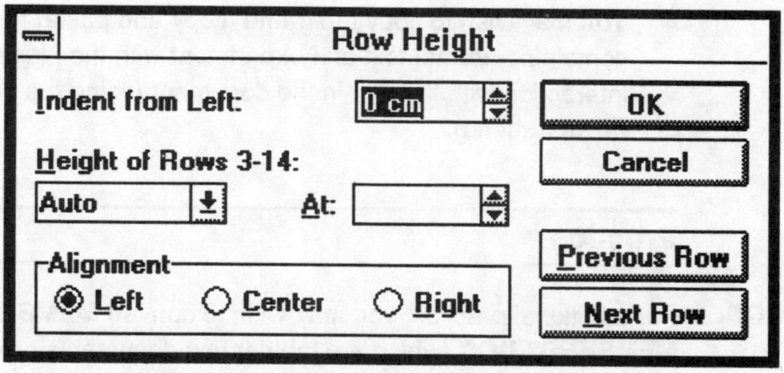

The *Height of Rows* drop-down list contains three options:

Auto (default) which adjusts the row height automatically according to the cell contents.

At Least sets a minimum row height according to the value entered into the *At:* text box.

Exactly sets a fixed row height according to the value entered into the *At:* text box.

The **Previous Row** and **Next Row** command buttons allow you to select further rows on which to operate if required.

Rows may be indented by entering an appropriate value in the *Indent from Left:* text box. Note: indents may also be adjusted by dragging the left indent marker on the Ruler when it is displaying the table scale.

The alignment of highlighted rows (or entire table) may be set in the *Alignment* area.

- Select to complete the operation(s).

EXERCISE 1 Experiment with setting: row height; paragraph spacing; indents; and alignment for the entire table and selected parts of the table.

20.9 Positioning a table

Once you have prepared your table, you may re-position it on the page as you wish by placing it within a frame. It will then behave much like any other graphic.

EXERCISE

1. Highlight the whole table in the **TABLE1.DOC** and select **Frame** from the **Insert** menu. This will place the highlighted selection inside a new frame.
2. Using a **Page Layout** view, highlight the frame.
3. If using a mouse, experiment with dragging, sizing and cropping the frame as you would with a normal graphic.

   If using the keyboard, select **Frame** from the **Format** menu and experiment with *Horizontal*, *Vertical* and *Size* options for the frame.
4. You may wish to copy the frame (copy and paste) to another document containing normal text and experiment with the placing of the frame and its interaction with the text in the document (using the **Frame** command from the **Format** menu).

Practice

EXERCISE For additional practice, you may wish to convert **MEMBERS.DOC** or **MEMBERS2.DOC** (which are tabular text documents produced on pages 99-101) into tables and experiment with the different options described above.

20.10 Inserting a new table

A new table may be inserted into a document in one of two ways:

Using a command

- Move the insertion point to where the table is to be inserted.
- Select **Insert Table** from the **Table** menu (ALT A I). The following dialogue box is displayed:

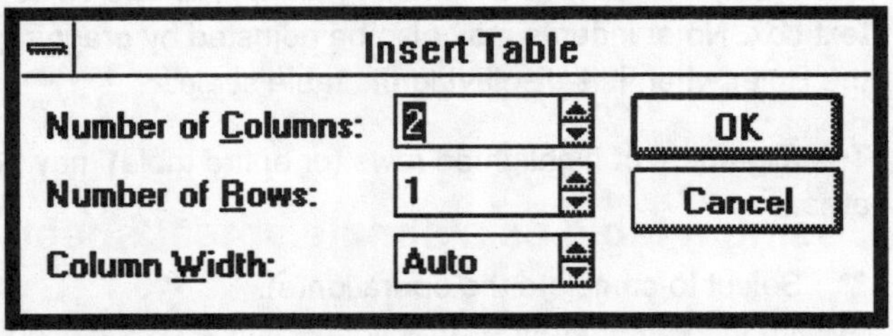

- Enter the *Number of Columns:*, *Number of Rows*: and alter the *Column Width:* if necessary.

- Accept to insert the table in the document.

Using the Table button in the Toolbar

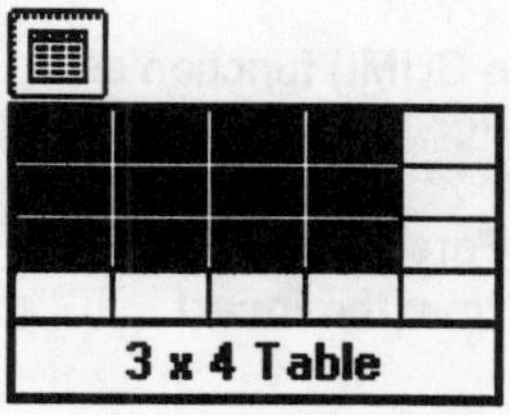

- Move the insertion point to where the table is to be inserted.
- Select the **Table** button in the Toolbar. A drop-down grid will appear.
- Drag out an area on the grid to select the appropriate number of rows and columns (maximum 5 columns, 4 rows).
- Release the mouse button to insert the table in the document.

EXERCISE

1 Open a new document and insert a table by selecting **Insert Table** from the **Table** menu. The table should have **6** rows and **3** columns.

2 Set a thin single line border around each cell (**Border** command in the **Format** menu).

3 Type the following into cell **[R1C1]** found at the top-left of the table: **Sales Figures : 1st Quarter**

4 Merge the cells in row 1 and centre the heading. Set the character formatting to something suitable and remove any unwanted, blank paragraphs.

5 Enter the additional information shown below using appropriate character and paragraph formatting (in the example, the figures were aligned by setting a decimal tab):

Sales Figures : 1st Quarter		
	Forecast	**Actual**
April	150700	175600
May	225400	164000
June	197000	215000
Totals		

6 Adjust the top border for the 'Totals' row so that it has a double-line border above it.

7 Save the document under a suitable name on the Samples Disk.

20.11 Using a table as a simple spreadsheet

Using the cell references mentioned earlier, it is possible to use a table to perform simple calculations.

Using the SUM() function

The figures in the second column will be totalled by using the SUM() function as part of a field expression.

EXERCISE 1 Move the insertion point to the cell at the bottom of the 'Forecast' column ([R6C2]) and insert the following expression field (**Field** from the **Insert** menu): = **SUM([R3C2:R5C2])**

Word for Windows provides a number of functions that may be applied to figures in a table. In this case, the **SUM()** function has been used to total up the contents of the cells referred to in the rest of the expression.

The colon (:) replaces the word 'to', therefore the [R3C2:R5C2] part of the expression means 'from row 3, column 2 to row 5, column 2 inclusive'. This is referred to as the *range*. The whole expression means: add up the numbers from row 3, column 2 to row 5, column 2 and place the result in the cell containing the insertion point.

With **Field Code**s displayed (**View** menu) the field will be displayed as: {=SUM([R3C2:R5C2])}

The result of the calculation will be shown in the table when field codes is de-selected.

2 In a similar fashion, set up a suitable field expression which will produce a total for the figures in the **Actual** column.

3 Save the document under the name of **TABLE2** on the Samples Disk.

Other functions

Other useful functions that you may like to try at this stage are as follows:

AVERAGE() Calculates the average of a range of numbers e.g. AVERAGE([R3C2:R3C3]).

COUNT() Counts the number of numerical entries within the range of cells e.g. COUNT([R1C1:R5C3]).

MAX() Finds the largest value within a range e.g. MAX([R6C2:R6C3]).

MIN() Finds the smallest value within a range e.g. MIN([R3C3:R5C3]).

For further information, use the **Help Index** to locate the help information for the expression =.

20.12 Graphing the data in a table

The information within a table may be easily displayed in the form of a graph using the Microsoft Graph program that is supplied with the main Word for Windows program.

To graph the data using the **mouse**

- Highlight all or part of the table containing the data.

- Select the **Graph** button in the Toolbar. A default graph of the data will be produced as the Graph program loads.
- Use the Graph program to modify the graph of the data.
- When ready, select the **Exit and Return** command from the Graph **File** menu to insert the graph immediately below the table.

To graph the data using the **keyboard**

- Highlight all or part of the table containing the data.
- Select the **Object** command from the **Insert** menu (**ALT I O**) and select the **Microsoft Graph** option in the *Object Type:* area of the *Object* dialogue box which appears.
- Use the Graph program to modify the graph of the data.
- When ready, select the **Exit and Return** command from the Graph **File** menu to insert the graph immediately below the table.

Using the Graph program, you may:

- Select from a broad range of graph types using commands in the **Gallery** menu.
- Add titles, labels, axes, gridlines and legends using commands in the **Chart** menu.
- Change colours, fonts, line and pattern styles and more using commands in the **Format** menu.
- View the graph at different zoom levels using commands in the **Window** menu.
- Change the data to be graphed using the commands in the **DataSeries** menu.
- Cut, copy, paste and move using familiar commands in the **Edit** menu.
- Use the **File** menu to import data into the Graph program, place a graph into a Word for Windows document and more.
- Obtain help using commands from the **Help** menu.

EXERCISE 1 Open the **TABLE2.DOC** document if necessary and highlight the cells **[R2C1:R5C3]**. This contains the labels and figures for the 'Sales Figures' (not including the totals).

2 Using one of the methods outlined above, load the Microsoft Graph program.

3 Experiment with the different menus and commands (briefly described above). Remember that the program contains a Help system if you require any further information about a specific command or option.

4 When ready, select the **Exit and Return** from the **File** menu. You will be asked whether you wish to update the graph in the document. Accept to insert the graph.

5 Place the graph into a frame if you wish to re-position it. An example is shown below:

Sales Figures : 1st Quarter

	Forecast	**Actual**
April	150700	175600
May	225400	164000
June	197000	215000
Totals	**573100**	**554600**

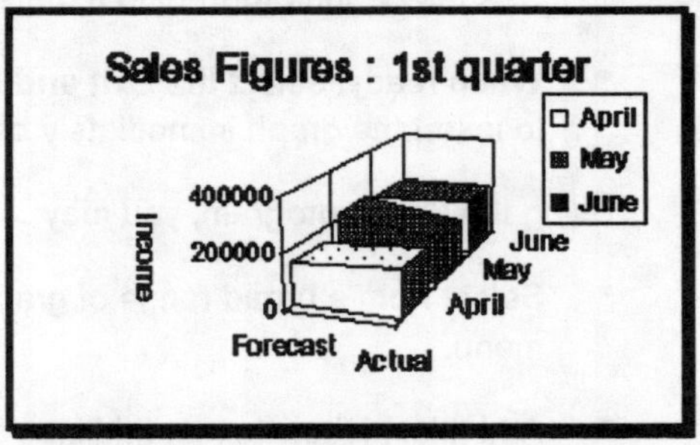

Should you wish to make changes to the nature of the graph, simply double-click on the graph or select the **Object** command from the **Insert** menu.

20.13 Consolidation exercise : An invoice

Wells Garage
Chinnor
Bucks
OK2 3MB
Tel. (0653) 110622
Fax. (0653) 110333

Wells Garage

SALES INVOICE

Invoice No: 623
Invoice Date: 27/10/95

Invoice To:	**Deliver To:**
Mr. J. Chatter Redways Longwick Staffs. ST1 6NP	Mr. J. Chatter Redways Longwick Staffs. ST1 6NP

Invoice No.	**Date of Invoice**	**Client Order No.**	**Sales Order No.**
	27/10/95	ST 65	654
623	**Account No.**	**Sales**	**No. of Parcels**
	AR 5	F. Gregory	6

Product Code	**Description/Serial No.**	**Quantity**	**Price**	**Totals**
4962	Thermostat housing	1	9.75	9.75
7864	Rear spring (5-leaf)	2	28.40	56.80
2021	Recon distributor	1	35.00	35.00
9843	Radiator exchange	1	49.95	49.95
7594	Track rod ends	2	8.45	16.90
5532	Water pump 803	1	17.00	17.00
6981	Rear axle U-bolts	4	1.95	7.80
3612	Front bumpers	1	43.50	43.50
			Total Value	236.70
			VAT @ 17.5%	41.42
			Total Due	278.12

Terms : 30 DAYS FROM DATE OF INVOICE   VAT NO. 359 7777 957

The sample invoice document above, was originally prepared as a template with the appropriate information omitted. This template was then loaded with a new document and the relevant details entered before printing. You may wish to prepare this invoice as a document only.

A combination of expressions using bookmarks and cell references was used to calculate all the figures in the 'Totals' column.

The invoice document contains a number of separate elements arranged into three separate areas of the page – the invoice heading block and two separate tables.

The following sections give notes for guidance, to assist in the preparation of a similar invoice template or document. You are encouraged to experiment with your own layout and formatting as you wish.

Invoice headings

This part of the page could have been defined as a *Section* consisting of three columns with appropriate spacing between them. The text could then have been typed with *column breaks* placed at the appropriate positions.

In reality, the text found towards the centre and right of the heading block was placed into frames and dragged into position.

The 'Invoice Date:' label was followed by the insertion of a **Date** field.

Appropriate character and paragraph formatting was then set for the text.

The **CAR1** graphic (found in the GRAPHICS subdirectory of the Samples Disk) was placed into another frame which was sized, cropped and again dragged into position. So that the graphic did not repel any text close to it, the *Distance From Text*: (**Frame** command from the **Format** menu) was set at 0 cm.

The {ASK} field code encountered on page 192, could be usefully employed in the entering of data within this invoice form. In addition, print-merging techniques could be used to print any number of individualised invoices.

Table 1

The first table consists of 3 rows and 4 columns, The height of the cells within the table was adjusted for each row by the inclusion of additional blank paragraphs as necessary.

The **Invoice No.** cell was merged with the one beneath it, creating one larger cell.

The central alignment of the cell labels was set.

The paragraphs for the address were indented, while those for the actual data values were centred within the cells. Appropriate character formatting was also set for the text (paragraph styles were set for each type of paragraph format, which ensured consistency).

Table 2

Table 2 consisted of 19 rows and 5 columns. with single line, outside and inside borders being set.

The horizontal and vertical **Borders** were removed for some rows and cells.

The character formatting for the text in row 1 was set appropriately and was centrally aligned. The spacing before and after the paragraph was set at 1 line, increasing the space between the text and the borders.

The alignment of the figures within columns 3 to 5 were set using decimal tabs.

R16C3:R16C4 (containing 'Total Value') were merged and likewise the cells containing 'VAT @ 17.5%' and 'Total Due'. The appropriate cell borders were set. The text within these merged cells was indented and their character formatting set appropriately.

All the cells in the last row were merged to hold the line of text at the bottom of the table. The text was typed and formatted.

The paragraphs within the cells in column 1, under the heading of 'Product code', were centred.

Calculations

The figures in the 'Totals' column were calculated using **expression** Fields, and the use of a combination of bookmarks and cell references.

For each row, the total is the **Quantity * Price**. The format of the result (and all other calculations) should be chosen as **#,##0.00** (i.e. two decimal places). Alternatively, you may wish to simply type the value into a cell.

The 'Total Value' calculation was easily performed by inserting the following **expression** Field into the appropriate cell: **SUM([R3C5:R15C5])**

Assuming that you have created a bookmark name representing the Total Value called **Value**, the VAT @ 17.5% amount may be calculated by entering the following **expression** field into the appropriate cell: **VALUE * 0.175**

Assuming that the VAT @ 17.5% amount is marked with the bookmark name of **VAT**, the 'Total Due' may be calculated by entering the following **expression** field into the appropriate cell: **VALUE + VAT**

21 Using multi-documents

Word for Windows provides a facility which allows you to display multiple views of a single document, within separate windows or in window panes. The same facility allows you to work on a number of different documents at the same time. Up to nine individual documents, or separate document views may be open on the screen at any one time.

When working with a long document, it may be useful to display various parts of the text on the screen. You might for example, want to check a section number referred to in the text or to move (or copy) a section of the document to a new position. The multi-document view facility allows you to display the part of the text with which you are currently working, with a number of additional sections being displayed at the same time.

The multi-document facility is useful where you need to check the relevant sections of a number of documents which have cross-referencing, or where you wish to copy text from one document to another.

Each document view may be displayed in its own document window with the normal window controls being available. In addition, each document window may be split into two separate views (*window panes*). This gives the potential for up to eighteen separate views of an individual document, or the display of nine separate documents, each of which may show two separate views (panes) of the text.

21.1 Splitting a document window into panes

You may wish to experiment with splitting document windows using the various methods described below. Any available document may be used.

When a document window is split, each pane contains its own set of scroll bars. Each pane may thus be scrolled independently.

You may alter a document in either pane but, since there are two views of the same document, any changes in one pane will be reflected in the other.

The document window may be split horizontally (or existing document window splits may be removed) in the following ways:

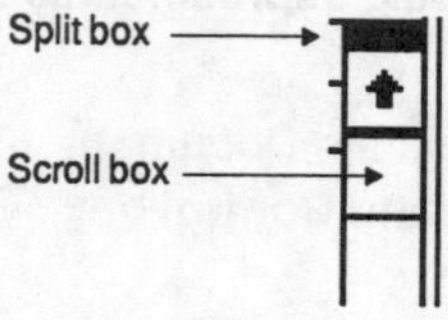

Using a mouse

At the top of the vertical scroll bar (if displayed), immediately above the upwards scroll arrow icon, is a thick black line called the **Split box**. Drag the **Split box** down the vertical scroll bar, to the desired split position.

An alternative method of splitting a document window with a mouse is to double-click on the **Split box** (this will split the document window into two similar sized parts).

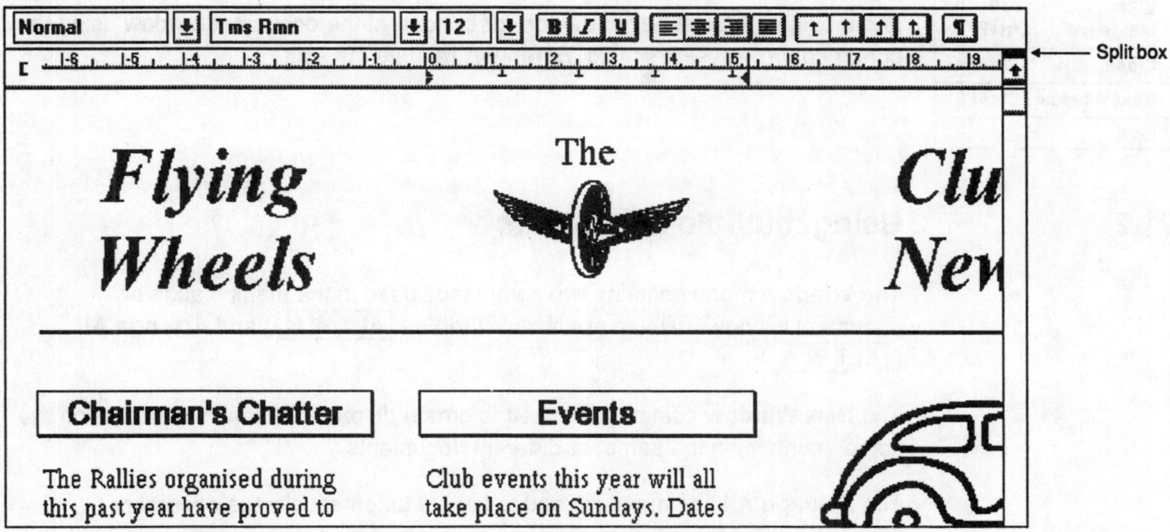

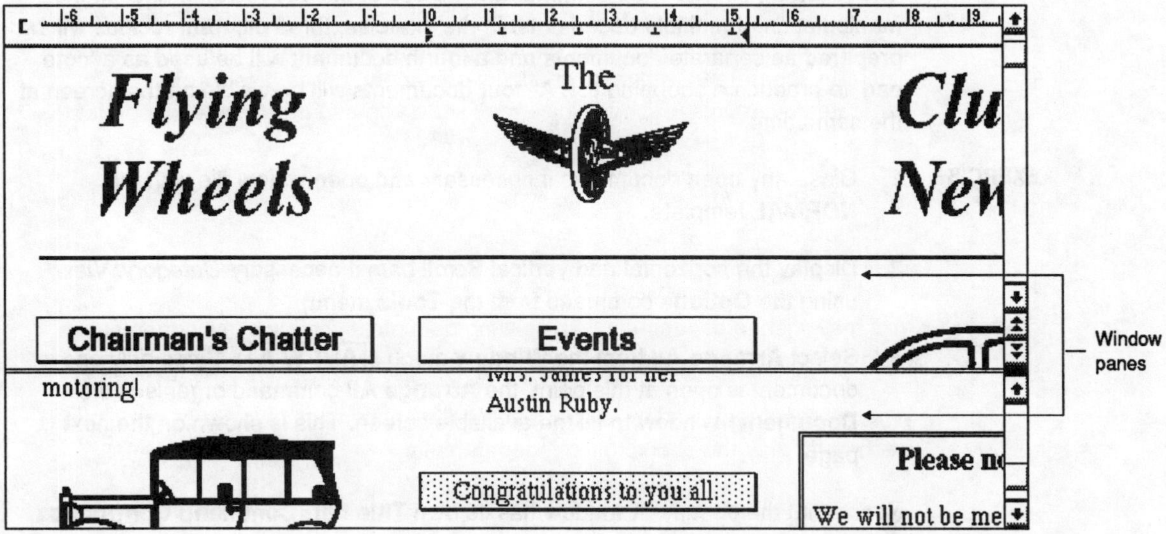

To remove a document window split *either:* drag the **Split box** to the top or bottom of the window, *or* double-click on the **Split box.**

Using a command

A document window may be split using the **Split** command from the **Document Control menu** accessed by clicking on the **Document Command Control box** (ALT - T).

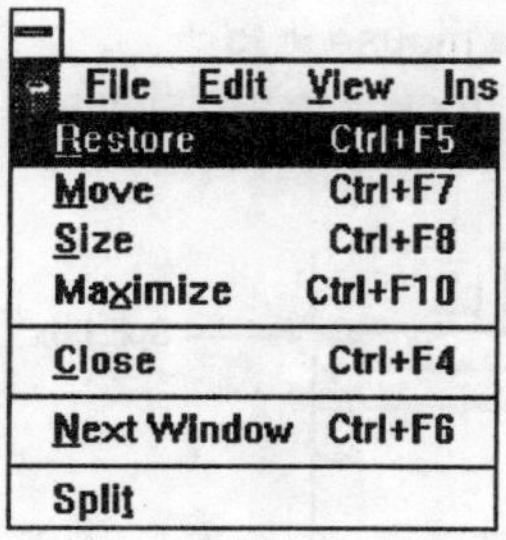

Use the up and down cursor control keys to move the **Split bar** to the required position and press Enter to fix the position of the split.

A document window split may be removed by issuing the same command again, and moving the **Split bar** to the top (or bottom) of the document window using the cursor control keys. Pressing Enter will remove the split.

21.2 Using multiple documents

The **Window** menu contains two commands used in the manipulation of document windows. These are **New Window** (ALT W N) and **Arrange All** (ALT W A).

The **New Window** command is used to create different document windows on the screen containing the same, or different documents.

The **Arrange All** command is used to lay out automatically the document windows on the screen according to a prescribed format. Any document window (including the Word for Windows application window) may, however, be moved or re-sized according to your requirements.

The following exercise will demonstrate the use of the above commands in the manipulation of multiple documents. In the exercise, three different recipes will be prepared as separate documents and a fourth document will be used as a 'note pad' to produce a shopping list. All four documents will be visible on the screen at the same time.

EXERCISE

1. Close any open documents if necessary and open a **New** file with the **NORMAL** template.

2. Display the horizontal and vertical Scroll bars if necessary *Category:* **View** using the **Options** command from the **Tools** menu).

3. Select **Arrange All** from the **Window** menu (ALT W A). Since only one document is open at this point, the **Arrange All** command organises the **Document1** window to fill the available screen. This is shown on the next page.

Notice that the document window has its own **Title bar, Command Control box, Ruler** and **Maximize button.**

The document window may be resized by dragging any horizontal or vertical window border. Alternatively, the window may be resized by dragging the **Window Size box** found at the bottom right-hand side of the window (this is only visible if both Scroll bars are displayed). This box allows you to resize the window horizontally and vertically in the same operation.

The document window may be moved to a new position by dragging the **Title bar.**

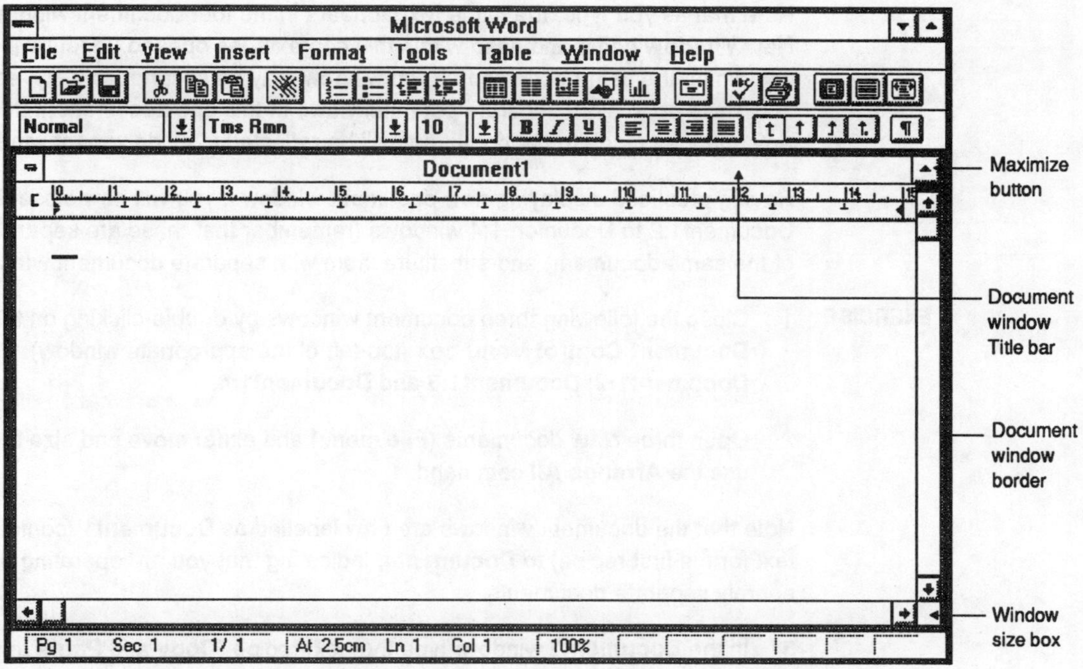

4 Select **New Window** from the **Window** menu (**ALT W N**) to add a new document window. This will lie on top of the first document window (which is slightly offset) with a title of **Document1:2** (meaning Document 1, window 2).

5 Add two more new document windows in the same way.

6 Rearrange the four document windows so that each is visible, using one of the two methods outlined below:

Either: select **Arrange All** from the **Window** menu (**ALT W A**). This will provide an automatic display of the open document windows.

Or: re-position and resize each document window in turn as described above, to produce a layout to suit yourself. An example is shown on page 235.

7 If you wish, remove the **Ruler** from each document window in turn by first selecting the appropriate window (point and click anywhere inside the window to activate it). This will give a larger area for viewing the text within the document windows.

8 In the **Document1:1** window, type:

GRANTHAM GINGERBREAD
100g butter
350g caster sugar
1 egg
250g self-raising flour
5ml ground ginger

Note that as you type, the same text appears in the four document windows. The **New Window** command used within this context, has opened up four windows containing the same document. Each window may be split horizontally, so you may have up to eight separate potential views of this one document at this stage. Any changes made to the document will be reflected in all document windows.

Having practiced displaying new document windows, you will now close the Document1:2 to Document1:4 windows (remember that these are separate views of the same document) and substitute them with separate document windows.

EXERCISE

1 Close the following three document windows by double-clicking on the **Document Control Menu box** (top-left of the appropriate window): **Document1:2; Document1:3** and **Document1:4.**

2 Open three **New** documents (**File** menu) and either move and size them, or use the **Arrange All** command.

Note that the document windows are now labelled as **Document1** (containing the text for the first recipe) to **Document4**, indicating that you are operating on four entirely separate documents.

3 In the **Document2** window, type the next recipe (**Copy** and **Paste** appropriate items from **Document1** if you wish):

GOOSNARGH CAKES
175g butter
225g plain flour
40g caster sugar
2.5ml caraway seeds

4 Type the following into the **Document3** window:

SHORTBREAD
150g plain flour
45ml rice flour
50g caster sugar
100g butter

According to how you arranged the document windows, the screen should appear similar to that shown on the next page.

5 Each document must be saved separately. Select the **Document1** window and save the document under the name of **GINGERBD.DOC.**

Select the **Document2** window and save the document under the name of **GOOSCAKE.DOC.**

Select the **Document3** window and save the document under the name of **SHORTBD.DOC.**

These file names will appear in the **Title bar** of the appropriate document windows.

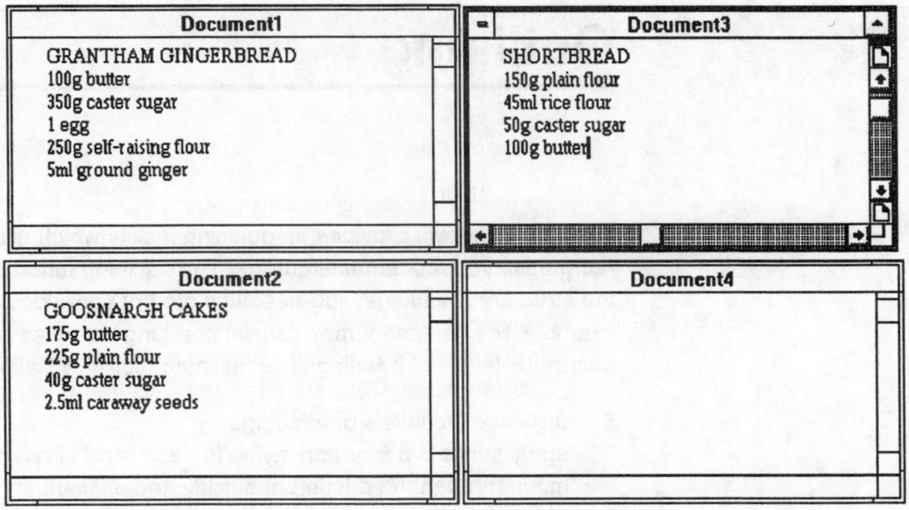

6 Use the text in the first three document windows to create a shopping list in the Document4 window. **Copy** and **Paste** as required.

7 Save the document in the **Document4** window under the name of **SHOPPING.DOC.** The screen should appear similar to that shown below (the size and positioning of the document windows are likely to vary):

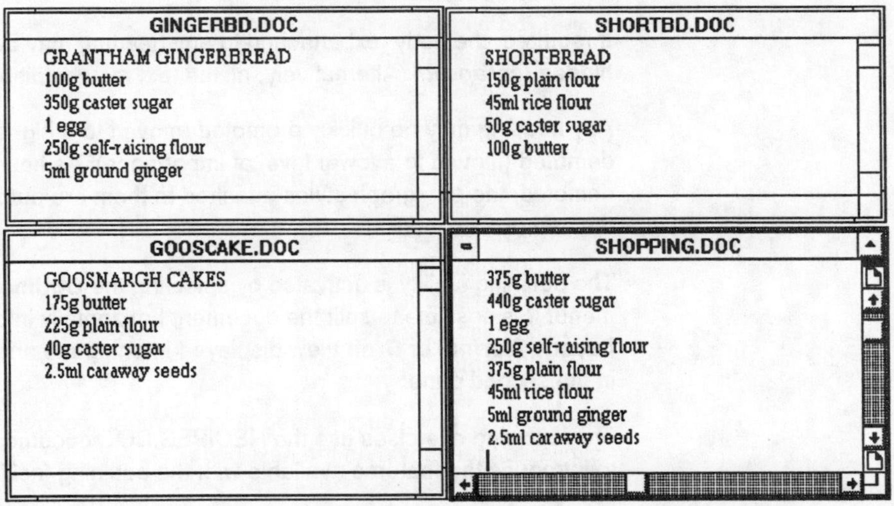

21.3 Practice exercise

Using separate document windows, **Copy** and **Paste** techniques, create another document (to be saved under the name of **RECIPES.DOC**) which contains all the text within the **GINGERBD.DOC**, **GOOSCAKE.DOC** and **SHORTBD.DOC** documents. The **RECIPES.DOC** document is to be used in the next chapter.

22 Outlining

Word for Windows provides an outlining facility which allows you to organise and reorganise your documents quickly. The outlining function allows you to establish the structure (headings, sub-headings etc.) of your documents easily. As an example, the document may consist of a long, complex report which contains numerous levels of heading. The outlining facility will allow you to:

- organise the levels of headings;
- apply suitable paragraph styles to each level of heading automatically;
- move through the document quickly and efficiently;
- generate entries for a table of contents automatically;
- automatically renumber headings if their positions change within the document.

An outline consists of various levels of **heading** (title) and **body text** (normal paragraphs of text placed under a heading). The outline may be made to display the various levels of heading and hence the structure of the document. Up to nine levels of heading may be accommodated.

If required, the body text attached to any heading may be displayed (*expanded*) or hidden (*collapsed*). Alternatively, all the text may be displayed.

Any heading may be quickly promoted (moved to a higher level of importance) or demoted (moved to a lower level of importance). As headings are promoted or demoted, the paragraph styles attached to them are automatically changed to suit the appropriate level.

The outlining facility is activated by selecting the **Outline** command from the **View** menu. It is possible to split the document horizontally into two panes with a **Page Layout, Normal** or **Draft** view displayed in one pane and an **Outline** view shown in the second pane.

The following exercises use the RECIPES.DOC document produced on page 234, to introduce the features available with the outlining facility.

In this case, the whole document will be prepared, with the outlining facility being applied afterwards. In reality, the outlining facility proves to be most useful when organising the structure of a new document, with the bulk of the text being entered after the organisation of the document has been defined.

22.1 Preparing the document

EXERCISE 1 Load the **RECIPES.DOC** document.

2 Edit the text so that it reads as follows (the degree symbol may be entered as a **superscript o** character format):

Family Cooking

GRANTHAM GINGERBREAD

Makes 30

Ingredients

350g caster sugar

1 egg

100g butter

250g self-raising flour

5ml ground ginger

Method

Whisk the butter and sugar together in a bowl until fluffy and pale. Gradually beat in the egg.

Sift the flour and ginger into the mixture and work until the dough is fairly firm.

Roll the dough into small balls the size of a walnut and space them apart on a buttered baking sheet.

Bake in the oven at 150°C (300°F) gas mark 2 for 40-45 minutes until crisp, well risen, hollow and lightly browned.

GOOSNARGH CAKES

Makes 30

Ingredients

175g butter

225g plain flour

40g caster sugar

2.5ml caraway seeds

Method

Rub the butter into the flour until it starts to bind together. Pat out into a shallow, lined tin (35 by 18cm).

Sprinkle liberally with the caster sugar mixed with caraway seeds.

Leave for 12 hours in a cool place and bake at 180°C (350°F) gas mark 4 for about 20 minutes. Cut into fingers and leave 24 hours before eating.

SHORTBREAD

Makes 8

Ingredients

150g plain flour

45ml rice flour

50g caster sugar

100g butter

Method

Sift the flour into a bowl and add the sugar. Work in the butter with your fingertips. Gradually work in the dry ingredients.

Knead well and pack into a 18cm sandwich tin.

Bake at 170°C (325°F) gas mark 3 for about 45 minutes until firm and golden.

3 Use the numbered list facility (see page 88) to number each of the paragraphs in the 'Method' section for each of the three recipes.

4 Save the document before continuing.

22.2 Using the outline facility to set heading levels

EXERCISE 1 Select **Outline** from the **View** menu. The screen display will change as shown below:

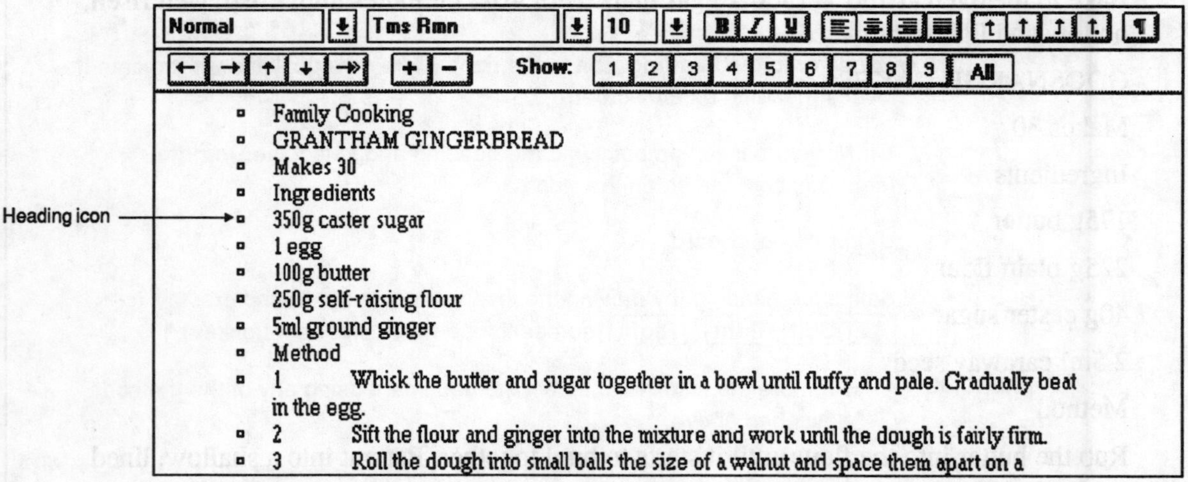

An **Outline Icon bar** will be visible at the top of the document window. The buttons on this bar represent the following functions:

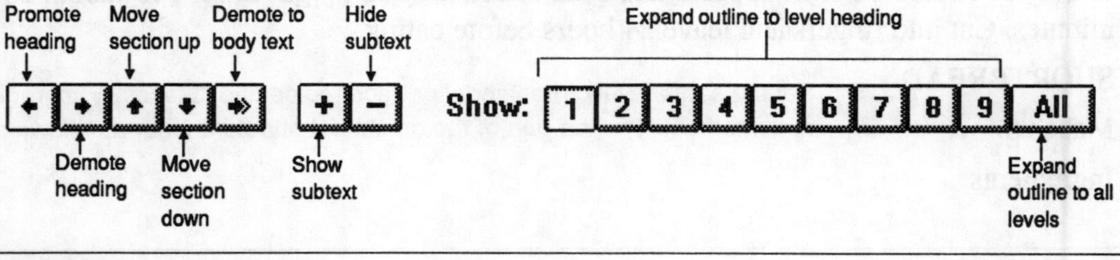

Note that each paragraph has an icon to its left. This symbol indicates that the text is classified as body text and has not been given a level of priority (heading).

Note also that the **All** button at this stage is active, displaying all the text in the document.

Promoting and demoting headings

Headings may be **promoted** in the following ways:

Using the mouse

Either: drag the **heading** icon to the left. A grey, vertical line will indicate the level of heading on the screen.

Or: Move the insertion point into the heading and select the **Promote** (left-pointing) button on the icon bar.

Using the keyboard

Select the heading (move the insertion point into it) and press **ALT Shift Left** (**Left** represents the left cursor control key).

Headings may be **demoted** in the following ways:

Using the mouse

Either: drag the **heading** icon to the right. A grey, vertical line will indicate the level of heading on the screen.

Or: Move the insertion point into the heading and select the **Demote** (right-pointing) button on the icon bar.

Using the keyboard

Select the heading (by moving the insertion point into it) and press **ALT Shift Right** (**Right** represents the right cursor control key).

EXERCISE

1. Promote the first line of text in the document using any of the methods described above.
2. Demote the next heading, 'GRANTHAM GINGERBREAD'.
3. Demote the next line ('Makes 30').
4. Promote 'Ingredients' to the same level of heading as the previous line. Similarly, promote 'Method'.
5. Set the same level of headings for each recipe title, 'Makes..', 'Ingredients' and 'Method'. The top part of the document should appear as shown on the next page.

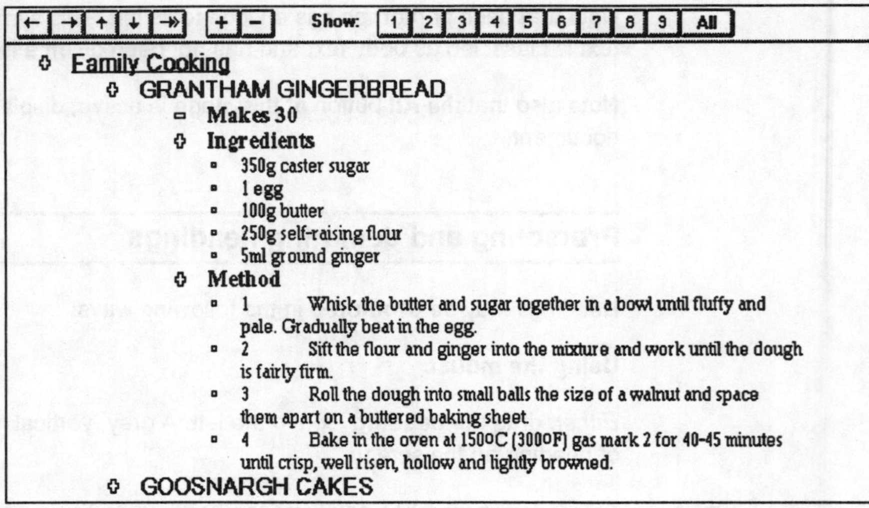

22.3 Using an outline

EXERCISE

1 Select the **Level 1** button in the Outline icon bar. This sets the lowest level of heading that you want to display (in this case 1). The screen should display only the first level heading as shown below:

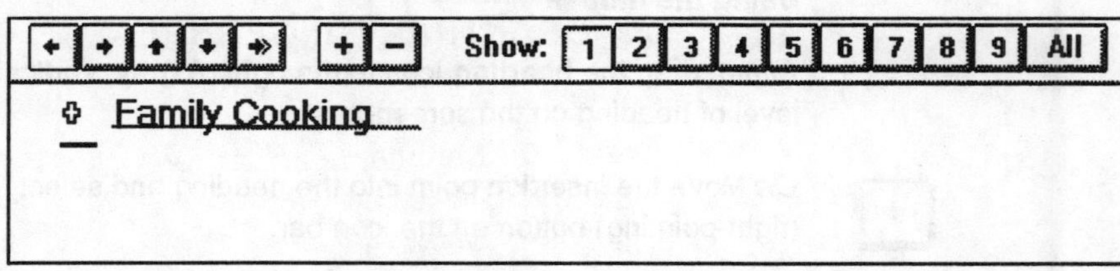

2 Select the **Level 2** button. The first and second level headings will be displayed:

3 Select the **Level 3** button. The first, second and third level headings will be displayed. This is shown on the next page.

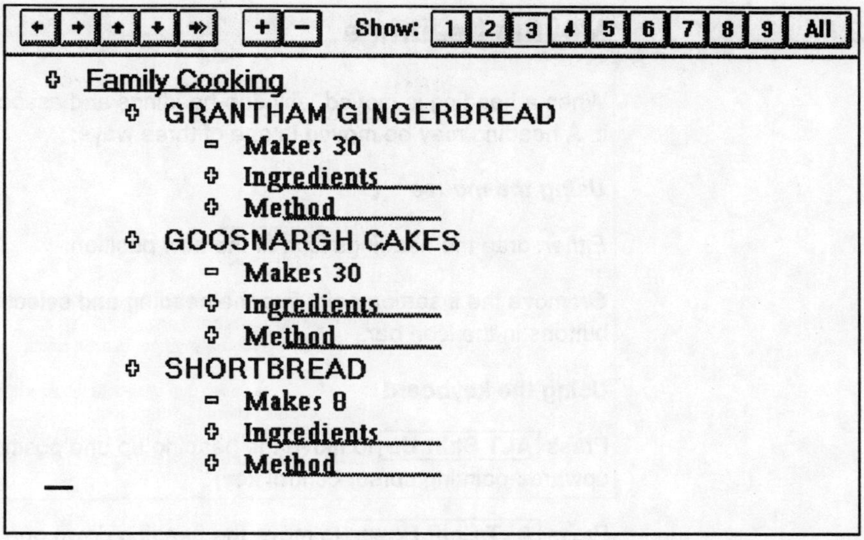

4 Move the insertion point into the **Ingredients** heading for **Shortbread** and select the + button (*or* double-click on the headings icon, *or* press [+] on the numeric keypad). This section will expand, to display the sub-text found under the heading as shown below:

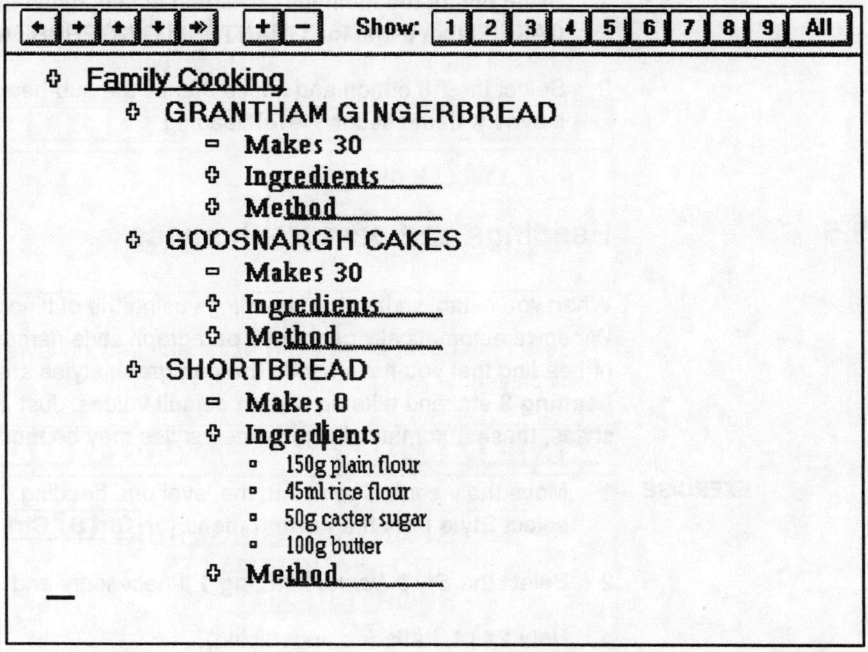

5 Select the – button (*or* double-click on the headings icon, *or* press [–] on the numeric keypad) to collapse the sub-text under the heading.

If you wish to display all the text at any point, select the **All** button.

The structure of a document is much more obvious when an outline has been set.

22.4 Moving headings

When a heading is moved, any sub-headings and associated text are moved with it. A heading may be moved in one of three ways:

Using the mouse

Either: drag the headings icon to the new position.

Or: move the insertion point into the heading and select the **Up** or **Down-arrow** buttons in the icon bar.

Using the keyboard

Press **ALT Shift Up** to move the heading up one position (**Up** represents the upwards-pointing cursor control key)

Press **ALT Shift Down** to move the heading down one position (**Down** represents the downwards-pointing cursor control key)

EXERCISE

1 Select the **Level 2** button to display the second level headings containing the recipe titles.

2 Using one of the methods described above, move the heading 'GOOSNARGH CAKES' above that for 'GRANTHAM GINGERBREAD'.

3 Select the **All** button and notice that all the sub-headings and sub-text have moved with the second level heading.

22.5 Headings and paragraph styles

When you establish levels of headings using the outline facility, Word for Windows automatically generates paragraph style names appropriate to the levels of heading that you have used. The paragraph styles are named **heading 1**, **heading 2** etc. and take up certain default values. Just like any other paragraph styles, these automatically generated styles may be modified.

EXERCISE

1 Move the insertion point into the level one heading ('Family Cooking') and select **Style** from the **Format** menu (*or* **Ctrl S** **Ctrl S**).

2 Select the *Style Name:* **heading 1** if necessary and set the following:

Helv 24 pt, italic (no underlining).
Paragraph *Alignment:* **Centred**
Spacing *Before:* **0** line
Spacing *After:* **1** line

3 Repeat the process for **heading 2, heading 3** and **Normal** paragraph styles, setting:

heading 2 style
Helv 14 pt, Bold.
Spacing *Before:* **2** lines
Spacing *After:* **1** line
Border: **Above, single line**

heading 3 style
Helv 12 pt, Bold.
Indentation *From Left:* **1cm**
Spacing *Before:* **0 li.**
Spacing *After:* **0 li.**

Normal style
Helv 10 pt.
Spacing *After:* **1 li**
Indents *From Left:* **4 cm**
Indents *From Right:* **0 cm**
Indents *First line:* **–1 cm**
Left *Tab Stop Position:* **4 cm**

The document will now be formatted. In **Page Layout** view the top part should appear similar to that shown below:

Family Cooking

GRANTHAM GINGERBREAD

Makes 30
Ingredients

350g caster sugar

1 egg

100g butter

250g self-raising flour

5ml ground ginger

Method

1 Whisk the butter and sugar together in a bowl until fluffy and pale. Gradually beat in the egg.

2 Sift the flour and ginger into the mixture and work until the dough is fairly firm.

3 Roll the dough into small balls the size of a walnut and space them apart on a buttered baking sheet.

4 Bake in the oven at 150°C (300°F) gas mark 2 for 40-45 minutes until crisp, well risen, hollow and lightly browned.

4 You may wish to insert a page break before the third recipe, to move it to the top of the next page.

5 Save and print RECIPES.DOC as required.

22.6 Generating a table of contents

Word for Windows offers two methods of automatically generating a table of contents. The easiest method is to use the headings defined in the document outline as a basis for the table of contents entries. The alternative method is to insert {TC} fields (table of contents fields) into appropriate positions within the text.

This section restricts itself to the generation of a table of contents using the document outline.

EXERCISE

1. Open **RECIPES.DOC** if necessary and insert a new line under the level one heading 'Family Cooking'. Move the insertion point into the newly created line.

2. Select **Table of Contents** from the **Insert** menu (**ALT I C**). The following dialogue box will be displayed:

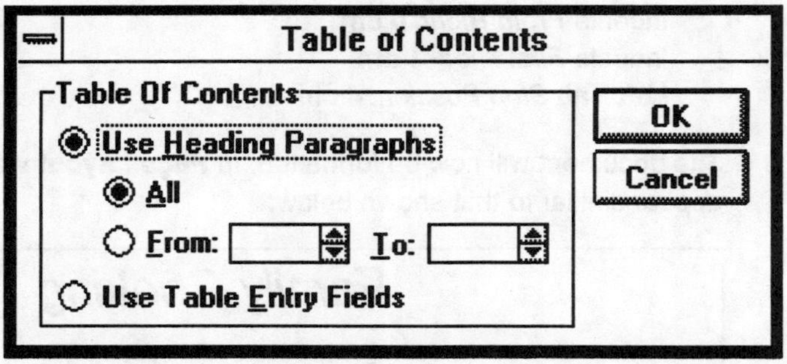

Use Heading Paragraphs instructs Word for Windows to use the headings defined in the document outline for table of contents entries.

Use Table Entry Fields instructs the program to use {TC} fields embedded within the text, for table of contents entries.

When *All* is selected, all nine levels of outline headings will be used for the generation of the table of contents.

From: specifies the highest level of heading that is to be included in the table of contents.

To: specifies the lowest level of heading to be included in the table of contents.

3. Select **Use Heading Paragraphs** if necessary and accept. A table of contents will be generated automatically. This is shown on the next page.

4. This table of contents contains headings that are not required. Cut the table from the document.

5. With the insertion point in the blank line under the level one heading, insert another table of contents, but this time, choose *From:* **2** and *To:* **2** for the outline heading levels to be included. A more sensible table of contents will be produced.

Family Cooking

Family Cooking 1

GRANTHAM GINGERBREAD 1

Makes 30 1

Ingredients 1

Method 1

GOOSNARGH CAKES 1

Makes 30 1

Ingredients 1

Method 1

SHORTBREAD 2

Makes 8 2

Ingredients 2

Method 2

Family Cooking

GRANTHAM GINGERBREAD 1

GOOSNARGH CAKES 1

SHORTBREAD 2

GRANTHAM GINGERBREAD

Makes 30
Ingredients

350g caster sugar

1 egg

When you insert a table of contents, paragraph styles are automatically generated (as with outline headings). The paragraph style are labelled toc 1, toc 2 etc. and may be modified in the same way as any other paragraph style.

6 Modify the table of contents paragraph styles to suit you.

7 Save and print the document as required.

23 Macros

A macro is an automated sequence consisting of a number of operations and actions within the Word for Windows program. This may include the highlighting and insertion of text, insertion point movement and the selection of menu or keyboard commands.

Word for Windows provides a powerful, flexible and, above all, easy to use programming language which may be used to automate commonly used sequences of operations and actions. This may make the whole process of document processing potentially even more flexible and efficient.

The Word for Windows macro language is called WordBasic and is similar in many respects to Microsoft QuickBasic. This book is not intended as a programming guide and thus will only demonstrate the basic tools available for the production and maintenance of macros, using simple examples. To get the most out of macros and their programming, it is useful to have access to the *Technical Reference* for WordBasic which is available from Microsoft Corporation. Word for Windows is however, supplied with an abridged version of the above text, in the form of a document, which is normally installed along with the program. The document (92 pages) is called TECHREF.DOC and may be located in the \WINWORD subdirectory of your hard disk. This is where the Word for Windows program resides.

As you have access to the TECHREF.DOC document, a description of the macro instructions will not be discussed in this chapter. Additional assistance is available from the Help system within the program. Further macro examples may be found in the TECHREF.DOC document and the MACROS.DOC (found in the same subdirectory).

Word for Windows also includes a facility for testing macros, allowing you to examine macros for errors. In addition, the program provides a Dialogue Editor which allows you to create your own dialogue boxes.

Each macro, simple or complex, is stored as a list of instructions (program) with its own unique macro name. Any macro may be made available to all documents (a *global macro*), or may be limited to one or more templates. In the latter case, Word for Windows may be customised for specific types of document.

The instructions making up a macro may be edited in a similar fashion to normal text. However, each instruction must be placed on a new line and should be followed by an **Enter** character.

Macros may be assigned to keyboard key sequences to suit you and, in addition, may be added to the menu system. These facilities offer methods of quickly accessing individual macros as required.

The **Tools** menu contains the available commands for the setting up, editing and running of macros.

In the exercises that follow, the principles of macros are explored by use of a simple process of transposition. The macro will be called **TRANSPOW** and its purpose will be to change the relative positions of two words in a sentence.

23.1 Defining a macro

The **Record Macro** command found within the **Tools** menu allows you to record the cursor movements, menu and keyboard commands that have been issued and certain mouse movements. These together form a macro that may be run when required.

Preparing the text

EXERCISE

1 Open a **New** document with the **NORMAL** template if necessary.

2 Type the following sentence:

This is a MACRO sample which is to be called TRANSPOW.

3 Place the insertion point immediately to the left of the word 'MACRO'.

Recording a macro

The word 'MACRO' is to be cut and pasted into position to the right of the word 'sample', thus transposing the two words. This involves:

- highlighting 'MACRO';
- selecting **Cut** from the **Edit** menu;
- moving the insertion point to the right of the word 'sample';
- selecting **Paste** from the **Edit** menu.

Note: When you are Recording a macro, movement of the insertion point and the highlighting of text is not possible with the mouse – keyboard commands must be used instead. The issuing of commands from the menu system with the mouse is however, permissible.

EXERCISE

1 With the insertion point still placed to the left of the word 'MACRO', Select **Record Macro** from the **Tools** menu (**ALT M C**). This will instruct the program to 'keep a note of' all the cursor movements and commands that are to follow. REC (for record) will appear in the Status bar and a dialogue box similar to that shown on the next page will be displayed.

Record Macro Name: allows you to give the sequence of instructions (macro) a name.

The *Shortcut Key* area allows you to define a keyboard sequence to a macro, allowing you to run the macro whenever you issue the sequence.

Description: allows you to add an optional comment describing the function of the macro. If a *Description:* exists, it will be displayed in the Status bar when the macro is selected.

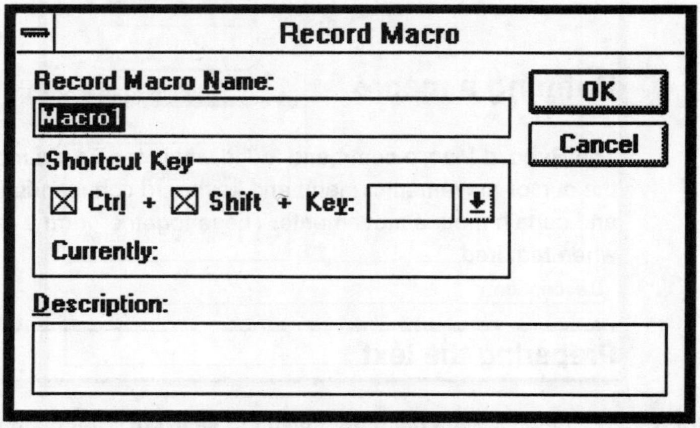

2 Type **TRANSPOW** inside the *Record Macro Name:* text box.

3 Type the *Description:* **Transpose two words.**

4 With the **Ctrl** and **Shift** check boxes selected as above, *either* type *or* select the letter **T** for the **Key:** *Shortcut Key* sequence. This will allow you to run the macro with the key sequence **Ctrl Shift T**. Accept when ready.

6 Press: **Ctrl Shift Right** to highlight one word to the right of the insertion point.

5 Select **Cut** from the **Edit** menu (**ALT E C** *or* **Ctrl X** *or* select the **Cut** button in the Toolbar) to cut the **highlighted** text.

6 Press **ALT Right** to move the insertion point one word to the right.

7 Select **Paste** from the **Edit** menu (**ALT E P** *or* **Ctrl V**, *or* select the **Paste** button in the Toolbar) to paste the cut text.

8 Select **Stop Recorder** from the **Tools** menu (**ALT O R**) to stop the TRANSPOW macro recording process. As you have been recording the macro, the order of the two words 'MACRO' and 'sample' will have been reversed in the text.

23.2 Running a macro

EXERCISE

1 Move the insertion point immediately to the left of the word 'sample'.

2 Select **Macro** from the **Tools** menu (**ALT O M**). A dialogue box similar to that shown on the next page will be displayed.

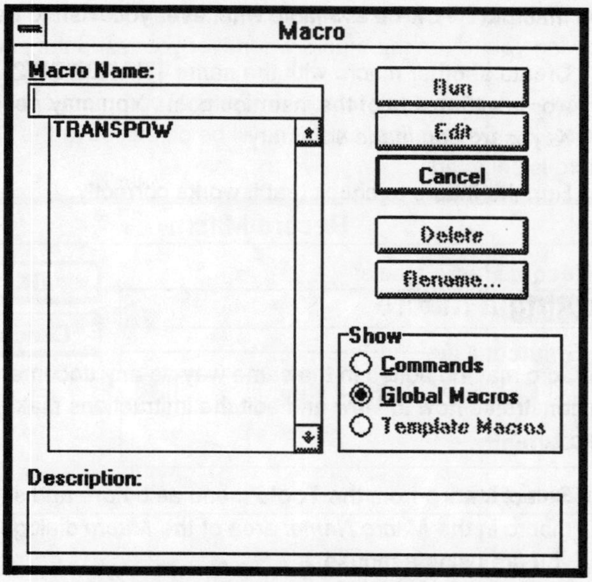

The *Macro Name:* area allows you to select the name of the macro that you wish to run.

When the **Commands** check box is selected in the *Show* area, all the Word for Windows commands are displayed along with the names of macros that have been supplied with the program, including those that you have created. If you were editing a template, the **Template Macros** check box would allow you to display all the macros that were attached to the current template.

When a macro has been selected, the **Rename**, **Delete**, **Run** and **Edit** command buttons become available.

The **Run** command button will allow you to run the chosen macro.

The **Rename** command button will allow you to give a macro a different name from that originally chosen.

The **Delete** command button will erase any selected macro.

The **Edit** command button allows you to edit a macro in the same ways as you would a document.

The *Description:* area displays any comment that was entered when the macro was created.

3 *Either* select **TRANSPOW** and select the **Run** command button *or* double-click on **TRANSPOW** to run the macro. The two words in the sentence will be changed back to their original positions.

4 Move the insertion point once again to the left of the word 'MACRO' and run the TRANSPOW macro, this time using the **Ctrl Shift T** shortcut key sequence. The two words will, once again, be transposed.

The macro will now be available whenever you wish to transpose two words.

EXERCISE 1 Create another macro with the name **TRANSPOW2** which will transpose two words either side of the insertion point. You may need to refer to *Appendix A* : Keyboard command summary.

2 Run the macro to check that it works correctly.

21.3 Editing a macro

A macro may be edited in the same way as any document. The following exercise demonstrates how to view and edit the instructions making up the TRANSPOW macro.

EXERCISE 1 Select **Macro** from the **Tools** menu as before and select the **TRANSPOW** macro in the *Macro Name:* area of the *Macro* dialogue box (only single-click if you are using a mouse).

2 Select the **Edit** command button from the *Macro* dialogue box. The instructions making up the macro will be displayed along with a *Macro icon bar* as shown below (paragraph marks have been displayed).

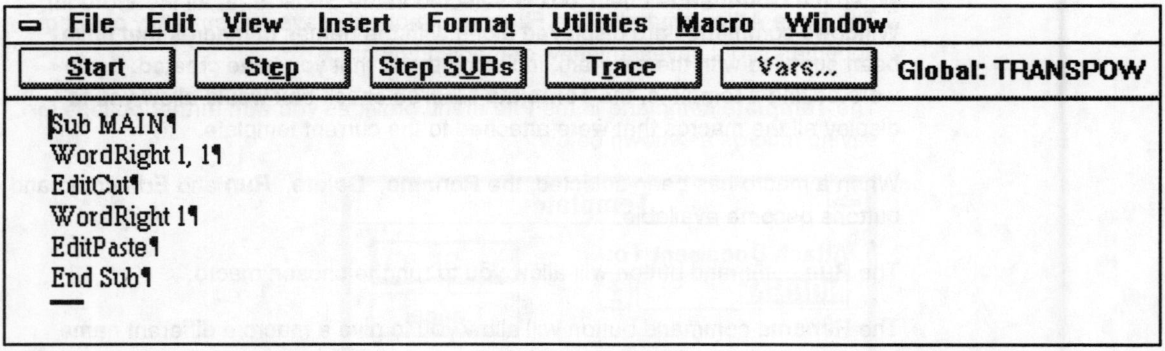

The Macro icon bar allows you to test your macro (and edit if necessary) while viewing the instructions making it up. The buttons provide program testing tools normally expected of programmers. However, since the example macro is very simple, the Macro icon bar will not be used. Should you wish to select any button from the icon bar using the keyboard, then press ALT Shift followed by the underlined letter found on the button.

3 Edit the instructions (as with any document) so that they read as follows:

Sub MAIN
WordRight 1, 1
EditCut
WordRight 1
EditPaste
EndOfLine
Insert " This macro transposes two words."
End Sub

4 Use the **Window** menu to display the original document.

5 Position the insertion point and run the **TRANSPOW** macro.

Two words will be transcribed and the sentence 'This macro transposes two words.' will be added to the end of the line.

This has demonstrated how to edit the instructions making up a macro. For a description of the instructions used, refer to the TECHREF.DOC document.

6 Before continuing, use the **Window** menu to display and edit the same macro again. Remove the two lines that were inserted earlier (EndOfLine and Insert...).

23.4 Saving macros

Any new or modified macros are not saved until the template in which they are stored, is saved. When you change any default values or create new macros, you are prompted with the message 'Do you want to save the global glossary and command changes?' before you exit from the Word for Windows program. New or modified macros will only be saved if you answer Yes to this question.

The **Save All** command in the **File** menu, not only saves all currently opened documents, but saves any new or modified macros.

The **Template** command in the **File** menu provides you with further options for saving macros as shown below:

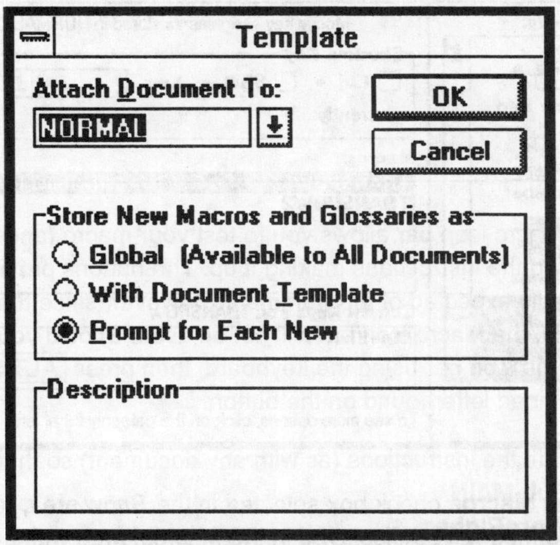

The *Store New Macros and Glossaries as* area provides three options:

- **Global (Available to All Documents)** literally makes new macros available to all documents irrespective of their template.

- **With Document Template** makes new macros available to documents using a specific template.
- **Prompt for Each New** displays the message 'Do you want to save the global glossary and command changes?' before exiting the program, giving you an opportunity of saving any new macros.

23.5 Assigning a macro to a key combination

You have already seen that macros may be easily assigned shortcut key combinations using the *Macro* dialogue box seen previously. These shortcut keys allow you to activate specific macros more efficiently. Throughout this guide, keystrokes for the keyboard control of the Word for Windows program at each stage have been indicated. Each of the keyboard combinations activates a macro supplied as part of the program. Collectively, these macros form the basis of the full program. Any macro that you develop and wish to use on a regular basis, may be assigned keystrokes determined by you. In addition, these keystrokes and those supplied as defaults with the program, may be redefined. You therefore have the capability to customise the program entirely if you wish.

In the exercise that follows, the **Options** command found in the **Tools** menu will be used to view all macros and their respective shortcut key combinations.

EXERCISE 1 Select **Options** from the **Tools** menu and select the *Category:* **Keyboard.** The familiar *Options* dialogue box will be displayed.

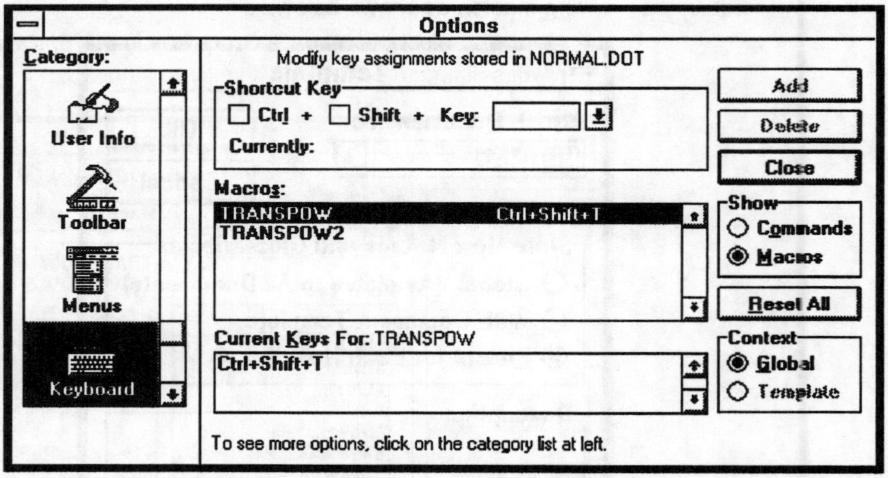

With the **Macros** check box selected in the *Show* area, the two macros that you have defined will be displayed in the *Macros:* area with any shortcut keys. The shortcut keys for the currently selected macro are also displayed in the *Current Keys For:* area.

The *Context* area allows you to select whether the selected macro is to be attached to a template or is to be offered to all documents. The **Template** option is unavailable if you are using the NORMAL.DOT template.

2 Select the **Commands** check box in the *Show* area. All the available commands and their shortcut keys will be displayed in the *Commands:* area.

3 Scroll down the list in the *Commands:* area and note that all the shortcut keys mentioned throughout this guide, are displayed. Note also that there are some commands without shortcut keys. You may allocate any shortcut keys that you wish to any of the commands, provided that the key combination is unique to a particular command.

4 If you wish, define a shortcut key code for a command, return to the document by selecting the **Add** command button and use the shortcut key for the appropriate operation.

5 Before continuing, you may wish to reset all the shortcut keys to their default values by selecting the **Reset All** command button found in the *Options* dialogue box.

23.6 Assigning a macro to a menu

As with assigning and re-assigning keystrokes to macros, the menu system may be modified to include additional macros and, in addition, other commands within the menus may be removed. This, once again allows you to customise the Word for Windows program.

In the following exercise, the macro TRANSPOW will be added to the **Edit** menu.

EXERCISE 1 Select **Options** from the **Tools** menu as before and select the *Category: Menus*. Select the **Macros** check box in the *Show* area if necessary. The *Menus* dialogue box will be displayed as below:

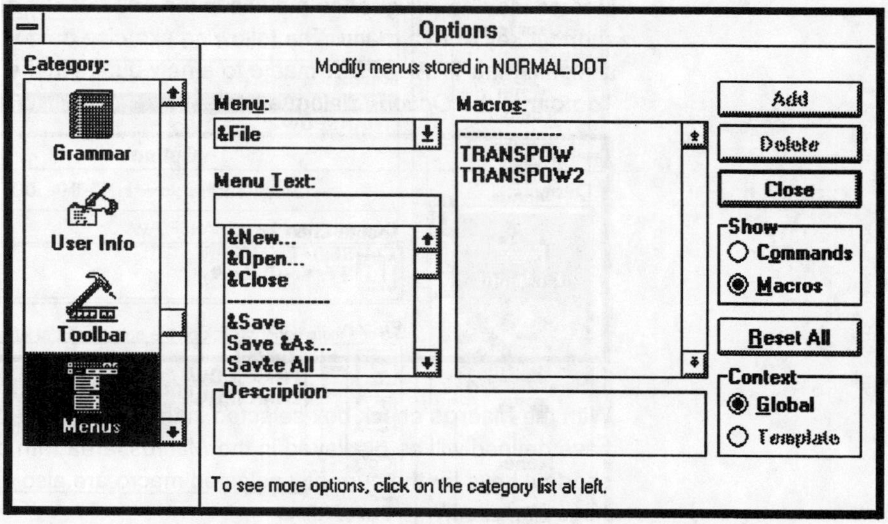

The *Menu:* text box allows you to select the name of the menu into which you wish to place a macro (command).

Menu Text: allows you to enter the text (command title) that is to be displayed in the menu. An ampersand (&) is typed before any letter that is to be underlined in the menu. The command may then be activated by the keyboard in the normal way. Avoid using a letter that is already in use by the menu. To assist with this, the commands currently installed in the chosen menu are displayed in the area below the *Menu Text:* text box.

The *Macros:* area allows you to select the name of the macro that you wish to add to, or remove from a menu.

2 Select **&Edit** in the *Menu:* drop-down list.

3 Select the **TRANSPOW** macro in the *Macros:* area. This will be appear in the Menu Text: text box.

4 Delete any text in the *Menu Text:* box and type **Transpose &Words**. Select the **Add** command button to add this command (macro) to the **Edit** menu.

5 Select the **Close** command button to return to the document.

6 Position the insertion point and display the **Edit** menu. Note that the **Transpose Words** command is now available in the menu and that the command may be activated by pressing **ALT E W** in the normal way.

7 Select the **Transpose Words** command. This will operate as before.

Other macros may be either added or removed from any of the menus as required.

23.7 Assigning a macro to the Toolbar

Macros may be assigned to buttons in the Toolbar just as they may be assigned a shortcut key or to a menu. The following exercise demonstrates this process by assigning the TRANSPOW macro to a new button in the Toolbar, using *Category:* **Toolbar** in the *Options* dialogue box.

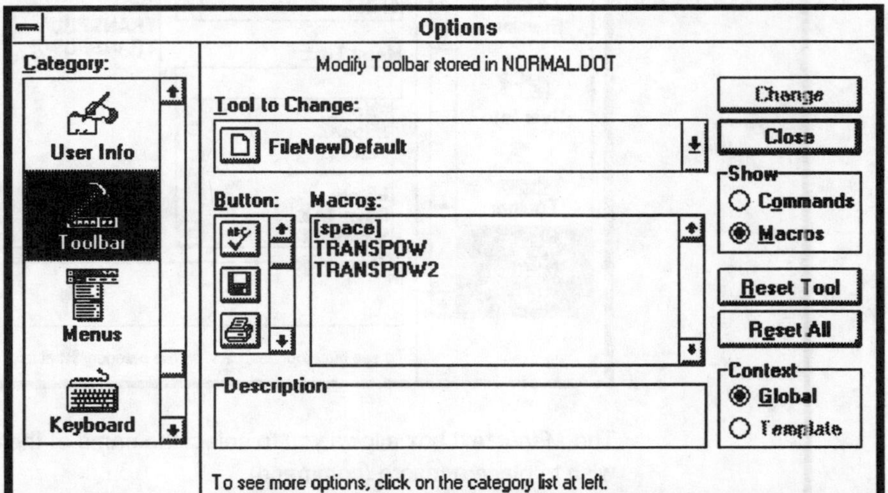

If no mouse is available, you may choose to omit this section.

EXERCISE

1 Select **Options** from the **Tools** menu as before and select the *Category:* **Toolbar**. Select the **Macros** check box in the *Show* area if necessary. The *Toolbar* dialogue box will be displayed as shown on the previous page.

2 Select the **Macros** option in the *Show* area if necessary. The macro names will appear inside the *Macros:* area.

3 Display the *Tool to Change:* drop-down list and select one of the **[space]** options (this is where a space currently appears in the Toolbar).

4 Inside the *Button:* list, select an appropriate button to be displayed in the Toolbar.

5 Select the **TRANSPOW** macro and select the **Change** command button.

6 Select the **Close** command button to return to the document. The new button should be visible in the Toolbar.

7 Check the correct working of the new button.

Should you wish to remove this button from the Toolbar and reset all the buttons to their default values, select the **Reset All** command button in the *Options* dialogue box for the Toolbar.

There are now six ways (provided you have carried out the last exercise) of activating the TRANSPOW macro:

- Selecting **Macro** from the **Tools** menu *or* ALT O M
- The shortcut key code: Ctrl Shift T
- Selecting **Transpose Words** from the **Edit** menu *or* ALT E W
- Selecting the **Transpose Words** button in the Toolbar.

Appendix A : Keyboard command summary

Alphanumeric keys

-	Hyphen
Alt -	Open Document Control menu
Alt Backspace	Undo last operation
Alt A	Open Table menu
Alt E	Open Edit menu
Alt F	Open File menu
Alt H	Open Help menu
Alt I	Open Insert menu
Alt O	Open Tools menu
Alt Spacebar	Open Word Control menu
Alt T	Open Format menu
Alt V	Open View menu
Alt W	Open Window menu
Alt Shift Down	Move selected paragraphs down (outline)
Alt Shift Left	Promote a paragraph (outline)
Alt Shift Right	Demote a paragraph (outline)
Alt Shift Up	Move selected paragraphs up (outline)
Alt Shift +	Expand text under a heading (outline)
Alt Shift *	Show all levels of heading (outline)
Alt Shift -	Collapse text under a heading (outline)
Alt Shift 1	Show level 1 headings (outline)
Alt Shift 2	Show level 2 headings (outline)
Alt Shift 3	Show level 3 headings (outline)
Alt Shift 4	Show level 4 headings (outline)

Alphanumeric keys *continued*

Alt Shift 5	Show level 5 headings (outline)
Alt Shift Keypad5	Demote to Body text (outline)
Alt Shift Keypad5	Apply Normal paragraph style
Alt Shift 6	Show level 6 headings (outline)
Alt Shift 7	Show level 7 headings (outline)
Alt Shift 8	Show level 8 headings (outline)
Alt Shift 9	Show level 9 headings (outline)
Alt Shift A	Show all in outline view
Alt Shift C	Close pane
Alt Shift D	Insert Date field
Alt Shift E	Step through macro
Alt Shift F	Show first line of text (outline)
Alt Shift F	Insert Merge field
Alt Shift O	Continue macro
Alt Shift P	Insert Page field
Alt Shift R	Trace macro
Alt Shift S	Start macro
Alt Shift T	Insert Time field
Alt Shift U	Step SUBS in macro
Alt Shift V	Show variables in macro
Backspace	Delete character to left of insertion point
Ctrl -	Optional hyphen
Ctrl =	Subscript (3 points below baseline)
Ctrl Backspace	Delete word left of insertion point
Ctrl Del	Delete word to right of insertion point

Alphanumeric keys *continued*

Ctrl Enter	Insert Page break
Ctrl Ins	Copy text or graphics to clipboard
Ctrl 0	No line space before paragraph
Ctrl 1	Single line spacing
Ctrl 2	Double line spacing
Ctrl 5	One and a half line spacing
Ctrl Keypad5	Highlight whole document
Ctrl A	All capitals
Ctrl B	Bold
Ctrl C	Copy text or graphics to clipboard
Ctrl D	Double underline
Ctrl E	Centre paragraph
Ctrl F	Set font
Ctrl G	Reduce hanging indent by one tab stop
Ctrl H	Hidden text
Ctrl I	Italics
Ctrl J	Justify text
Ctrl K	Small capitals
Ctrl L	Left align text
Ctrl M	Reduce left indent by one tab stop
Ctrl N	Indent from the left margin by one tab stop
Ctrl O	Line space before paragraph
Ctrl P	Set font point size
Ctrl Q	Remove paragraph formatting
Ctrl R	Right align text
Ctrl S	Set paragraph style
Ctrl S Ctrl S	Display Style box
Ctrl T	Set hanging indent to one tab stop
Ctrl U	Underline
Ctrl V	Insert contents of clipboard

Alphanumeric keys *continued*

Ctrl W	Word underline
Ctrl X	Delete selected text and send to clipboard
Ctrl Y	Show the automatic styles in the Styles dialogue box
Ctrl Z	Undo last action
Ctrl Shift Down	Highlight to end of paragraph
Ctrl Shift Left	Highlight to start of word
Ctrl Shift Right	Highlight to end of word
Ctrl Shift Up	Highlight to start of paragraph
Ctrl Shift *	Display all non-printing characters
Ctrl Shift -	Non-breaking hyphen
Ctrl Shift =	Superscript (3 points above baseline)
Ctrl Shift End	Highlight to end of document
Ctrl Shift Enter	Insert Column break
Ctrl Shift Home	Highlight to beginning of document
Ctrl Shift Spacebar	Insert non-breaking space
Ctrl Spacebar	Reset character formatting
Ctrl Tab	Insert tab (Tables)
Del	Delete character to right of insertion point
Enter	Insert paragraph break
Shift Down	Highlight one line down
Shift End	Highlight to end of line
Shift Home	Highlight to start of line
Shift Left	Highlight one character to left
Shift PgDn	Highlight one screen down
Shift PgUp	Highlight one screen up
Shift Right	Highlight one character to right
Shift Up	Highlight one line up

Cursor control keys

Down	Move down one line
Alt Shift Down	Move selected paragraphs down (outline)
Ctrl Down	Move down one paragraph
Ctrl Shift Down	Highlight one paragraph down
Shift Down	Highlight one line down
End	Move to end of line
Alt End	Move to end of row (Table)
Ctrl End	Move to end of document
Ctrl Shift End	Highlight to end of document
Home	Move to beginning of line
Alt Home	Move to beginning of row (Table)
Ctrl Home	Move to start of document
Ctrl Shift Home	Highlight to start of document
Shift Home	Highlight to beginning of line
Left	Move one character left
Alt Left	Move one word left
Alt Shift Left	Promote heading (outline)
Ctrl Left	Move one word left
Ctrl Shift Left	Highlight one word left
Shift Left	Highlight one character left
PgDn	Move down one window
Alt PgDn	Move to bottom of column (Table)
Ctrl PgDn	Move to bottom of window
Ctrl Shift PgDn	Highlight to bottom of window
Shift PgDn	Highlight one line down
PgUp	Move up one window
Alt PgUp	Move to top of column (Table)
Ctrl PgUp	Move to top of window
Ctrl Shift PgUp	Highlight to top of window
Shift PgUp	Highlight one window up
Right	Move right one character
Alt Right	Move one word right
Alt Shift Right	Demote heading (outline)
Ctrl Right	Move one word right

Cursor control keys *continued*

Ctrl Shift Right	Highlight one word right
Shift Right	Highlight one character right
Up	Move up one line
Alt Shift Up	Move up one paragraph
Ctrl Up	Move selected paragraphs up (outline)
Ctrl Shift Up	Highlight one paragraph up
Shift Up	Highlight one line up

Field keys

Alt Shift D	Insert Date field
Alt Shift F	Insert Merge field
Alt Shift P	Insert Page field
Alt Shift T	Insert Time field
Alt Shift F9	Simulate double-clicking a field
Ctrl F9	Insert blank field
Ctrl F11	Lock a field (prevent updates)
Ctrl Shift F7	Update linked information
Ctrl Shift F9	Replace field with last contents
Ctrl Shift F11	Unlock field
F9	Update selected fields
F11	Go to next field
Shift F9	Switch beteen field codes and field results
Shift F11	Go to previous field

Function keys

F1	Help
Alt F1	Move to next field
Alt Shift F1	Move to previous field
Shift F1	Get Help on a command/key combination/screen area
F2	Move
Alt F2	File: Save As
Alt Shift F2	File: Save
Ctrl F2	Enlarge font

Function keys *continued*

Ctrl Shift F2	Shrink font
Shift F2	Copy
F3	Expand Glossary name
Ctrl F3	Cut text or graphics to the Spike
Ctrl Shift F3	Insert from and clear the Spike contents
Shift F3	Change case of letters
F4	Repeat last action
Alt F4	Close the Word window
Ctrl F4	Close active document window
Shift F4	Repeat last Find or Goto command
F5	Goto
Alt F5	Restore Word window
Ctrl F5	Restore document window
Ctrl Shift F5	Insert Bookmark
Shift F5	Move to previous insertion point position
F6	Move to next pane
Alt F6	Move to next document window
Alt Shift F6	Move to previous document window
Ctrl F6	Move to next document window
Ctrl Shift F6	Move to previous document window
Shift F6	Move to previous pane
F7	Spell check
Alt F7	Move Word window
Ctrl F7	Move document window
Ctrl Shift F7	Update source for Include field
Shift F7	Thesaurus
F8	Extend highlight (selection)
Alt F8	Size Word window
Ctrl F8	Size document window
Ctrl Shift F8	Column mode
Shift F8	Shrink highlight (selection)

Function keys *continued*

F9	Update field
Alt F9	Minimize Word window
Alt Shift F9	Simulate a double-click
Ctrl F9	Insert blank field
Ctrl Shift F9	Unlink field
Shift F9	Switch between field codes and field results
F10	Activate Word menu bar
Alt F10	Maximize Word window
Ctrl F10	Maximize document window
Ctrl Shift F10	Activate Ruler
Shift F10	Activate icon bars in: annotation/outline/header & footer/macro
F11	Move to next field
Ctrl F11	Lock field
Ctrl Shift F11	Unlock field
Shift F11	Move to previous field
F12	File: Save As
Ctrl F12	File: Open
Ctrl Shift F12	File: Print
Shift F12	File: Save

Header & Footer Icon bar keys

Shift F10 C	Close
Shift F10 D	Insert Date
Shift F10 L	Link to previous
Shift F10 P	Insert page number
Shift F10 T	Insert time

Numeric keypad keys

Keypad*	Show all levels (outline)
Keypad+	Expand outline
Keypad-	Collapse outline
Alt Keypad5	Highlight entire Table
Alt Shift Keypad5	Apply Normal paragraph style
Ctrl Keypad5	Highlight entire document

Outline keys

Alt Shift Down	Move selected paragraphs down
Alt Shift Left	Promote paragraph
Alt Shift Right	Demote paragraph
Alt Shift Up	Move selected paragraphs up
Alt Shift +	Expand text under heading
Alt Shift -	Collapse text under heading
Alt Shift n	Show up to heading level n (1 to 9)
Alt Shift Keypad5	Demote to body text
Alt Shift A	Show all text
Alt Shift F	Show first line of body text

Ruler keys

Ctrl Shift F10	**Make the Ruler active then:**
Left	Move the rule cursor a small distance left
Right	Move the rule cursor a small distance right
1	Left tab alignment
2	Centre tab alignment
3	Right tab alignment
4	Decimal tab alignment
Ctrl Left	Move the rule cursor a larger distance left
Ctrl Right	Move the rule cursor a larger distance right

Ruler keys *continued*

Del	Delete tab
End	Move the rule cursor to the right end of the Ruler
Enter	Exit and apply settings
Esc	Exit and cancel settings
Home	Move the rule cursor to the left end of the Ruler
Ins	Set tab
F	Set first line left indent
L	Set left indent
R	Set right indent

Table keys

Down	Move one row down
Left	Move one column left
Right	Move one column right
Up	Move one row up
Alt Keypad5	Highlight entire table
Alt End	Move to last cell in current row
Alt Home	Move to first cell in current row
Alt PgDn	Move to last cell in current column
Alt PgUp	Move to first cell in current column

Appendix B : Mouse operations

Highlighting text

Any text	• Drag across the text from left to right (or right to left) and up and down. • Place the insertion point at one end of the text that you wish to highlight; hold down the Shift key and click on the opposite end of the text.
Word	Double-click on the word.
Line	Click in the selection bar to the left of the line of text.
Multiple lines	Drag in the selection bar to the left of the lines of text.
Sentence	Hold down the Ctrl key and click anywhere inside the sentence.
Paragraph	Double-click in the selection bar to the left of the paragraph.
Multiple paragraphs	Double-click and drag in the selection bar to the left of the text.
Document	Hold down the Ctrl key and click anywhere inside the selection bar.
Column	Hold down the right mouse button and drag.

Mouse shortcuts

Tabs dialogue box	Double-click on any tab stop in the Ruler.
Paragraph dialogue box	Double-click on anywhere in the upper half of the Ruler.
Go To dialogue box	Double-click anywhere on the Status line.
Options dialogue box	Double-click anywhere on the Toolbar (except a button).
Section Layout dialogue box	Double-click on any section break in the document.
Footnote pane	Double-click on the footnote reference mark in the document.
Page Setup dialogue box	In Page Layout view, double-click on the corners of the page (outside of the margins)
Character dialogue box	Double-click anywhere on the Ribbon (except for a text box or button).

Print Merge Setup dialogue box	Double-click on the Print Merge icon bar.
Symbol dialogue box	Double-click on any inserted symbol.
Macro dialogue box	Double-click anywhere on the Macro Editing icon bar (except for a button)
Split current document window into two panes	Double-click on the split box.
Maximize window	Double-click on the window Title bar.
Annotations pane	Double-click on any annotation in the document.
Edit an embedded object	Double-click on the embedded object (picture, graph, equation, WordArt etc.)

Mouse pointers

The pointer (referred to as an 'I-beam') is in the document area.

This pointer appears in print preview when it is positioned over an object that you may drag. This pointer also appears when dragging out a new frame.

The pointer is positioned over a menu, scroll bar, Ribbon, Ruler or Toolbar. It is also used as the sizing arrow for pointing and dragging, the sizing and cropping handles of embedded objects.

The pointer is either positioned in the selection bar used for selecting various sections of text, or is placed inside a table selection bar.

The Word for Windows program is busy.

This pointer appears when you press **Shift F1** to activate context sensitive Help system. You may position the pointer over a command or any other region of the screen and click to obtain help on the item.

The pointer is either positioned on the **Split box** in the vertical scroll bar, or the Split command from the **Document Command Control** menu has been selected.

The pointer is positioned on a horizontal or vertical window border. Drag a horizontal border to change the vertical height of the window and a vertical border to change the window width.

The pointer is placed over a window border corner. Drag to adjust the horizontal and vertical borders in one operation.

The pointer appears when either the title bar of a window is being dragged (moving the window to a new position), or the **Move** or **Size** commands have been selected from the **Word Command Control** menu.

The pointer has been positioned over a frame, indicating that it may be dragged to a new position (**Page Layout** view). Alternatively, this pointer will appear when it is positioned over a selection symbol in **Outline** view, indicating that the heading may be dragged to a new position.

The pointer is positioned over a side frame or object handle, indicating that it may be dragged horizontally, resizing (or cropping) the frame or object. Alternatively, this pointer appears when a heading in **Outline** view is being dragged (left or right) to a new level.

The pointer is positioned over the top or bottom frame (or object) handle, indicating that it may be dragged vertically, resizing (or cropping) the frame or object. Alternatively, this pointer appears when a heading in **Outline** view is being dragged (up or down) to a new position.

The pointer is positioned over a corner frame or object handle, indicating that it may be dragged diagonally, resizing (or cropping) the frame or object.

The pointer is positioned over a column in a table. Click to select the column.

This pointer appears when text (or a graphic) is being dragged to a new position in the document ('drag and drop').

Appendix C : Buttons and icons

Default Toolbar

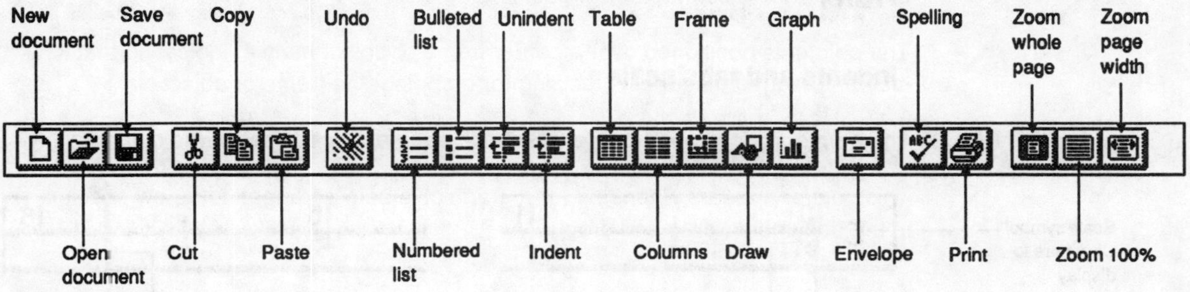

Data file Toolbar

Ribbon

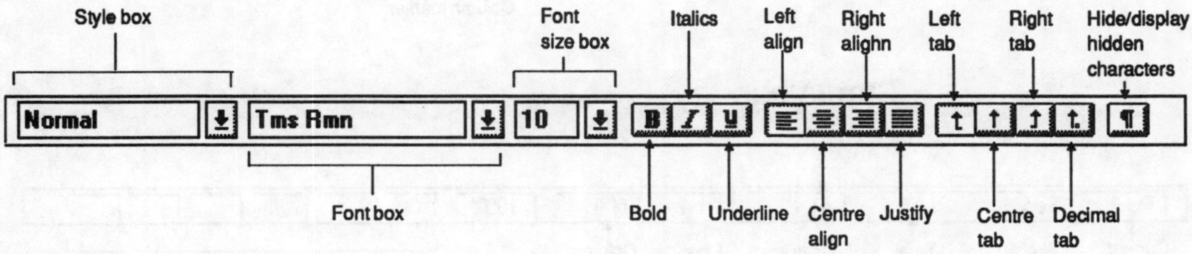

Outline icon bar

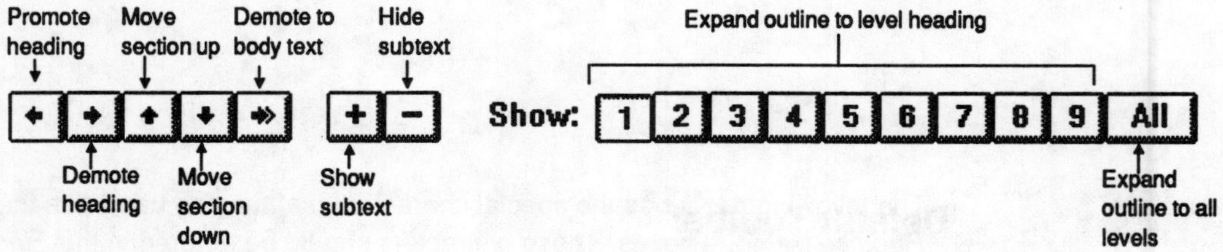

Ruler

Indents and tabs scale

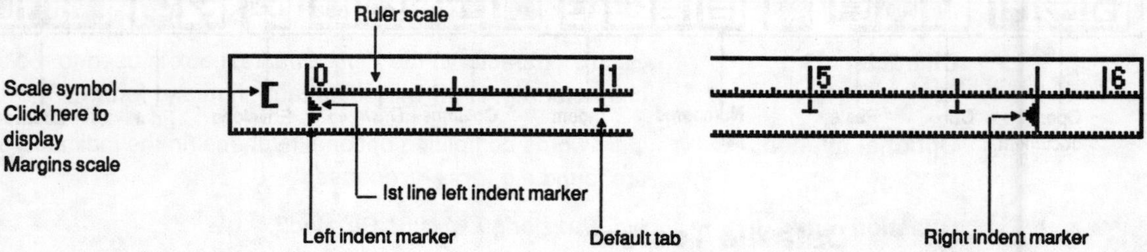

Margins scale

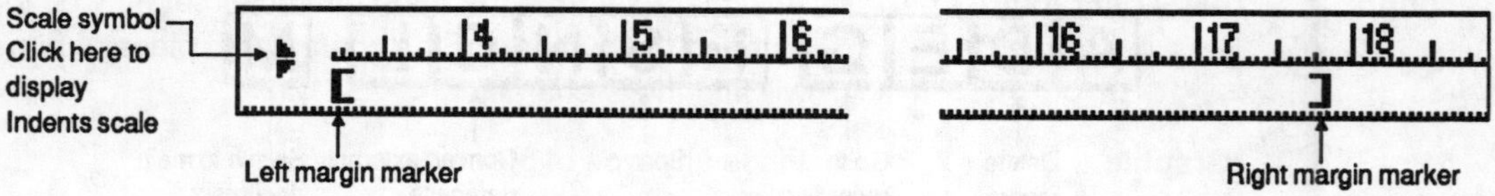

Table columns scale

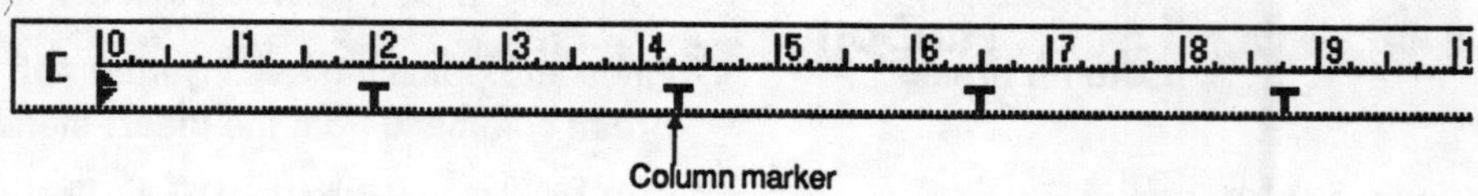

Status bar

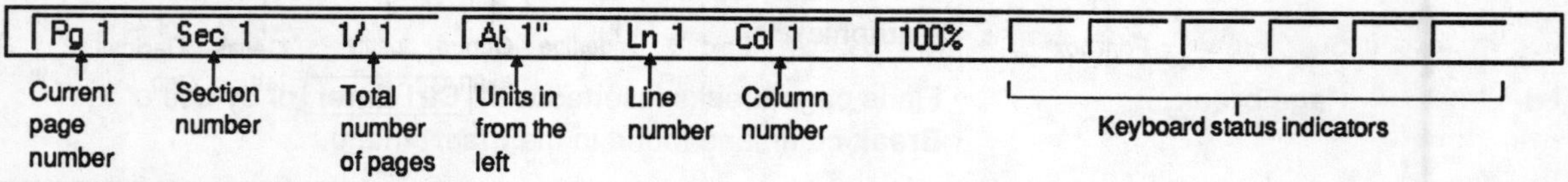

Appendix D : Find and replacement characters

The following describes the special characters that may be used with the *Find* and *Replace* dialogue boxes. These characters should be entered in the *Find What* and *Replace With* text boxes in the normal way.

The '^' (*caret*) character referred to below, is entered as **Shift 6** on most keyboards.

Character	Find or replace	
?	**Character**	Each ? character in the *Find What* text box is used to replace any character e.g. **f?rm** will locate farm, firm and form.
^-	**Optional hyphen**	Only words containing optional hyphens (in the indicated position) are found e.g. **pre^-processed**.
^?	**Question mark**	e.g. **Puzzled^?** will find Puzzled?.
^^	**Caret**	e.g. **X^^2** will find X^2.
^~	**Non-breaking hyphen**	Finds non-breaking hyphens inserted with **Ctrl SHIFT -** e.g. **riff^~raff** will find riff-raff.
^0nnn	**ANSI character**	Any character from the ANSI character set may be found by entering the number for the character in place of nnn e.g. **^0210** will find the Ô character.
^1	**Graphic**	Finds any type of graphic.
^2	**Footnote reference mark**	Used only in the *Find What* text box to locate any automatically generated Footnote reference mark.
^5	**Annotation mark**	Used only in the *Find What* text box to locate any annotation mark.
^14	**Column break**	Finds any Column break inserted with **Ctrl Shift Enter** or the **Break** command from the **Insert** menu.
^19	**Field**	Finds any field code. Field codes must be displayed on the screen.
^c	**Clipboard contents**	Replaces search text with the contents of the clipboard. This code is used in the *Replace With* text box only. It provides a way by which the maximum entry of 255 characters in the *Replace With* text box may be increased by use of the clipboard (this includes a graphic).
^d	**Page break**	Finds page breaks inserted with **Ctrl Enter** or by use of the **Break** command found in the **Insert** menu.

Character	Find or replace	
^d	**Section break**	Finds section breaks (and page breaks) inserted by use of the **Break** command from the **Insert** menu.
^m	**Search text**	Uses the contents of the *Find What* text box in the replacement e.g. if the *Find What* text box contains **facilities** and the *Replace With* text box contains **advanced ^m**, the result will be 'advanced facilities'.
^n	**Line break**	Finds line breaks inserted with [Shift Enter]
^p	**Paragraph break**	Finds paragraph breaks inserted with [Enter] e.g. if the *Find What* text box contains **^p^p** and the *Replace With* text box contains **^p**, two paragraph marks will be replaced by one.
^s	**Non-breaking space**	Finds non-breaking spaces inserted with [Ctrl Shift Spacebar].
^t	**Tab**	Finds tab characters inserted with the [Tab] key.
^w	**White space**	Finds any number and combination of tabs, normal and non-breaking spaces.

Appendix E : Readability scales

When the **Show Readability Statistics** option is selected as a default value from the *Options* dialogue box (*Category:* **Grammar**), a *Readability Statistics* information box is automatically displayed when the grammar-checking process is completed. The following provides a brief description of the *Readability:* scales displayed in the *Readability Statistics* information box:

Passive Sentences

The percentage number of passive sentences found in the document is displayed. An example of a passive sentence is "The document was word-processed by John." whilst an example of an active sentence is "John word-processed the document". Excessive use of passive sentences can make text more difficult to read (and understand).

Flesch Reading Ease & Grade Level

These are based on the average number of words per sentence and the average number of syllables per 100 words. A value for average text is based on approximately 17 words per sentence and 147 syllables per 100 words.

Difficulty level	Flesch Reading Ease	Flesch Grade Level
Very easy	90-100	4
Easy	80-90	5
Fairly easy	70-80	6
Average	60-70	7-8
Fairly difficult	50-60	9-10
Difficult	30-50	11-14
Very difficult	0-30	15-16

Flesch-Kincaid

This scale assigns a grade level which is approximately equal to the Flesch Grade Level.

Gunning Fog Index

This index is based upon the length of sentences and the number of words consisting of more than one syllable, within sentences. The higher the score, the more difficult the text is to read.

Index